D1237785

DISCARDED

The G20 Macroeconomic Agenda
India and the Emerging Economies

EDITED BY
PARTHASARATHI SHOME

CAMBRIDGE
UNIVERSITY PRESS

CAMBRIDGE
UNIVERSITY PRESS

Cambridge House, 4381/4 Ansari Road, Daryaganj, Delhi 110002, India

Cambridge University Press is part of the University of Cambridge.

It furthers the University's mission by disseminating knowledge in the pursuit of
education, learning and research at the highest international levels of excellence.

www.cambridge.org
Information on this title: www.cambridge.org/9781107051102

First published 2014

Printed in India by Sanat Printers, Kundli, Haryana

A catalogue record for this publication is available from the British Library

Library of Congress Cataloging-in-Publication Data
The G20 macroeconomic agenda : India and the emerging economies /
edited by Parthasarathi Shome.
     pages cm
Includes bibliographical references and index.
Summary: "Discusses the role India has played in the success of the G20 process and
delineates the possible barriers to India's enhanced involvement in the G20 and in global
governance in general"– Provided by publisher.
ISBN 978-1-107-05110-2 (hardback)
1. Group of Twenty countries. 2. International economic relations. 3. International
finance. 4. Economic policy. 5. India--Foreign economic relations. 6. Economic
development–India. 7. Economic development--Developing countries. I. Shome,
Parthasarathi, 1950-
HF1359.G267 2014
339.509172'4--dc23
2013048005

ISBN 978-1-107-05110-2 Hardback

Contents

List of Tables and Figures

List of Tables

List of Figures

List of Appendices

Preface

As the premier forum for global economic governance, the Group of 20 nations (G20) was successful in warding off the global economic crisis of 2008–09 and preventing it from becoming a full-blown depression. In its wake, the G20 initiated a series of financial sector reforms as the crisis originated from that sector. Indeed, financial sector behaviour continues to be the most crucial link to the vulnerability of global commodity price rise and volatility. The G20 managed to achieve unprecedented global cooperation – by bringing together the G7 and newly emerging economies – for improved global macroeconomic management. They opted for stimulus packages to loosen a liquidity crunch, initiated a series of measures to identify and check global macroeconomic imbalances, introduced measures to check frictions in global monetary arrangements and enhance financial safety net and supported the use of capital controls under certain extenuating circumstances. With these initiatives, the G20 enjoyed considerable initial success.

As the global economy recovered in 2010, the G20 expanded its brief to include a development agenda, in particular, achieving food security, controlling commodity price volatility, recycling global savings to boost infrastructure investment and enhancing energy and environmental sustainability. Thus, the G20 agenda since the outbreak of the 2008–09 global financial crisis was broadened and currently includes not only financial sector reforms and regulation and global macroeconomic coordination and reforming international financial institutions (IFIs), but also a list of pillars of development as well as energy security and environmental sustainability.

The G20 has also had a discernible effect on the global geopolitical balance – on the role of emerging markets in global governance and in agenda setting. For example, a sub-group comprising Brazil, Russia, India, China and South Africa (BRICS) found itself in the position of being thrust into a forward role in global economic discussion and policy making. In particular, China's role became central to the concerns of the G20. And India, which was one of the fast-growing emerging economies that came off unscathed by the crisis despite extensive integration with the global economy, was well placed to influence the G20 in its functioning as a global steering committee.

Nevertheless, despite the emergence of BRICS, there was no scholarly volume on emerging economy concerns and perspectives set in the context of G20 reform initiatives and impasses. This need is addressed here, by assessing the progress of the G20 as well as the unresolved concerns in the aforementioned financial and macroeconomic areas with a focus on India while, leaving for the future, the particular issues pertaining to the development agenda. The volume discusses the role India has played in the success of the G20 process and, more importantly, delineates the possible barriers to India's enhanced involvement in the G20 dialogue, and in global governance in general.

The organization of the book corresponds to the major themes of the G20 agenda. The introductory chapter comprising Section 1 on the evolution, functioning and prospects of the G20 by Parthasarathi Shome, succinctly explores the historical purpose and evolution of early global governance groupings such as the G7 and G8. It then sets the tone for the book by providing a brief description of the historical necessity for the G20, and the evolution of its agenda on financial sector reforms and macroeconomic management. It also mentions the G20's development agenda, its relations with formal multilateral institutions, its performance and the future outlook.

Section 2 on financial sector reform and regulation explores the progress of G20 financial sector reform initiatives – global standards such as Basel III and macroprudential framework and tools and discusses issues where there is less success such as reducing capital flow volatility, alternative tools for self-insurance and greater exchange rate flexibility. On the quality of reform initiatives, this section explores issues such as the lack of attention on shadow banks, systemically important financial institutions, excessive focus on standards and capital buffers and marked neglect of in-built perverse incentives for overt risk-taking by financial institutions. On India's reform strategy, it explores the cost of Basel III and the need for complementing international reform initiatives with domestic financial sector reforms – such as opening up the financial sector for entry and competition, issues related to the incentive structure of public sector banks and developing a credit registry.

This section includes two chapters, the first on financial regulation and the G20 and the options for India by Ashima Goyal and the other on financial sector reforms under G20 and ramifications for Indian banks by Poonam Gupta.

Section 3 on global macroeconomic coordination and reforming international financial institutions is the largest section. It discusses the effectiveness of the G20 Mutual Assessment Process (MAP), especially the need for an independent review committee for better transparency in assessing the progress and hence the credibility of the process, reforming the governance structure, quota and voice of IFIs, and the nuances of successful capital control strategies followed by emerging markets using both tax and non-tax instruments. It also discusses issues pertaining to the international monetary system (IMS) including the pitfalls of a dollar-dominated IMS, the cost, benefit and likelihood of moving to alternative systems such as a Special Drawing Rights (SDR)-based system or a multicurrency system, the role of regional financial safety net arrangements and India's interest in regional arrangements in the context of financial safety, regional economic power and IFI governance.

Thus, the first chapter in Section 3 by David Vines is on the G20MAP, global rebalancing, and sustaining global economic growth, and includes India's role in supporting cooperation among global macroeconomic policymakers. The next chapter is by T. N. Srinivasan on the reform of international financial institutions. Parthasarathi Shome, Jyotirmoy Bhattacharya and Shuheb Khan follow on assessing the success of capital control instruments. Renu Kohli addresses the matter of mitigating risks in the IMS from dominance of the dollar and India's stance with respect to it. Alok Sheel takes up the challenges in IMS reforms from the perspective of emerging markets. Finally, how India should view the emergence of the regional grouping of the Chiang Mai Initiative is analysed by Sheetal Chand.

In conclusion, the G20 remains an important international body to take the global economy out of the prevailing recessionary environment and also pursuing forward-looking structural reforms at a global level. As the global economy remains mired in uncertainties – stemming from the Euro crisis, lacklustre economic performance in the US and slowing of major emerging economies – this volume fills the need for a collection of analytical research papers from the perspective of emerging economies and takes stock of the performance of the G20 thus far. It also points towards unresolved issues and the future course of action in global financial and macroeconomic stance.

Individuals and institutions have to be thanked for the success of this effort and its publication. This includes the Indian Ministry of Finance which financed this research as a segment of an overarching project on the G20 with the Indian Council for Research on International Economic Relations (ICRIER) where I was Director and Chief Executive, when I headed the project. Francis Rattinam Xavier managed the project through challenges that such a large project posed in its daily functioning with diligence and efficiency, coordinating its various aspects. Santosh Gupta provided secretarial help and support in reference enquiry. It is hoped that the readership will find this work useful in assessing the successes and future challenges of the G20 process.

New Delhi   Parthasarathi Shome

Section 1
Introduction

The G20: Evolution, Functioning and Prospects
A Concise Review

Parthasarathi Shome[1]

Introduction

Global economic governance, both policy coordination and international regulation, from the 1960s was organized by small networks outside the formal global governance institutions. It was, in effect, a 'minilateralism'[2] of a dominant few that used soft law as well as a loose coordination mechanism characterized by rules voluntarily agreed and monitoring and enforcement to achieve desirable results. The group of a handful provided the political critical mass for addressing the most urgent needs of the global economy and imparting a sense of urgency in the global governance agencies that had the formal mandate to tackle such issues. Informality and flexibility were central to the success of the arrangements.[3] The G7 was one such dominant network in the latter part of the twentieth century.

The balance of global economic power in terms of GDP and international trade in the early 2000s had become more dispersed, with a need for recognition of this new balance. The formal Bretton Woods system, its mandate, and mode of operation had become somewhat wanting in this new world order of the 2000s. Its inability to recognize or expand the role of emerging economies meant that they could not cope with changing times. Even the dominant triad of the G7 – United States, Japan and Europe – could not adequately counter interconnected challenges including macroeconomic imbalances, development imbalances or the provision of global public goods, in particular, energy, commodities and environmental sustainability.

Emerging economies, with superior growth performance in recent years, increasingly began calling for a place at the negotiating table. The Asian economic crisis of 1997–98 and the global crisis of 2008–09 finally resulted in modifications in the way global economic governance was organized. The formal governance system – the UN Security Council, the International

Monetary Fund (IMF) and the World Bank – were not adequately suited for resolving emerging crises as they primarily reflected the preference of the old world order, hence were increasingly unable to enjoy the confidence of the emerging economic powers. The need of the hour was a truly global network that adequately reflected the new political and economic multipolarity, and to synthesize a more representative balance of power with a transparent framework for global economic governance. Thus was born the G20 Finance Ministers and Central Bank Governors' Network in 1999 after the Asian crisis and the G20 at the Leaders' level in 2008 with the onset of the global crisis.The emergence of the G20 recognizes the fact that, in an increasingly integrated world economy, problems become, more often than not, global. This, in turn, demands global solutions involving all stakeholders, including the newly emerging market economies.

This chapter attempts to succinctly explore the origin and development of the G20, the evolution of its agenda, its relations with formal multilateral institutions, its performance and the future outlook for the group.

G-x: Purpose, Evolution and Shortcomings

Informal groups (G-x) emerged as a result of changing global scenarios especially when formal coordination mechanisms lagged behind or failed. In the 1970s, following the collapse of the Bretton Woods exchange rate arrangements, together with twin oil crises and subsequent stagflation in the global economy, formal mechanisms were too slow to conjure up quick solutions. Emergence of the G-x (G10/G7/G8)[4] functioned as an effective mechanism for the handful of advanced economies to cope with new challenges.

The aim of these informal mini-lateral processes, in the context of complex global economic interactions, has been to provide political and strategic leadership and, in the process, function as the inner core of a more formal multilateral process, i.e., the Bretton Woods system. The G-x provides an informal vision, a sense of direction and a political stance for needed actions to the formal decision-making bodies. In the late 1970s, the G7 emerged as such a platform for coordinating macroeconomic policies among advanced industrial countries, setting international standards, e.g., Financial Stability Forum (FSF), and promoting international trade and development aid. It further expanded to include non-core issues such as environment, energy, food security and terrorism (Alexandroff, 2010).[5]

As the G7 expanded to include Russia to become G8, it became the global steering committee through the 1990s when a series of market crises hit the global economy. After the crises, it was clear that the global steering committee that did not include systemically significant developing countries would be inadequate for future crisis resolution or prevention. There was a need for a wider outreach to include emerging economies. Hence, in 1999, an informal network of finance ministers and central bank governors for 20 countries (G20) was established.

G20 Finance Ministers and Central Bank Governors' Network

The first G20 communiqué noted that the purpose of the network was to create a platform for informal dialogue on economic and financial issues to encourage cooperation among systemically important advanced as well as emerging economies to achieve stable and sustainable global economic growth.[6] The initial mandate reflected crisis prevention as the central objective. However, the G20 increasingly expanded its agenda to include combating the challenges of globalization for emerging economies, curbing terror financing in the aftermath of the 9/11 terrorist attack on the World Trade Centre in New York City and ensuring the effectiveness of development aid, in addition to the development of domestic financial markets, regional economic integration and resource security (Group of 20, 2008).[7]

As indicated in its first communiqué that the G20 would dialogue 'within the framework of the Bretton Woods institutional system',[8] the heads of Bretton Woods institutions, i.e., the Managing Director of the IMF, the President of the World Bank and the Chairpersons of the International Monetary and Financial Committee and Development Committee of the IMF and World Bank, were granted ex-officio status to participate in the discussions.

Selecting the countries was informal. Though economic weight was argued to be the guiding principle, the size of the economy, neither in terms of absolute size nor in terms of Purchasing Power Parity (PPP) calculations could be easily translated to the inclusion in G20 membership. Apparently, other factors such as countries' systemic importance measured in terms of their global integration, ability to contribute to global governance and fair geographical representation played a significant role (Jokela, 2011).[9] Factors such as political stability and ideological proximity were also apparently considered, with some observers reasoning that the G20 was a mere 'reflex of the G7 world' (Wade, 2009). Wade stated that:

[G20 countries] were selected by Timothy Geithner at the US Treasury in a transatlantic telephone call with his counterpart at the German Finance Ministry, Caio Koch-Weser. Geithner and Koch-Weser went down the list of countries saying, Canada in, Spain out, South Africa in, Nigeria and Egypt out, and so on; they sent their list to the other G7 finance ministries; and the invitations to the first meeting went out.[10] (p. 553)[11]

Be that as it may, apart from the inclusion of systemically important emerging economies in the global governance process, which was a watershed moment in itself, the G20 in its initial years enjoyed moderate success in building consensus on global financial matters. These included understanding on setting standards and codes to enhance transparency in the global financial system, introducing a framework for debt restructuring and initiating reforms at the Bretton Woods institutions, especially quota and representation reforms. In the early 2000s when the Asian market crisis was already behind, the initial impetus of G20 was lost as there were no new major non-G7 agenda, and quota and representation reforms were close to an impasse.

The critics argued that, even in its initial phase, the G20 had stayed under the shadow of its senior cousin, the G7. The G20 communiqués closely followed the communiqués of the G7 and, if there were any conflict, the G7 preferences prevailed (Martinez-Diaz and Woods, 2009; Martinez-Diaz and Woods, 2010).[12] In another study, Martinez-Diaz (2007), taking G24[13] communiqués as representative views of non-G7 countries, showed that the G20 communiqués were dominated by the G7 preferences and that non-G7 countries in G20 were silent and neutral.[14] Further, some critics argued that the existence of the G20 nipped any radical alternatives to be undertaken by the emerging markets. For example, major emerging economies, such as China and India, were cautious in G20 meetings. Thus, a perusal of the literature reveals that there has been a significant number of detractors to the G20 process.

G20 at Leaders' Level: Changing Political Climate

The decade following the inception of the G20 witnessed drastic geopolitical changes, increasing global interconnectedness and new growth poles. It was increasingly difficult for the G7, whose economic weight declined relatively, to provide global governance without effectively involving major emerging powers. Calling on the G20 to replace or fill in the shoes of the G7 was not straightforward. A G8 outreach programme, the Heiligendamm process, was initiated in 2007 at a G8 summit in Heiligendamm, Germany. The new G8

+ 5 included Brazil, China, India, Mexico and South Africa. However, the outreach programme was criticized by emerging economies as their inputs were not sought. The Indian Prime Minister Dr Manmohan Singh expressed his apprehension as,

> [T]he expanded group (*G-8* + *China, India, Brazil, Mexico and South Africa*) is not cohesive since the countries included for purposes of outreach do not participate fully in the proceedings, or the preparations, and the expanded group therefore does not have a composite identity. Second, these groupings do not have any special legitimacy within the UN System.[15]

The report of a High-Level Panel on threats, challenges and change constituted by the United Nations stated that,

> While the annual meetings of the G8 group at a head of state or government level fulfill some of the characteristics required to give greater coherence and impetus to the necessary policies, it would be helpful to have a larger forum bringing together the heads of the major developed and developing countries. One way of moving forward may be to transform it into a leader's group – the G20 group of finance ministers, which currently brings together States collectively encompassing 80 per cent of the world's population and 90 per cent of its economic activity, with regular attendance by the International Monetary Fund, World Bank, WTO and the European Union.[16] (p. 88)

As the global economic crisis escalated in 2008, the need for involving emerging economies to effect meaningful coordinated solutions and impart confidence in the markets was met through the G20's representative power and legitimacy achieved through its high proportion in global GDP, trade and finance.

If the 1997 Asian crisis highlighted the extent of financial integration of emerging market economies and the need, through global dialogue, to take their views, the 2008 global crisis exposed the inadequacies of the existing formal global governance arrangements and the inevitability of a more pronounced role of emerging economies in structuring frameworks for solving global problems. The newly emerging geopolitical scenario culminated in designating 'the G-20 as the premier forum' for international economic cooperation at its Pittsburg Summit.[17]

Martinez-Diaz and Woods (2009) argued that emerging economies have also used their experience with the G20 summitry to accumulate institutional knowledge of the G-x process. They built up capacity at their respective ministries – usually finance and external affairs – to deal with G20 issues. They indicate that, 'ten years of practice in the G20 finance network means that the emerging economies have come into the G20 Leaders' network much better prepared for global summitry than they were in 1999.

G20 Agenda and Concerns

When the G20 Leaders' first Summit was convened, the need of the hour was to restore the confidence in the global financial system which was at the root of the global crisis. In the Washington Summit held on 14–15 November 2008, a 47-point action plan was agreed upon to identify the vulnerabilities exposed by the crisis and to improve regulation to adequately strengthen the financial sector. The Leaders also agreed to resist any protectionist tendencies. By the second Leaders' Summit held in London on 2 April 2009, a global recession had set in. The Leaders agreed on coordinated fiscal and monetary stimulus measures to check the recession and recapitalize the international financial institutions (IFIs) and multilateral development banks (MDBs) to assist developing countries cope with the crisis. Financial sector regulation was taken up by expanding the erstwhile FSF to include the dynamic emerging markets in the Financial Stability Board (FSB). It was mandated to coordinate financial sector regulation initiatives along with the IMF and Bank of International Settlements (BIS).

The Pittsburgh Summit held on 24–25 September 2009, marked the watershed moment in the G-summitry initiatives for global governance as Leaders designated the G20 as the premier forum for international economic coordination. The G20 expanded its agenda by laying out the 'Framework for Strong, Sustainable and Balanced Growth' to coordinate global recovery by reducing global imbalances. Voice and representation reforms at IMF to adequately reflect the new world order was assured. Financial sector regulation initiatives progressed further as measures to identify and regulate systemically important financial institutions (SIFIs) were endorsed. The Toronto Summit on 26–27 June 2010 further consolidated the initiatives of previous summits.

The Seoul Summit, the first Leaders' Summit chaired by a non-G7 country on 11–12 November 2010, delivered on many of the commitments previously made and initiated a whole set of new agenda and items to include the concerns of emerging and developing countries. Basel III norms proposed by the Basel Committee on Banking Supervision (BCBS) were endorsed. Transferring 5 per cent IMF quotas to dynamic emerging economies from over-represented countries was agreed upon. The IMF introduced two new lines of credit for the enhancement of global financial safety nets, a Flexible Credit Line (FCL) and a Precautionary Credit Line (PCL). Constructive steps were initiated under the Framework for Strong, Sustainable and Balanced Growth, as Leaders agreed to develop guidelines to measure and devise solutions to check destabilizing movements in indicators. Embarking on a new path, Leaders also endorsed the Seoul Development Consensus for Shared Growth. This is explained in the next section.

Expanding the Agenda: Development Consensus

The initial Leaders' summits were dominated by issues such as policy coordination to ward off impending recession. They put in place meaningful financial sector regulation and attempted to reorient the global economy towards reducing global imbalances, a rather G8-like agenda. However, those were the need of the hour to quickly restore confidence in the global economy. With the backdrop of coordinated stimulus packages, the global economy fared better than expected in 2009 and recovered well in 2010 (WEO, 2010).[18] It was felt that time was ripe for the G20 to transform itself into a global steering committee rather than a limited crisis containment group and look beyond macroeconomic and financial sector issues.

Many emerging economies expressed the need for expanding and reorienting the agenda to include developmental issues that are intrinsic to traditional macroeconomic factors (Shome and Rathinam, 2011).[19] As emerging economies were expected to contribute to global growth, introducing a development agenda would have been complementary to existing G20 objectives, especially for 'strong, sustainable and balanced global growth'. A strong development agenda in the form of global cooperation for investment in infrastructure, food security, freer international trade and human resource development was perceived to be integral to boosting the growth performance of emerging and developing countries. It was also felt that the formal multilateral arrangements lacked impetus in dealing with these crucial issues. Instead, the G20 was well placed to provide the political momentum to achieve these goals.

The South Korean G20 presidency, seeing itself as a bridge between the G7 economies and the emerging world, steered the G20 agenda towards development goals. Strongly backed by the emerging economies, a comprehensive framework for a 'Development Consensus for Shared Growth' was agreed at the Seoul Summit. It must be admitted, however, that some detractors believed there was a certain measure of incrementalism as the early financial stability focus of the G20 moved on to include additional objectives. Shome (2011)[20] pointed out that the nine pillars of development that emerged

> …challenged the singular focus that is needed to address the most crucial faultlines that should be addressed for restoring stability in financial flows. The lesson is that, in the prevailing era, the widely accepted concerns of global governance appear to embrace so many aspects and issues that they compete with the central issues that demand singular attention for achieving systemic correction. The broadening of objectives assuages the developing countries that claim recognition of their long-term structural concerns as a group. However, it carries the danger, and perhaps the reality, of diluting the immediacy of instituting strong and meaningful global indicators that should automatically trigger tightening/loosening macroeconomic–financial and fiscal–policies that most advanced economies should be implementing now. (pp. 94–95)

India is one of the active supporters of a development agenda for both bringing in new items on board as well as reorienting the focus of existing concerns to address issues of development. The Indian Prime Minister, for example, stated that channelling global savings into infrastructure investment in emerging economies will 'not only address the immediate demand imbalance, it will also help to address developmental imbalances'[21] by stimulating domestic demand and imports in emerging economies. This will not only lead to faster growth in emerging economies but also to a speedy global recovery. China also backed the development agenda to 'narrow the development gap and promote common growth' and 'further unleash the development potential of emerging markets and developing countries, and boost the economic growth of developing countries in order to stimulate aggregate global demand.'[22]

The G20 Leaders in Seoul in November 2010 set up a high-level panel on infrastructure investment with recommendations for 'financing infrastructure needs, including from public, semi-public and private sector sources, and identify, with multilateral development banks, a list of concrete regional initiatives'.[23] The panel recommended the G20 to build local capability especially PPP units to prepare bankable projects, an effective enabling environment for the model to work and ways for MDBs to effectively support the development of PPPs.

The latest Summit at Cannes on 3–4 November 2011, was however, overshadowed by the imminent Euro crisis. The Leaders agreed on a Cannes Action Plan for Growth and Jobs which necessitated country-specific reform measures. In a significant move on the financial sector front, 29 global and systemically important financial institutions (G-SIFIs) were identified for closer scrutiny. The Summit also streamlined the Development Agenda by agreeing to focus more on food security and financing for infrastructure. The discussion paper issued by the most recent 2012 Mexican presidency of the G20[24] reiterates that the G20 focus will be primarily on commodity price volatility and food insecurity due to insufficient growth in supplies as well as price volatility, though it also includes green growth in its agenda.

Assessment of Achievements

The early achievement of the G20 was crisis management. After the Lehman collapse, the resultant liquidity crunch had escalated the US housing market crisis into a full-blown global financial crisis. The confidence crisis in the financial markets spilled over to the real economy. A globally coordinated policy response was required to restore confidence.

The G20 economies agreed to introduce Keynesian counter-cyclical policies, i.e., monetary and fiscal stimuli as were suited to their individual needs. Support came in the form of unprecedented bail-out packages and recapitalization of banks and financial institutions. The G20, as a whole, set in place a package of about USD 5 trillion in the belief that it would prevent the global financial sector from collapsing. All industrial as well as emerging economies agreed to stimulate their economies. They also collectively agreed to recapitalize the international financial institutions to assist the crisis-laden economies. Interestingly, the G20 did its best to ensure that the national policies of its members were not detrimental to the recovery of others. The Leaders agreed to avoid premature withdrawal of stimuli and to exit from those policies in a coordinated way.

A complete assessment of the outcomes of the heterodox, demand-propelled policies is yet to emerge. One of the fundamental causes of the crisis, where there was universal consensus, was lax regulation of financial institutions, an unregulated shadow banking system and 'too big to fail' SIFIs. The G20 acted decisively on reregulating the financial sector. Though Basel II norms were not fully satisfactory, Basel III norms on capital, leverage and liquidity standards were more stringent than in the former Basel II and were endorsed by the G20 despite sharp criticism and resistance from the finance industry. The new norms were expected to raise the quality and quantity of bank capital and liquidity, check build-up of leverage and maturity mismatches and initiate counter cyclical buffers that could be drawn down in adverse times (FSB, 2010).[25] Implementation of these norms are said to be in progress (FSB, 2011),[26] but there is some concern that it has been slower than optimal.

The G20 came up with a more coordinated view on global imbalances. There are two sides to the global imbalances issue: the first is the surplus generated by the export-led strategy of selected countries with the help of managed exchange rates; the second side is that large surpluses of those economies have corresponding lack of savings and leveraged consumption in deficit countries. The G20 Mutual Assessment Process (MAP) was introduced to identify systemically important countries that are running imbalances on both sides. The 2011 G20 Summit at Cannes agreed that the solution should come from individual countries given their individual circumstances as they have different global shares in imbalances and are at different stages of economic growth (G20, 2011).[27]

Lack of adequate emergency financing was one of the causes of reserve build-up by many of the Asian countries. After the Asian crisis experience when they found themselves without adequate cover, they realized that having adequate reserves would be the first line of defence against market speculation and also for ensuring national policy independence. The IMF, with the guidance of the G20, acted swiftly to introduce new credit lines as mentioned earlier, that could be accessed by member countries without too many strings attached. Reflecting the dwindling capital base of the IMF vis-à-vis its growing global capital needs, the G20 recapitalized the IMF, first by $750 billion and then again by $250 billion.

Looking Forward

The G20 to a large extent succeeded as a firefighting committee in 2008–09, though it has not been fully successful as a lightning rod for anticipating and preventing crises such as the newest Euro crisis, for which unusual financial indicators need to be put in place, based on, among others, potential flight capital, volatility of capital flows and stock markets and interest-rate spreads that tend to precede or are associated with financial crises.[28] However, its role in averting the Euro crisis in 2011 has been less active. The next major transformation would be for the G20 to switch over to a global steering committee role that fits the new global economic order. In a two-paced post-crisis world, it has to balance traditional G7 issues such as macroeconomic policy coordination and new developmental concerns on the one hand, with longer term green (and other sustainability) issues on the other. The G20 in the past proved quite capable of transformation as it had successfully updated its agenda in the post-crisis scenario.

Nevertheless, inclusion of the development agenda and, more than a year from the inclusion, the G20's performance on the development pillars have received mixed reviews. First, as the G20 Leaders Summit itself is a work in progress which was elevated to this level to deal with the frailty of global recovery, introducing a development agenda is feared to overburden the network's ability to perform its primary function of enhancing financial stability. Second, the development pillars are thought to be too many for a nascent network to deal with.[29]

Many of the developmental issues are politically sensitive for which it is difficult to arrive at a consensus. The 2011 French presidency and the 2012 Mexican presidency have streamlined the agenda to concentrate more on infrastructure investment, food security, commodity price volatility and green growth. On the other side, it is countered that developmental inequalities are at the heart of macroeconomic inequalities, such as trade deficits and surpluses, that the G20 is grappling with. How effectively emerging countries manage to forge a credible coalition, despite diverse preferences, in successfully setting the G20 agenda in the years to come, has also emerged as an issue with the most successful among them – Brazil, Russia, India, China and South Africa (BRICS) – forming a subgroup to articulate and act upon the emerging group's concerns. As the G20 presidencies will be with non-G7 countries until 2015, it appears that the development agenda will continue to play a significant role. This is fine as long as the focus on stability and containment of volatility in global financial and commodity markets remains central to the G20 agenda.

Conclusion

The G20 as a crisis-related committee has been relatively successful. However, it is too early to assess its performance as a global steering committee. The G20 is mandated to work within the Bretton Woods system, i.e., use the knowledge and capacity of the existing formal economic multilateral institutions and the UN system and also involve other regional bodies. It has marked a beginning in a new multilateral world order, which would eventually lead to reforming the formal global governance system and institutions. However, it has also evoked criticisms of the group's legitimacy, 'minilateralism' of a few rather than a more equitable multilateralism and its relatively slow performance in some aspects of global governance. Given that the G20 is more legitimate than its predecessors and has been effective in containing the immediacy of the 2008 global economic crisis, it is the only viable, if ad hoc, initiative that is available and functioning and will remain so until the UN and the Bretton Woods system are more fundamentally reformed.

Endnotes

[1] The author appreciates the assistance received from Francis Rathinam. All opinions are, however, the author's.

[2] Naím (2009) who coined the word 'minilateralism' stated that it is a process of bringing the 'smallest possible number of countries needed to have the largest possible impact on solving a particular problem'. Naím, M. 2009. 'Minilateralism: The Magic Number to Get Real International Action', *Foreign Policy*, July/Aug 2009.

[3] A network is based on an informal relationship rather than any formal abilities in rule-making, enforcing or arbitrating when disputes arise. It is used for information-sharing, agenda-setting, consensus-building, norm-setting and monitoring voluntary implementation (Martinez-Dias and Woods, 2009).

[4] The Group of Ten (G10), the first of the G-x, was established in 1962 by Belgium, Canada, France, Germany, Italy, Japan, Netherlands, Sweden, United Kingdom and United States with Switzerland as an associate country. The G10 was instrumental in effecting General Arrangements to Borrow (GAB) at the IMF, creation of the Special Drawing Rights (SDR), signing the Smithsonian Agreement and establishing the Basel Committee (BCBS) for setting banking standards. The Group of Seven (G7) was established in 1975 by Canada, France, Germany, Italy, Japan, United Kingdom and United States at the level of finance ministers and central bank governors. With the inclusion of Russia, it was expanded to the Group of Eight (G8) in 1998. The European Union (EU) was a permanent attendee in G7/G8 summits since 1977.

[5] Alexandroff, Alan. 2010. 'Challenges in Global Governance: Opportunities for G-x Leadership', *Policy Analysis Brief*, The Stanley Foundation, US.

[6] G20 Communiqué, G20 Finance Ministers and Central Bank Governors Meeting, 15–16 December 1999, Berlin, Germany.

[7] G20. 2008. 'The Group of Twenty: A History'. G20.

[8] Canada.1999. 'New G-20 Forum: Backgrounder'. Canada, Department of Finance.

[9] Jokela, Juha. 2011. 'The G-20: A pathway to effective multilateralism?' *Chaillot Papers* 125, European Union Institute for Security Studies, Paris.

[10] Wade, R. 2009. 'From global imbalances to global reorganizations'. *Cambridge Journal of Economics* 33: 539–562.

[11] In the event, the members of the G20 were Argentina, Australia, Brazil, Canada, China, France, Germany, India, Indonesia, Italy, Japan, Republic of Korea, Mexico, Russia, Saudi Arabia, South Africa, Turkey, United Kindom, United States and European Union.

[12] Martinez-Diaz, L. and N. Woods. 2009. 'The G20: The Perils and Opportunities of Network Governance for Developing Countries'. GEG Policy Brief; Martinez-Diaz, L and N. Woods. 2010. eds. 'Networks of Influence? Developing Countries in a Networked Global Order'. Oxford University Press, New York.

[13] The Group of Twenty-Four (G24) was established in 1971 to represent the interests of developing countries in monetary and development finance issues in international negotiations. The G24 members include: Algeria, Arab Republic, Argentina, Brazil, Colombia, Congo, Côte d'Ivoire, Egypt, Ethiopia, Gabon, Ghana, Guatemala, India, Iran, Lebanon, Mexico, Nigeria, Pakistan, Peru, Philippines, South Africa, Sri Lanka, Syrian, Trinidad and Tobago and Venezuela.

[14] Martinez-Diaz, L. 2007. 'The G-20 After Eight Years: How Effective a Vehicle for Developing-Country Influence?' Global Working Papers, No. 12, The Brookings Institution.

[15] Singh, Manmohan. 2009. 'PM's vision of how the world is governed in the 21st century'. 7 July, New Delhi.

[16] United Nations. 2008. 'A More Secure World: Our Shared Responsibility', Report of the High-Level Panel on Threats, Challenges and Change, United Nations, New York.

[17] G20. 2009. 'The Leaders Statement'. The Pittsburgh Summit, 25 September.

[18] WEO. 2010. 'Rebalancing Growth'. *World Economic Outlook*, IMF, April.

[19] Shome, Parthasarathi and F. Rathinam. 2011. 'India's Expectations from G20' in M. Metzgar, eds. 'Global Financial Stability: A Dialogue on Regulation and Cooperation'. Deutsche Gesellschaftfür Internationale Zusammenarbeit (GIZ), 99–116.

[20] Shome, Parthasarathi. 2011. 'Governance: History, Contemporary Debate and Practice', in S. Kochhar. ed. *Policy Making For Indian Planning – Essays on Contemporary Issues in Honour of Montek S. Ahluwalia*, Skoch Development Foundation, New Delhi.

[21] Manmohan Singh's remarks at the Plenary Session of the G20 Summit, 12 November 2010, Seoul, Republic of Korea.

[22] Jintao, H. 2011. 'Promote Growth Through Win-Win Cooperation', speech delivered by the Chinese President at the G20 Summit, France.

[23] G-20 Leaders' Declaration, Seoul, 12 November 2010.

[24] G20. 2012. 'Discussion Paper'. Mexico's Presidency of the G20, January.

[25] FSB. 2010. 'Progress of Financial Regulatory Reforms', 9 November.

[26] FSB. 2011. 'Progress in implementing the G20 Recommendations on Financial Regulatory Reform: Status report by the FSB Secretariat', The Financial Stability Board, 4 November.

[27] G20. 2011. 'The Cannes Action Plan for Growth and Jobs', 4 November.

[28] Shome, Parthasarathi. 2012. 'Fiscal Stimuli and Consolidation', in Olivier Blanchard, David Romer, Michael Spence and Joseph Stiglitz. eds. *In the Wake of the Crisis*. The MIT Press, Cambridge, London.

[29] The G20 in the Seoul Summit committed to 'resolve the most significant bottlenecks to inclusive, sustainable and resilient growth in developing countries, low-income countries (LICs) in particular: infrastructure, human resources development, trade, private investment and job creation, food security, growth with resilience, financial inclusion, domestic resource mobilization and knowledge sharing'. The G20. 2010. 'Framework for Strong, Sustainable and Balanced Growth'. G20 Seoul Summit, 11–12 November.

Section 2
Financial Sector Reforms and Regulation

2 Financial Regulation and the G20: Options for India

Ashima Goyal[1]

Introduction

The global financial crisis generated a number of ideas for improving financial regulation. There was some action, but as the crisis fades, the onus is on the G20 to sustain the momentum. It made real contributions towards a coordinated macroeconomic stimulus that prevented another Great Depression, but then was divided by the two-speed recovery and therefore asymmetric exit from the stimulus. The Euro debt crisis may enable a refocus on financial fragility. But instead of just fire-fighting the target should be on preventive measures and bringing stability over the longer period.

The advanced economies (AEs) still have large unemployment and poor domestic demand. Most emerging markets (EMs) continue to have high unemployment or low productivity employment but inflationary pressures are strong. Early hardening of commodity prices due partly to the large liquidity pumped into markets during quantitative easing (QE) by Central Banks in the AEs aggravated inflation. Since improvements in financial regulation are slow and incomplete, the risky search for yields that contributed to the crisis continues. The alternative view that higher consumption in EMs is driving commodity prices is not tenable. Aggregate consumption remains larger in the AEs where growth is low, while commodity price rise in the six months from November 2010 to March 2011 was the steepest in history. Moreover, the supply response that set in by 2013 due to artificially higher prices, led to prices falling, showing EM demand did not justify high prices.

Making trading profits to rebuild destroyed wealth, and cheapening currencies in order to increase export demand, are the recovery strategies of the AEs. Thus, the focus is on imbalances as a fundamental cause of the crisis, since large reserves in an EM may prevent its currency from appreciating.

But EMs see QE-induced appreciation or volatility in their currencies as unfair and requiring intervention. QE also leads to fluctuating risk-on risk-off capital flows into EMs.

While imbalances are a source of stress and need to be reduced, they persisted for more than a decade and yet did not create the dollar crisis that had long been predicted. It was the US financial sector that imploded instead, largely because of weak regulation and high leverage. It is urgent that the G20 focuses on improving financial regulation, but it is being diverted on the divisive issue of macroeconomic policies. We show financial sector weaknesses may themselves have contributed to imbalances, so that a better quality of financial integration may itself reduce reserve accumulation and imbalances.

A G22 was set up after the East Asian crisis. Then also there were many suggestions for financial reform, but AEs were not affected, and the financial interests they represented were too strong. So reforms towards international benchmarks were largely carried out only in EMs (Goyal, 2002). If a few of the suggested reforms had been implemented, perhaps the financial implosion could have been averted. The Independent Evaluation Office (IEO) of the IMF has pointed to the tendency to group think that prevented action on many emerging pre-crisis financial risks.

This time G20 has a stronger mandate. Since it is a better balance of finance exporting and importing countries, there is a chance for real financial reform, provided the focus remains on financial regulation. The chapter outlines the major reform initiatives underway and the position of G20 countries with respect to them. It identifies gaps in ideas and in implementation from the Emerging and Developing Economies' (EDEs) point of view. It discusses the feasibility of 'broad pattern regulation' (Goyal 2013) including innovative taxes on the financial sector, which could contribute to financial stability and reduce risks, even while moving away from a sole focus on capital adequacy.

The structure of the chapter is as follows: After a brief survey of G20 history and achievements in Section 2, Section 3 turns to positions on financial regulation in the G20 and in the individual G20 countries and Section 4 takes up the major lacunae in the regulatory responses before Section 5 concludes.

G20: History, Achievements and Expectations

Although the G20 has no legislative mandate and does not represent all countries unlike the UN, it has more influence after the global financial crisis (GFC). Due to the rapid growth of EMs it now stands for 85 per cent of world income. The implementing and monitoring agencies for policy decisions such as Bank for International Settlements (BIS), the IMF and the Financial Stability Board (FSB) are also seeing more representation from EDEs, although many more governance changes are required.

After the initial successes there were some achievements, but also increasing divisiveness, largely over macroeconomic exit and imbalances. Commentators either dismiss the G20 as an unwieldy talking shop or have excessive expectations from it. But since the international monetary system at present has inadequate means of managing spillovers between countries, regular talking to each other is useful in itself and may eventually lead to better understanding and greater coordination. Goyal (2005) had pointed out that gradual adjustment was feasible and was the best way to reduce imbalances. A dollar crisis was not certain but was probable, and better coordination was one way to reduce the probability of such a crisis. G20 is delivering that coordination.

The mutual assessment process[2] (MAP) agreed with the IMF is a good illustration of coordination possibilities. It started in Pittsburgh, during the third summit (2009), with aggregation of country information to develop global scenarios and identify collaborative policy actions for better global outcomes. The second stage was conducted at the country and regional level. At the Seoul Summit (2010) each G20 member identified specific policy actions for themselves towards achieving collective objectives. A new Integrated Surveillance Decision (2013) enhanced Article IV consultations to add multilateral to bilateral surveillance to also cover spillovers from member countries' policies that may impact global stability. Even without legal commitments, this can bring peer pressure to bear on imbalance-creating countries. Greater weight can be given to domestic concerns over international spillovers, but the latter can make a case for multilateral coordination on capital controls or partial internalization of the risks of volatile capital flows by lenders. It will be a major step towards symmetry if the onus for capital flow volatility is put on source countries also instead of the current system where the entire burden of adjustment is borne by recipient countries.

But macroeconomic issues lead to too much unhealthy finger pointing. The focus on imbalances is repeating the pre-crisis neglect of financial regulation. The latter is likely to be less divisive with more common interests and greater possibility of moving ahead together.

To leverage the G20's greater diversity, countries like India must be willing to bring different points of view to the debate. It may help if Asian countries or the BRICS group of countries develop a common position which they can push for. Examining the evolving positions of individual G20 countries may contribute to discovering such a position on financial regulation.

Financial Regulation and the G20

Different types of market failure justify regulation. This section traces the GFCs to these failures, draws out the implications for regulation and finally assesses the G20 stance and individual country's actions in this context.

Market Failures, Crisis and Regulation

Fundamental failures in financial markets are subject to asymmetric information leading to exclusion and arbitrage across asset types and markets; large systemically important financial institutions (SIFIs) that are 'too big to fail' and excess volatility or pro-cyclicality. There are also regulatory failures that include delay and either laxity or overzealousness. Reform, to be successful, must reverse the disincentives legal and institutional reform created, as well as mitigate fundamental failures by improving transparency, competition and reducing incentives for excessive risk-taking.[3] Information available not just to regulators but also to other market participants would improve market discipline.

Moreover, implementation, to the extent possible, should not rely on discretionary regulatory decisions. Principal-based rules, based on the principles causing market failure, can allow the flexibility to context of a principle-based approach and yet reduce delays and regulatory forbearance. They are like rules since they are triggered by objective criteria related to principles (for example, prompt corrective action clauses based on well-defined financial prudential parameters), thus reducing regulatory discretion and delay.

Special attention is required for SIFIs and to the arbitrage by which entities and transactions escape regulation, creating the shadow banking system. There are strong cross-border relationships between institutions and markets. Harmonization of general standards, while retaining operational flexibility, could prevent regulatory arbitrage and competitive risk taking (see Box 2.1). Special capital penalties, oversight and insurance premiums on SIFIs will create disincentives for marginal contributions to systemic risk. Competition policies may aim to prevent firms from getting too big. Concentration margins could be charged for banks that lend predominantly to a closed circle of big finance.

Box 2.1: Why Universal Standards are Important

The game theoretic payoff structure[4] below shows why either universal standards or taxes would help reduce pro-cyclicality. Table 2.1 depicts the actions, equilibria and payoffs. The first number is the payoff to a bank from its operations in a country and the second to the country. Note that the payoffs are to the country, but a regulator takes the action. Consider the first two columns of payoffs. Suppose a bank can make *risky* or *safe* investments. As an example consider a Korean MNC bank choosing between a risky short-term dollar carry trade and a strategy of raising local retail deposits to invest locally.

The regulator can either *do nothing* or make emergency funds available under a *bail out* incase of a crisis. There are two *Nash equilibria*, the first where the bank selects *safe* investments and the regulator does not have to take any action, and the second where a *bailout* follows *risky* loans. But if the bank moves first, it will choose the risky strategy. The expected bailout raises returns from the risky strategy thus creating moral hazard. The regulator will have to bailout since the country does so badly under no action. The unique *Subgame Perfect Nash Equilibrium* then is (8, 3).

Table 2.1: The Effect of Regulation on Risk

		Regulator/Country		
		No action	**Bailout**	**Taxes**
		1	2	3
Bank	Safe	(7,4)	(7,4)	
	Risky	(4,0)	(8,3)	(5,2)

But if the rules of the game are changed to introduce short-term transaction taxes that fall on risky activities, column three of payoffs is added. In this game, the bank will prefer to make *safe* loans. The taxes make the bank's payoff relatively higher under safe loans. Now the unique Nash equilibrium is (7, 4), with the creditor making *safe* loans and the regulator *doing nothing*. The probability of a crisis falls. In equilibrium zero taxes are raised since the risky activity is not chosen. The regulatory strategy just has to be available and announced. It does not actually have to be used. Both the country and the bank are better off in this case.

Now consider a number of banks choosing between the strategies. Competition among banks forces the choice of risky strategies. That is why universal standards are so powerful. If a bank is assured its competitor will not choose risky strategies that may allow it to make more money or be able to arbitrage taxes, it will not choose those strategies either. Once the first mover chooses a risky strategy the regulator is forced to bail out.

G20 Positions

An early G20 (2009) report on regulation came out with 25 recommendations largely in line with the above principles. They included a national focus on financial stability, oversight of all SIFIs, countercyclical macro-prudential norms, comprehensive international standards to be applied consistent with the national context and incentives for financial stability from micro-conduct regulation. Improving incentives is also important to compensate for regulatory limitations. G20 positions on detailed regulations evolved over time.

On capital requirements, the Basel III agreement is given in Box 2.2; on securitization originators should retain a part of the risk of the underlying asset; standardized over-the-counter (OTC) derivatives should shift to exchanges; tools are to be created for crisis resolution; countries are to shift towards simplified global accounting standards; credit rating agencies (CRAs) and hedge funds are to be subjected to regulatory oversight with enhanced supervision and disclosure; variable pay for senior executives is to be deferred; IMF surveillance is to be expanded and regulatory systems also are to monitor macro-prudential risks.

The new Basel III norms were accepted in the G20 Seoul 2010 meeting, and the Dodd–Frank (DF) Act (2010) passed in the US. Box 2.2 and 2.3, respectively, outline these reforms. These, together with EU initiatives, form the template for global reforms. The basic weakness of both is complexity, inadequate macro-prudential reform and insufficient attention to the shadow banking system. Complexity implies lack of universality that creates scope for cross-border arbitrage, including by SIFIs. Large areas of discretion imply a question mark over implementation. So reforms fall short of satisfying the principles above and the requirements of G20. They also do not come to grips with excess global liquidity, volatility of capital flows and uneven access of EMs to global finance.

Box 2.2: Basel III and Global Minimum Capital Standards

Basel III of the Basel Committee on Banking Supervision (BCBS) seeks to increase capital buffers, restrict leverage and cover systemic liquidity and funding risk (BIS 2010a).

The minimum common equity requirement is increased from 2 per cent of risk-weighted assets to 4.5 per cent by 1 January 2015. Tier 1 higher quality capital requirement including common equity will increase to 7 per cent by January 2018, including a capital conservation buffer of 2.5 per cent to cover future liabilities.

A macro-prudential countercyclical buffer is to be introduced as an extension of the conservation buffer. It is to come into effect during periods of systemic risk due to excess credit growth, conditional on national circumstances, within a range of 0 to 2.5 per cent of common equity or other loss absorbing capital.

Additional collateral would be required for derivative contracts if the institution's credit rating is downgraded. A proposed Liquidity Coverage Ratio (LCR) to meet liquidity risk covering all wholesale funding, off-balance sheet commitments; any short-term deposit withdrawal; a Net Stable Funding Ratio (NSFR) to cover longer term funding risks and possible haircuts by reducing short-term funding and stronger regimes for SIFIs have been further delayed and have been pushed to 2019. The proposed reforms, including dates, are still being negotiated.

A leverage ratio (3 per cent) is also imposed for the first time. It implies that 3 units of Tier I capital must be held against 100 units of the book value of assets including off-balance sheet items. So the accounting or balance sheet leverage, which is the inverse of the leverage ratio, is limited to 1/0.03 or 33.3 to 1, which was the level in Bear Sterns when it failed. Moreover, lack of clarity in the definition of assets offers potential to escape the limits.

The Basel Committee and the FSB continue to examine combinations of capital surcharges, contingent capital, bail-in debt and strengthening of resolution regimes to reduce risk in and from SIFIs.

Box 2.3: Dodd–Frank Wall Street Reform and Consumer Protection Act.

The new US law enhances consumer protection and regulation of OTC derivatives and creates a resolution authority. The focus is on reducing risk from SIFIs, increasing transparency and accountability in derivative trade, raising regulatory oversight and creating a Financial Stability Oversight Committee (FSOC) to coordinate regulators.

Since the government has been given resolution authority over SIFIs, it can also treat investment banks and bank holding companies as it would an insolvent bank, providing alternatives to sending them into bankruptcy or bailing them out. But this may only worsen the moral hazard problem.

Dodd–Frank can force firms with a tangential relationship with big banking such as mainstream swap dealers into greater transparency, information sharing, reporting and auditing. Technologies and trading solutions are available to enable regulatory ongoing compliance. Direct access from own trading platform to clearing house systems and straight-through processing remove the need to reconstruct data after the event and eliminates layers of risk by removing redundant data keying and duplication. Enhanced risk management capabilities can actually create new opportunities.

But, instead of using technology to enforce tighter regulations, the Act exempts loans, spot foreign exchange or commodities and also repurchase and reverse repurchase agreements or securities lending transactions required for liquidity management. FX swaps are exempted on the grounds the FX market works well, and settlement risk is well provided for (Kuttner, 2011). Banks can invest in hedge funds, private equity funds, treasuries, bonds of government-backed entities and municipal bonds.

This illustrates the major problem with the Act. While it enables regulators to make strict rules implementation it is too dependent on the perceptions and quality of individual regulators and political pressures. For example, dealers could use exclusions for FX swaps to structure swap transactions so as to avoid regulation, thus expanding shadow banking and creating systemic risks. The latter are the concern of macro-prudential regulation, which Dodd–Frank makes the responsibility of a 15-member FSOC, chaired by the treasury secretary, with the Fed as the most influential participant, since it houses the executive and research arms. The FSOC can, however, override the recommendations of the new independent consumer protection agency housed at the Fed. But the FSOC could get mired in turf wars among regulators making systemic regulation the weakest link in Dodd–Frank, as also in Basel III.

Without rules to initiate prompt corrective action against a troubled financial firm or set a maximum level of allowable leverage for all assets (it used to be 12 to 1 before pre-crisis legislative loopholes were created) or ensure all complex financial derivatives without exception are traded transparently, there is no warrantee that the action will be adequate.

Weaknesses in the Regulatory Response

While commentators have welcomed the changes as in the right direction, these changes have been widely criticized as being too little, too slow, too narrow and too dependent on individual country and regulatory discretion.[5] Hanson et al. (2011) argue that low Basel standards could be boosted by some type of contingent capital. This gives automatic conversion of debt into equity based on a pre-existing contract, reducing reliance on regulatory discretion. Countercyclical buffers may not be built without automatic triggers. To force banks to raise new equity and expand credit, their option to adjust through asset shrinkage may have to be closed.

Shin (2011) argues the focus should be on preventing risky behaviour rather than on the loss-absorbing or shock-insulating role of buffers. The emphasis on the liability side allows risks to be taken on the asset side. Finally, the narrow focus on banks implies arbitrage will continue to drive more financial intermediation into the shadowbanking sector. Investment banks carry out banking functions such as issuing debt, but face minimal oversight since they do not take deposits. More corporate and consumer loans could be securitized and held by highly leveraged investors, such as hedge funds, not subject to bank-oriented capital regulation. Hansen et al. (2011) suggest imposing minimum haircut requirements at the level of asset-backed securities and not only on banks. Then short-term leverage will be constrained for all investors taking a position in credit assets mitigating the shadow banking problem. A simple loan to value ratio can more effectively constrain leverage than risk-based buffers since opportunistic action affects risk.

Macro-prudential policy needs to prevent credit booms and busts. Credit cycles arise since agents tend to under price risk in an upswing and become too risk averse in a downswing. Agents also do not internalize the spillovers they create for others and for the financial network. This is why micro-prudential policy, which reduces financial imbalances in individual financial institutions, is inadequate for systemic risk.

Monetary policy may also be an inefficient tool for calming the credit cycle, if at the same time it tries to moderate the business cycle. The frequency and amplitude of business and credit cycles can be quite different.[6] Applying one instrument, the policy rate, to address multiple objectives cannot be satisfactory.

Macro-prudential policies increase the long-term cost of giving credit during booms and reduce these costs during busts. Examples of macro-prudential tools include pro-cyclical regulatory ratios such as capital adequacy requirements that are raised over a cycle when there is above-average growth of credit expansion and leverage, and wherever there is mismatch in the maturity of assets and liabilities. Thus institutions borrowing short and lending long would need higher capital reserves. Time-varying margins or haircuts could be applied on certain financial transactions between banks and shadow banks or hedge funds. Countercyclical surcharges on liquidity requirements would lean against the collective under-pricing of liquidity risk during credit booms. Market-to-market procedures that enhance pro-cyclicality also need to be changed. Remuneration packages could be linked to long-term performance. Simple loan-to-value ratios can effectively decrease leverage while reducing the element of discretion in judging a cycle (BOE, 2009; Goyal, 2010a).

High leverage, which is extremely susceptible to a fall in asset values, was a consequence of light pre-crisis regulation. Investment banks borrowed short in wholesale retail markets, leveraged the borrowing many times and lent long. Leverage in Bear Sterns, when it failed, was 33: 1, compared to 15:1 for a commercial bank.

Since deposit-taking banks are no longer the only financial intermediaries, their deposit liabilities (equivalent to broad money) underestimate the size of leveraged balance sheets, which now must include those of the shadow banking sector. Even for banks mainly funded by deposits, banks' liabilities to foreign creditors are not counted as money, but they expand balance sheets (Shin and Shin, 2010).

In the US especially, securitization and capital markets dominate traditional banking. After the 1980s, the money stock is unable to explain much of US macroeconomic fluctuations since excess liquidity no longer corresponds to excessive growth of the money stock. Deposits are now not the most volatile component of aggregate financial liabilities. In such a world, money is a less useful basis on which macro-prudential policy can be designed.

Since credit spillovers occur not only across banks but also across borders, macro-prudential policies require international regulatory cooperation and information sharing to reduce credit externalities. Countercyclical regulatory policy needs to be implemented mainly by the 'host' rather than the 'home' country, since cycles differ across countries. Regulatory discretion in synchronizing cycles with macro-prudential regulations requires strong national accountability to ensure that the regulations are implemented.

Actions in G20 Countries

How do positions on financial regulation in the G20 countries themselves compare with general principles of intervention against market failure?[7] Have the weaknesses identified affected paths of regulatory reform? We start with the AEs and then consider the EMs in G20. The first set consists of Australia, Canada, France, Germany, Italy, Japan, United Kingdom, United States and European Union and the second includes Argentina, Brazil, China, India, Indonesia, Mexico, Russia, Saudi Arabia, South Africa, South Korea and Turkey.

Smaller countries are largely following the G20 guidelines: regulating CRAs and hedge funds, converging to Basel III and international accounting standards, introducing reporting for OTC derivatives, skin in the game, resolution regimes and some kind of consumer protection and issuing guidelines on a sound remuneration system, which reflects the FSB principles. That is, remuneration should not create incentives for inappropriate and excessive risk-taking.

Advanced Economies

The DF Act exemplifies the US stance (Box 2.3). The EU has more emphasis on rules while the US has left more to regulatory discretion.[8] The US is stronger in moves for consumer protection. It is more ready to allow failure of big banks than Europe for which banks are national champions. Since EU banks have more than a quarter of assets abroad, more cross-border regulation is required there. Cross-border issues dominate SIFI issues (Goldstein and Veron 2011; Bertelsmann Foundation, 2010).

Exemptions vitiate the ban on proprietary trading by deposit-taking banks the Volcker rule seeks. A 2011 UK Independent Commission on Banking proposed stronger ring fencing of retail banking, prohibiting trading book activities. But financial activities required to fulfil treasury functions are still exempt. In the EU, the 2012 Liikanen Report proposed milder ring fencing, without full separation of investment and retail banking, in order to support the European universal banking model. Proprietary trading (with some exceptions to allow client servicing within narrow position risk limits) was to be hived off to a legally separate unit in the same bank holding company.

Europe wants to further soften these proposals so that banks do not have to separate key market-making business. France and Germany are also trying to dilute Basel III capital requirements and fighting for other delays to win respite for troubled European banks in need of recapitalization. Italian banks, for example, have given their end-2010 capital position and need about a 40 billion Euro boost for Basel III compliance. In Australia, high-quality liquid assets may fall short of meeting Basel III requirements.

The outflow calculations determining the LCR and the quality of liquid assets banks have to carry were moderated in 2013, and the implementation date was further postponed. Apart from government bonds and top quality corporate bonds even equities, lower quality BBB corporate bonds and discounted top quality mortgage-backed securities are now allowed in liquidity buffers. This has steeply reduced banks' liquidity shortfall. The collateral requirement for OTC derivatives has also been softened.[9]

In other respects EU wants stricter regulation. In 2013, as part of its ongoing Capital Requirements Directives (CRD4) the European parliament sought to limit bank bonuses to one time the base salary. Shareholder approval would be required for bonuses to increase to two times the base salary. This comes on top of earlier initiatives that reduced bonus pools and linked individual awards to longer term outcomes, by using bail-in bonds or equity subject to clawbacks. There will also be centralized regulation of banks with assets greater than $200 billion, as part of strengthening the Eurozone.

Belgium, Germany, Estonia, Greece, Spain, France, Italy, Austria, Portugal, Slovenia and Slovakia agreed to levy a financial transaction tax of 0.1 per cent on stock and bond trades and 0.01 per cent on derivatives transactions. The tax would apply to financial institutions with headquarters in the tax area or who trade on behalf of a client in the tax area or for an instrument issued in the tax area but traded anywhere in the world. There are exemptions for the trades of central banks (CBs) and pension funds. The move is strongly resisted by the US and UK business groups who fear double taxation. There are attempts to dilute it towards the UK system of electronic stamp duties on equity that has worked well.

Like the US, most countries have set up some kind of coordination committees across regulators that are responsible for macro-prudential policy. Since the CB has more knowledge of the macro and credit cycle, it typically has a dominant role in the committee. In the UK the CB is to have a financial-policy committee, charged with identifying threats to the financial system, in addition to its monetary policy committee. In EU countries, supervisory responsibilities of the French and German CBs have been increased. A new Council for Financial Regulation and Systemic Risk has been set up to advice the French government on systemic risk. Europe has a new European Systemic Risk Board (ESRB) made up of national regulators and central bankers.

Regulators will have to share much more information, for example on financial interconnections and maturity mismatch of banks' assets and liabilities. The European Central Bank (ECB) will have to rely on national regulators for information, and the latter can ignore its advice. American bank supervisors will have to change their philosophy and way of working. Creating coordination boards is not the same as making them effective. They may only further delay response.

Although the Canadian system is also based on principles rather than specific rules, a hard-to-arbitrage asset-to-capital ratio helped prevent gaming of the system. Proprietary trading did not create a financial problem. Even so, quantitative aspects that in some respects are more stringent than Basel III are being phased in. The gross leverage ratio limit and loan-to-value (LTV) restrictions for residential mortgages are examples of effective macro-prudential regulation. Such broad-pattern regulation may be the way forward to compensate for the discretion, re-negotiation and delays in capital adequacy.

Emerging Markets

Turning to EMs, Brazilian banks already hold 11 per cent of combined Tier 1 and Tier 2 capital, above the level required by Basel III – so big changes may not be needed. Conservative prudential regulations, such as liquidity buffers from high reserve requirements and effective supervision for banks and markets mitigate risks. Unlike US-UK, the OTC market comprises only 20 per cent of derivatives trades. Standardized contracts are traded on the Brazilian exchange, BM&Fbovespa, and all OTC derivatives transactions involving financial institutions are mandatorily registered at a central registry. This is now the goal for advanced markets. Regulators have full access to information. CRAs are not currently regulated in Brazil but a stocktaking exercise is going on.

Similarly, in China OTC foreign exchange derivatives and some OTC RMB interest rate derivatives are traded on an electronic platform, and those interest rate derivatives not so traded are reported to authorities. In India also derivative markets are tightly regulated. There are various restrictions on futures traded on exchanges. In any OTC derivative contract, one party to the contract must be an RBI-regulated entity. A Central Counterparty Clearing (CCP) ensures good reporting, clearing and settlement. OTC derivatives positions have to be based on real exposures. Both countries are making progress on converging to international regulatory standards on transparency and governance.

Over the years, Indian banks have improved structurally. High growth and legal reform that made debt recovery easier led to non-performing assets falling to historic lows, notwithstanding some reversal after the GFC. Most of the banks follow a retail business model and their dependence on short-term or overnight wholesale funding is limited, reducing market risk. Banks have sufficient liquid assets to be able to meet the new standards. But as an EM with low credit ratios India can expect to see these rise with growth.[10] Because of skill and data gaps that limited the use of risk-based regulations, the move away from microeconomic controls during liberalizing reforms took the form of broad-pattern regulation such as caps on credit to some sectors, position limits and limits on exposure to different types of risk. This turned out to have good incentive properties compared to Basel II. There is a case, therefore, for using these as a partial substitute for capital buffers.

Loan to value and provisioning ratios are countercyclical. For example, a provisioning coverage ratio for banks of 70 per cent of gross non-performing assets augments provisioning buffers in good times. Changing sectoral provisioning requirements was more effective than varying risk weights, since they directly impact the profit-and-loss account of banks. With the latter there was scope for arbitrage, for example, if average capital adequacy ratios were above the minimum.

Commercial banks' statutory liquidity ratios (SLR) that force them to hold government debt are still high. The RBI is of the view that these should not be counted as leverage in calculating commercial banks' leverage ratio. They also contribute to liquidity, since the RBI can only provide liquidity against such acceptable collateral. But the BCBS regards the SLR as a statutory requirement that cannot be reduced. But asking Indian banks to maintain liquid assets over and above on already high SLR would reduce their competitiveness (Goyal, 2014).

India and Indonesia set up a Financial Stability and Development Council chaired by the Finance Ministers. A Financial Sector Legislative Reform Commission established to clean up and modernize Indian financial legislation has also submitted its report.

Russia's financial market is not well developed but it aims to improve regulation while giving financial market participants a favourable tax climate. Argentina's financial system is in bad shape. The financial sector operates on market-based risk assessment but there are severe legal, regulatory and government failings. The country fails to comply with most international standards for combating money laundering and terror financing.

Mexico already complies with most of the capital adequacy requirements, and new Basel standards will be reached within the agreed timeframe. New initiatives include a Securities Market Law, mechanisms for early detection of potential imbalances, a revised Corporate Governance Code and Payment Systems, measures to increase access to banking services and a Financial System Stability Board.

Korea has planned to standardize OTC derivatives, establish a CCP clearing house and introduce consumer financial protection. Both Korea and Indonesia are reintroducing prudential capital controls. The average leverage ratio of larger domestic banks at 4.6 per cent far exceeds the 3 per cent minimum leverage ratio, but the Korean Financial Supervisory Service will put more restrictions to reduce leverage through derivatives and increase long-term funding. Indonesia plans to intensify and expedite financial inclusion initiatives.

South Africa follows, internationally, the best practice in financial regulation and is introducing a consumer protection act. The current leverage ratio is far more conservative than the proposed change, but compliance with new global liquidity standards requires structural changes to give banks access to more long-term financing such as by allowing pension funds to buy long dated bank debt.

In Saudi Arabia, common equity and retained earnings dominate banks' capital, and they are far above Basel III requirements. Liquidity ratios and loan/deposit ratio ceilings are conservative. Counter-cyclical buffers are to be applied to banks. There is no SIFI bank.

Comparing EMs to AEs

The same post East Asian crisis pattern seems to be emerging now. In some respects EMs are actually closer to international standards and keener to follow them. The advanced financial centres are the ones seeking special treatment, as they continue to struggle with the fallout of their past practices. This is against the dominant perception that there are two kinds of financial systems: modern transparent and efficient in AEs and relationship-based crony capitalism in EMs. It is true that EM banks are distant from mature markets in terms of scale (Tables 2.2 and 2.3), so financial deepening and inclusion remain a priority for them. The tables show Indian banks to be taking on more international positions.

Table 2.2: International Positions by Nationality of Ownership of Reporting Banks. Amounts Outstanding (USD billion)

End-September 2010		
Total positions		
Parent country of bank	Assets	Liabilities
AEs		
Australia	421	751.3
Canada	885	749.3
France	4,443.80	4,233.70
Germany	4,552.80	3,598.40
Italy	1,025.70	1,046.70
Japan	3,637.70	2,039.80
UK	4,570.20	4,492.00
US	4,043.20	4,570.30
EMs		
Argentina	NA	NA
Brazil	202.3	223.8
Chinese Taipei	258.5	275.9
India	142.1	168.5
Indonesia	NA	NA
Mexico	44.8	45
Russia	NA	NA
Saudi Arabia		NA
South Africa	78.6	78.3
South Korea	222.2	225.1
Turkey	163.4	196.5

Source: Table 8A from http://www.bis.org/publ/qtrpdf/r_qa1103.pdf#page=7, accessed in January 2011.

Table 2.3: Banks: Exposures and Claims (USD billion)

	Consolidated foreign claims and other exposures of reporting banks-ultimate risk basis On individual countries by sector and type					Consolidated claims of reporting banks – immediate borrower basis On individual countries by maturity and sector			
	Consolidated crossborder and local claims in all currencies		Other exposures (not included in foreign claims)			Consolidated cross-border claims in all currencies and local claims in non-local currencies			
	Total Foreign claims	Of which cross border claims	Derivatives contracts	Guarantees extended	Credit commitments	Total foreign claims on a contractual basis	Total international claims	Maturities up to and including one year	Total foreign claims on an ultimate risk basis
AEs									
Australia	543.6	263.8	83.9	130.2	86.1	635.5	354.7	129.5	621.9
Canada	427.0	212.0	83.1	88.4	64.4	574.7	367.4	219.7	589.6
France	1271.0	1076.0	402.0	453.1	206.0	1848.1	1669.8	1044.8	2009.4
Germany	1819.7	1180.5	601.7	446.1	214.3	2131.2	1507.3	748.2	2399.4
Italy	990.7	532.8	141.0	270.5	82.0	1242.3	770.3	267.0	1253.3
Japan	875.7	341.5	140.1	208.0	76.7	1135.3	673.1	547.0	1173.2
UK	3068.9	1338.7	991.7	1584.9	581.2	3716.5	2553.9	1692.6	3705.5
US	5292.4	2455.8	1145.2	720.7	961.4	5505.9	2667.9	927.6	5613.0
EMs									
Argentina	33.6	10.6	0.1	20.8	4.8	37.9	19.1	10.5	36.7
Brazil	468.6	182.0	12.0	65.0	94.8	477.7	195.5	99.1	500.2
China	320.8	188.8	15.3	43.5	24.6	421.7	321.5	238.9	421.4
India	258.2	155.9	13.4	31.3	18.1	287.9	191.7	110.6	298.2
Indonesia	71.9	41.4	1.9	16.9	12.8	97.3	69.2	41.7	73.9
Mexico	331.4	68.4	26.0	49.8	79.3	344.4	94.2	32.4	333.9

Consolidated foreign claims and other exposures of reporting banks-ultimate risk basis On individual countries by sector and type					Consolidated claims of reporting banks – immediate borrower basis On individual countries by maturity and sector			
Consolidated crossborder and local claims in all currencies		Other exposures (not included in foreign claims)			Consolidated cross-border claims in all currencies and local claims in non-local currencies			
Total Foreign claims	Of which cross border claims	Derivatives contracts	Guarantees extended	Credit commitments	Total foreign claims on a contractual basis	Total international claims	Maturities up to and including one year	Total foreign claims on an ultimate risk basis
EMs								
Russia	172.4	97.3	4.8	89.3	17.5	192.1	138.0	59.5	182.3
Saudi Arabia	47.7	45.2	5.0	11.4	8.0	52.7	48.6	32.6	51.3
South Africa	124.6	30.7	11.3	23.3	14.3	128.9	34.9	15.0	127.9
South Korea	336.7	159.5	21.3	68.3	24.7	368.7	224.5	143.3	362.9
Turkey	144.1	72.2	4.9	83.4	21.2	173.1	111.4	55.5	164.3

Source: Table 9A and 9C from http://www.bis.org/publ/qtrpdf/r_qa1103.pdf#page=7, accessed in January 2011.

Goldstein and Veron (2011) argue that since Asian financial centres are developing, hegemonic voices are absent making it difficult to reach agreement on regulation. But this is overstated since EMs are willing to change their regulations towards those of AEs but the latter need to show more movement towards some of the practices EMs are already following. These were regarded as conservative, but may now show the way to a stable future.

Market-based standards such as Basel II increased risk taking instead of containing leverage. Robust global standards, which investment banks need most, should draw on the experience of different regions. Such standards can be consistent with financial development and the space to adjust to local issues, as more insular aspects of domestic financial sectors vary across countries.

The highly bank-based regulatory stance of the BCBS is a problem for EMs since their financial systems are bank dominated, may already have strong regulation and taxes yet have to reach scale. Moreover, the shadow banking system that plays a large part in volatile flows to the region escapes regulation. Ideally, the regulator package should be redesigned and lightened for banks, yet be spread more widely to also cover shadow banks.

Regarding macro-prudential regulation EMs seem to have more specific countercyclical rules in place compared to AEs, which rely on coordination and regulatory discretion. China, India and Korea all have countercyclical capital adequacy rules. Argentina has a cap on loan-to-deposit ratios. AE banks need more time compared to EM banks to meet Basel III capital requirements. Moreover, cross border flows create problems for EMs, which are examined in the next section.

EM Concerns: Global Liquidity and Cross Border Flows

Figures 2.1 and 2.2 show the highest volatility in private capital flows to EMs came from interbank flows. Tables 2.2 and 2.3 and Figures 2.3 and 2.4 show international positions by nationality of banks and by their location in countries. On all counts the US and the UK banks are the largest. Therefore, these countries, and their banks, are the source of the largest and the most volatile cross border flows to EMs.

Figure 2.1: Capital Flows, Reserves, Debt

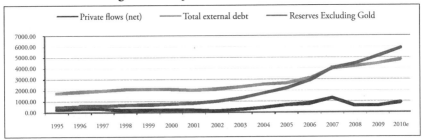

Figure 2.2: Volatile Constituents of Capital Flows

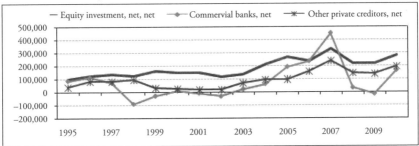

Figure 2.3a: External Positions of Reporting Banks in Developed Countries: Assets (Total 13516.2 USD billion)

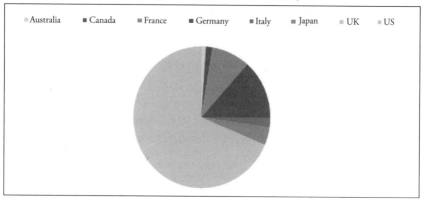

Figure 2.3b: External Positions of Reporting Banks in Developed Countries: Liabilities (Total 12261.5 USD billion)

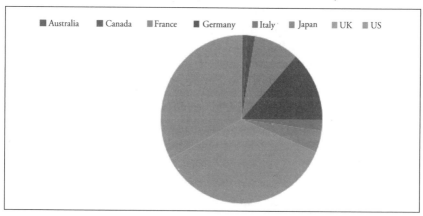

Figure 2.4a: External Positions of Reporting Banks in Emerging Markets- Assets (Total 2778.91 USD billion)

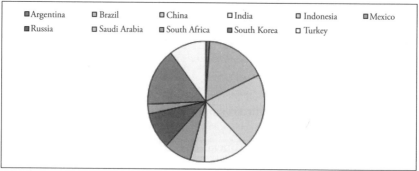

Figure 2.4b: External Positions of Reporting Banks in Emerging
Markets – Liabilities (Total 2151.18 USD billion)

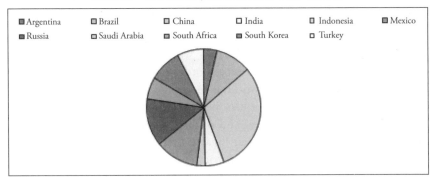

Multinational banks either borrow cross border in various financial centres (Swiss and US banks) or source extensive local funding abroad (Canadian and Spanish banks have expanded in Latin America and in the United Kingdom). In a decentralized funding model intra group funding has a low share and the role of the central treasury in allocating and distributing funds is limited. Local assets are largely funded locally. Among the G7, Spanish banks are the most decentralized, followed by Italian, Australian and UK banks. Swiss and US banks also tap funds in multiple locations but might use those deposits in cross border intra group funding, as do German and Canadian banks. Japanese and, to a lesser extent, French and German banks fund most of their foreign activity from their home offices, given a large domestic deposit base (BIS 2010b).

Although the foreign exchange market infrastructure was resilient during the crisis, cross-currency maturity mismatches created problems. For example, European banks typically held long-dated less liquid US dollar-denominated assets funded by short-dated USD borrowing and FX swaps.[11] The US dollar as the reserve currency is the funding currency for global banks. Around 160 foreign banks raise about one trillion dollars of wholesale dollar funding in US capital markets to send 600 billion dollars to head office. These interoffice assets of foreign bank branches in the US increased steeply since the 1990s (Shin, 2011).

During the GFC, intra group positions and local claims and liabilities in local currencies dropped less sharply than cross-border claims – local funding was more resilient. Decentralized banks were less exposed to disruptions in international wholesale funding and swap markets. EM banks were more resilient. Their local currency operations are based more on retail and corporate lending on the asset side, funded by deposits on the liability side. But even with traditional banking, if capital accounts are open, US liquidity creation affects balance sheets through portfolio flows, foreign liabilities of the banking sector and other types of dollar carry trade.

So, while BIS (2010b) thinks banks will increase local funding Shin and Shin (2010) disagree. When cross-border flows are profitable they will happen. They document the working of the dollar carry trade in Korea. Foreign bank branches sold dollars borrowed from headquarters to buy Korean Won on the spot market and simultaneously bought dollars in the forward market. Before the FX swap created matured, the foreign banks held Won-denominated fixed income instruments, thus lending at the higher Korean interest rate.

Local banks held claims on Korean firms, arising from the hedging of long-term dollar receivables by shipbuilders. They borrowed short in dollars for maturity transformation of the long-term dollar assets. This maturity mismatch, even without a currency mismatch, led to sharp depreciations of the Won in 2008 and 2010. Assets were not usable to meet maturing dollar liabilities.

US monetary policy is the second reason as to why cross currency funding can be expected to persist. Although the US is the largest net debtor it is a substantial net creditor for the global banking system. Its borrowing is long, as central banks invest in treasury securities, but lending is short through commercial banks. This lending facilitates cross-border spillovers in US monetary policy, making the latter global monetary policy. Portfolio decisions of the global banks that equalize returns across regions carry dollar liquidity across borders. Under asymmetric exit, low US interest rates encourage an active dollar carry trade. European banks that financed purchases of longer-term mortgage-backed securities through short-term wholesale market borrowing were in trouble as wholesale markets froze after the Lehman crash.

Dollar funding flows to EMs show up as banking sector capital flows in the balance of payment accounts. Disaggregated capital inflows to EMs from the Institute of International Finance (IIF) that are shown in Figures 2.1 and 2.2 show these banking sector flows to be the most volatile, displaying pro-cyclical booms and deleveraging surges.

Shin (2011) defines non-core liabilities of the banking sector as non-deposit liabilities and shows these peaked in Korea before the financial crises in 1997 and in 2008. The rapid build-up in foreign currency liabilities and debt security liabilities of Korean banks from 2003 to 2007 were the mirror image of rising foreign banks net interoffice accounts in the US.

A New York branch fundraising wholesale dollars from money market mutual funds and sending the funds to the home office overseas, issuing a mix of time deposits of various maturities in lieu of short-term claims on the home office, would violate intra group exposure limits and liquidity standards such as LCR and NSFR of the BCBS if they were applied on a standalone basis without recourse to intra group funding. Pure fundraising would then become unviable. Global banks would have to decentralize liquidity management also if local regulators impose requirements exceeding the global standard, such as a strict form of self-sufficiency restricting intra group transfers. Limiting intra group transfers could increase liquidity costs and trap liquidity pools within financial groups (BIS 2010b). But these norms are to kick in with some delay and may not be applied uniformly due to renegotiation. If the proposed Basel III liquidity norms cannot reduce cross-border flows, an alternative would be a prudential tax that reduces pro-cyclical expansion of banks' non-core liabilities (Shin, 2011).

Moreover, the share of portfolio flows in capital flows may increase, as financial markets partially substitute for banks' internal markets and cross-border lending. Macro-prudential levies that apply at the level of financial transactions can reduce such arbitrage – for example, a financial transaction tax to reduce carry trade through portfolio flows.

The US and the UK continue to be the largest in components of international debt (Table 2.4), but since OTC dominates in these mature markets, Asia has a high share in derivatives traded in exchanges (Table 2.6). India is third among EMs in corporate issuance of international debt securities and third also in short-term debt securities (those with residual maturity of one year; see Table 2.5) and in domestic debt of governments. US issuance of debt securities exceeds that of every other country by a large multiple. It only yields first place to Japan for domestic debt securities of governments (Table 2.5). Regulations have to be designed to cover the many dimensions of financial markets in order to prevent arbitrage. Indian banks and corporates are exposed to international risks, and the Asia-Pacific region has seen a risky growth of derivative trade, which should be somewhat moderated for more balanced financial development.

Table 2.4: International Debt (USD billion)

International debt securities by nationality of issuer			International money market instruments – all issuers By residence of issuer	International debt securities – all issuers By residence of issuer
	Corporate issuers	Govern ments		
	Amounts outstanding	Amounts outstanding	Amounts outstanding	Amounts outstanding
	Dec-10	Dec-10	Dec-10	Dec-10
AEs (Total)	**3214.3**	**1818.4**	**869.0**	**24078.0**
Of which % of each country:				
Australia	0.9	1.0	5.5	2.4
Canada	5.3	6.5	0.1	2.7
France	13.0	3.4	10.0	7.9
Germany	3.9	16.6	11.3	8.5
Italy	3.3	13.9	0.0	4.7
Japan	1.7	0.2	0.2	0.8
UK	9.1	5.3	21.4	15.2
US	50.3	0.6	11.0	27.4
EMs (Total)	**309.4**	**565.5**	**6.2**	**1148.5**
Of which % of each country:				
Argentina	1.1	8.4	1.6	4.9
Brazil	8.9	9.2	29.0	10.2
China	3.0	1.0		2.1
India	9.7		0.0	2.5
Indonesia	1.0	3.2		2.0
Mexico	12.4	8.0	0.0	8.1
Russia	8.5	5.4		5.7
Saudi Arabia	NA	NA	NA	NA
South Africa	2.8	1.8	–	2.4
South Korea	13.2	1.3	66.1	11.9
Turkey	0.2	7.9		4.2

Source: Calculated from Tables 11, 12C and 14A from http://www.bis.org/publ/qtrpdf/r_qa1103.pdf#page=7, accessed in January 2011

Table 2.5: Domestic and Short-term International Debt (USD billion)

Domestic debt securities by sector and residence of issuer			International debt securities. With remaining maturity up to one year
Financial institutions	Corporate issuers	Governments	All issuers
Amounts outstanding	Amounts outstanding	Amounts outstanding	Amounts outstanding by sector and residence of issuer
Sep-10	Sep-10	Sep-10	
AEs			
Australia 616.1	41.0	310.4	127.6
Canada 261.5	156.3	970.7	78.2
France 1207.7	295.3	1,695.50	302.0
Germany 784.7	349.0	1,555.50	428.5
Italy 730.5	376.2	1,974.80	109.0
Japan 1206.4	855.9	11,212.80	28.1
UK 321.9	21.3	1,343.80	522.3
US 11523.9	2888.3	10,746.10	979.4
EMs			
Argentina 3.1	6.4	48.9	
Brazil 461.7	10.0	821.9	7.0
China 859.0	493.1	1,616.90	3.9
India 75.1	24.9	606.8	6.0
Indonesia 4.7	5.5	97.2	–
Mexico 140.8	33.3	239.4	5.0
Russia NA	NA	NA	NA
Saudi Arabia NA	NA	NA	NA
South Africa 34.0	25.3	107.6	0.5
South Korea 271.9	366.1	480.6	23.5
Turkey –	–	238.6	2.0

Source: Tables 16B and 17B from http://www.bis.org/publ/qtrpdf/r_qa1103.pdf#page=7, accessed in January 2011

Table 2.6: Derivative Financial Instruments Traded on Organized Exchanges. By Instrument and Location. Number of Contracts in Millions

	Contracts outstanding	Turnover	Contracts outstanding	Turnover
	Dec-10	2010	Dec-10	2010
	Futures		Options	
All markets	**85.2**	**6346.7**	**139.0**	**5812.2**
Interest rate	63.3	2546.1	62.1	653.0
Currency	5.3	1406.3	2.9	56.4
Equity index	16.7	2394.3	74.0	5102.7
North America	**43.5**	**2160.9**	**39.3**	**627.6**
Interest rate	36.5	1177.9	19.3	269.1
Currency	1.3	234.8	0.6	12.0
Equity index	5.7	748.2	19.4	346.6
Europe	**17.1**	**1988.4**	**62.4**	**720.4**
Interest rate	9.0	931.3	16.9	256.0
Currency	1.5	145.6	0.1	1.6
Equity index	6.6	911.5	45.4	462.7
Asia and Pacific	**6.2**	**1641.2**	**8.2**	**4226.3**
Interest rate	3.0	119.2	0.0	5.0
Currency	1.0	913.0	0.3	6.2
Equity index	2.2	609.0	7.8	4215.1
Other Markets	**18.4**	**556.2**	**29.1**	**237.8**
Interest rate	14.8	317.8	25.9	122.8
Currency	1.5	112.8	1.8	36.7
Equity index	2.1	125.6	1.4	78.4
Memorandum items				
Commodity contracts	40.7	2675.4	22.1	154.8
US markets	30.4	663.9	20.5	137.0
Other markets	10.3	2011.5	1.7	17.7

Source: Table 23B from http://www.bis.org/publ/qtrpdf/r_qa1103.pdf#page=7, accessed in January 2011.

One consequence of volatile cross-border flows is high foreign exchange reserves. The relationship between the two is explored in the next section.

Reserves and Global Imbalances

Arguments on crisis causality

There is a school of thought that blames high saving Asian economies and the reserve they accumulated and placed in US treasuries as the fundamental cause of the crisis. It is said to have triggered risky innovation to satisfy demand for high-rated assets. Bernanke (2005) pointed to this 'savings glut' as the reason for low long interest rates, even after policy began raising short rates. But he (Bernanke *et al.* 2011) admitted that financial innovation-driven cross border flows from Europe were exceptionally large. It was not only Asian central banks (CBs) that were investing in the US. CB investments were more stable. Even so, the cause of the crisis was not so much the inflows as the inability of the US financial sector to handle them because of poor regulation. Others have argued that world savings had actually fallen during this period; finance-fuelled consumption booms and asset bubbles caused the inflows (Liabson and Mollerstrom, 2010). It is the financial sector that must be set right to mitigate such future risks.

Exchange rate adjustment alone will also not resolve reserve imbalances. EMs need to manage their exchange rates. They cannot have full floats since their narrow markets would otherwise be subject to excess volatility aggravated by capital movements. Moreover, the real exchange rate has to be relatively depreciated to the extent the average real wage is lower in an EM. Countries with large current account surpluses do need some revaluation, but only moral suasion is possible now. After the US abrogated the Bretton Woods agreement on fixed exchange rates in the 1970s, countries became free to follow what exchange rate regime they choose; there was no enforceable agreement with the IMF.

Reasons for rising reserves

High reserve accumulation seen after the 1990s has been ascribed to either mercantilist motives of preventing exchange rate appreciation or to the precautionary motive, especially in EMs after the East Asian crisis.

The discussion is dominated by China, which has almost 3 trillion dollars of reserves and a large current account surplus so the exchange rate may be undervalued. But it is not true that all countries with rising reserves have a current account surplus. Among the G20 countries with rising reserves and a deficit are South Africa, Mexico, Israel, India and Brazil. Therefore, the mercantilist motive is ruled out for these countries.

But the precautionary motive is also in trouble. The countries whose reserves were based on inflows did not use the reserves during months of the global financial crisis when outflows were large, preferring to depreciate exchange rates instead (Aizenman, 2009). There is a tendency to add to reserves but not to let them fall, suggesting a hoarding motive.

Annual data for the G20 clearly show that except for US, UK, Euro Area, Chile and Argentina, reserves have tended to increase steadily since the 1990s, which was the period of large inflows (Figure 2.5). The figures show countries in the 0-50 USD billion range of reserves to be Chile, Argentina, Canada and South Africa. Those in the 0-200 range were Thailand, Turkey, Mexico, Israel and Indonesia. India, Brazil, Korea and Hong Kong were in the 0–300 range and Russia, Saudi Arabia and Japan in the 0–1200 range.

Figure 2.5: Rising Thresholds, in FX reserves

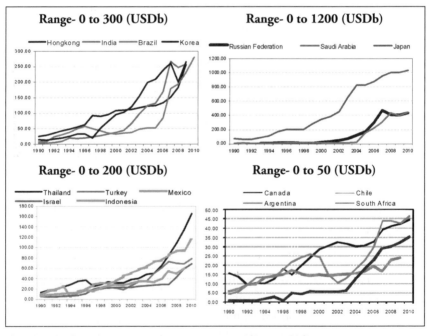

The data also suggest that reserves show a rising threshold except for countries in an inner financial circle.[12] The explanation may therefore lie in the nature of financial integration combined with rising capital flows.

Countries without reliable access to crisis liquidity may fear market interpretations of a fall in reserves, which may set off a downward spiral. Rating agencies give too much weight to measurable aspects, so they tend to downgrade a country whose reserves fall.[13] If reserves are regarded as a signal of strength, they cannot be allowed to fall.[14] Their precautionary use is limited then only to the signal. There are other psychological pressures such as bettering one's own past record and keeping up with the Jones's (namely China).

Policy alternatives to reduce reserves

Reserves are an expensive form of self-insurance and although they may not be able to sustain an undervaluation of the currency in terms of fundamentals, they do tend to reduce nominal appreciation.[15] Therefore, capital-account management policies that reduce short-term inflows are a substitute for costly reserve accumulation.

Such policies may even be necessary to reduce short-term liabilities that may otherwise expand due to the complacency created by reserves. This happened to Korea. From 2004 to 2008 the Korean external short-term debt/GDP ratio increased from 7.5 per cent to 20 per cent, while the overall external debt/GDP increased from 23 per cent to 50 per cent, without significant change in the high reserves/GDP ratio. During the first stage of the 2008-global liquidity crisis, short-term dollar funding dried up; Korea's reserves of more than 200 billion USD declined by about 25 per cent. But markets calmed only after a swap agreement with the Fed. The Chang Mai swap initiative also proved inadequate because of the link of larger loans to borrowing from the IMF, which was not politically acceptable. In this period the expansion of non-deposit liabilities of foreign banks formed 60 per cent of the short-term liabilities of all Korean banks. The dollar carry trade, which resumed as US interest rates fell and the Fed pumped in liquidity, also created instability in the Won during 2010.

Aizenman (2009) argues bank intermediation facilitated by short-term external borrowing in hard currency exposes the economy to balance sheet vulnerabilities. Such a crisis induces fire-sale effects – costly premature liquidation of tangible investments. If foreign currency reserves are limited, the deleveraging pressure bids up the price of foreign currency, requiring each bank to liquidate more of its investment. Because of competitive financial intermediation each bank overlooks the impact of its deleveraging on the liquidation costs of all the other banks. These macro fire-sale externalities reduce the marginal social benefit of borrowing below the private benefit and increase the marginal social benefit of hoarding reserves above the private one. External borrowing creates an externality in the shape of a potential deleveraging crisis. A Pigovian tax-cum-subsidy scheme reduces the private benefit from borrowing, forcing borrowers to internalize the externality they create. In effect, these borrowers then are made to co-finance the precautionary hoarding of reserves. They show that optimal external borrowing and reserves require two policy instruments – an external borrowing tax and a subsidy in the form of FX reserves. If fiscal revenue from the borrowing tax exceeds the cost of funding the reserves, the tax would fund the subsidy. Any type of tax on inflows implicitly subsidizes the costs of reserves held, funding the accumulation of reserves by the activities that create the need to self-insure by these reserves.

All other available alternatives have some inadequacies. For example, swap lines are giver-and not user-driven, typically of short duration and are limited by moral hazard considerations. Mutual vulnerabilities and interests may be a precondition for their availability. Credible changes in IMF governance are required for its support to become acceptable in East Asia after the crisis experience. Sequenced capital account liberalization as in India, with equity before debt, does force foreign capital to share risk but the controls have costs and restrict the functioning of markets.

To the extent surges in capital flows do not reflect local fundamentals but are based on leveraging and deleveraging cycles, letting the currency appreciate in response to inflows may create further distortions. Shin (2011) argues that macro-prudential policy is required to reduce the build-up of non-core banking sector liabilities and therefore reduce vulnerabilities to sudden stops. A levy on the foreign exchange denominated liabilities of the banking sector, with a higher rate applying to short-term liabilities, would work as an automatic stabilizer, since the base of the levy is larger during booms. This overcomes delays from political impediments under discretionary policy. It does not disturb the core intermediation function of the banking while reducing pro-cyclical liabilities that were major drivers of the GFC. The levy would also function as a market-friendly type of capital control, reducing the need for quantitative controls and for reserve accumulation. Reserve imbalances due to volatile inflows would reduce. Any effect it might have on exchange rates and trade imbalances is additional to its financial stability role.

Tax-based reversals of capital account convertibility: Post GFC there is a reversal of capital account convertibility in many EMs aimed at reducing short-term inflows given global excess liquidity.[16] Brazil imposed a 2 per cent tax on foreign inflows. Indonesia is lengthening its debt maturity and imposing limits on banks' net FX open positions. Prudential measures include implementation of a minimum one-month holding period for CB certificates of all maturities, and introduction of a non-securities monetary instrument in the form of term deposits.

Korea has imposed restrictions on the use of banks' foreign currency loans, and FX derivatives are limited to 0.5 capital base for local and 2.5 for foreign banks. The government is considering various measures from a 'Tobin' tax on foreign exchange transactions, a tax on capital flows, further limits on derivative positions and, most controversially, the reintroduction of a 14 per cent withholding tax on foreign bondholders' earnings. It is to impose a bank tax on foreign currency wholesale funding by maturity, with a maximum cap of 50 basis points – 20 basis points for less than one year, 10 basis points for 1–3 years maturity and 5 basis points for longer than three years.

Wider Effects of Taxes

The above sections show taxes can substitute to some extent for capital adequacy; macro-prudential delays; can create incentives that encourage countercyclical behaviour; reduce ill effects of QE; design market-based capital controls; reduce inflow volatility and share the cost of holding reserves.

Taxes are automatically countercyclical since the tax base expands in good times and they can be designed to fall more on highly leveraged activities, thus providing good forward-looking incentives (IMF, 2010). Non-standard tax treatment across assets must, however, be carefully thought through. Its mobility made finance under taxed (Table 2.7), but new technology is changing that. Disinterested estimates of the effect of such taxes on borrowing cost are quite low. Table 2.8 shows financial taxes applied in select G20 countries.

Table 2.7: Corporate Income Tax (CIT) Paid by the Financial Sector (%)

	Period	Share of corporate taxes	Share of total tax revenue
Italy (max)	2006–2008	26.3	1.7
Argentina (min)	2006–2008	6.0	1.0
Unweighted Average		17.5	2.3
Note: Italy had the maximum share of corporate taxes paid by the financial sector and Argentina the minimum.			

Source: IMF. 2010. IMF Staff estimates based on G20 survey.

Table 2.8: Special Financial Sector Taxes Levied/Planned in G20 Countries

AEs	
Australia	Australia had a bank debit tax for cash withdrawals between 1982 and 2002–05, but is now concerned about the competitiveness of its domestic institutions with foreign entrants. No bank levies anticipated.
European Union	Provisional plans envisage ex-ante fund for orderly wind-downs funded by levy on banks and built on harmonized system of national funds.
France	Temporary tax of 50 per cent on excess bonuses paid in 2009. A tax on high-risk activities of large banks to finance rescue fund was considered in 2011.
Germany	Banking sur-tax to compensate for crisis costs.
Italy	Permanent tax on financial sector bonuses and stock options exceeding three times the base salary.
Japan	A securities transaction tax (STT) was abolished in 1999. A change in the tax system on cross-border transactions is aimed to promote participation from foreign investors in the Japanese securities markets. These are designed to increase securities lending and to change international taxation principles from an 'entire income principle' to an 'attributable income principle'.
UK	The stamp duty on secondary sales of shares and trusts holding shares raised over the three years on average about 40 per cent as much as the CIT on financial institutions. A bank levy is to be imposed at the rate of 0.05 per cent of global balance sheet in 2011, rising to 0.075 per cent in 2012. Stamp duty on stock market transactions (0.5 per cent). Surtax on bonus pay – temporary bank payroll tax 2009–10.
US	Funds needed for liquidation in crisis resolution to come from Treasury, clawed back from industry ex-post. The Government wanted in 2010 to impose a 0.15 per cent tax on the liabilities of large financial institutions as a financial crisis responsibility fee.
EMs	
Argentina	Credits and debits on current accounts have been taxed since 2001. This raises significantly more than CIT on financial institutions. The Banco del Sur levies part of its funds through an FTT.
Brazil	Until the end of 2007, Brazil levied a bank debit tax that raised about three times the amount raised by the CIT on financial companies. In 2009 Brazil announced a 2 per cent tax on foreign purchases of fixed-income securities and stocks. Banco del Sur levies part of its funds through an FTT.
China	Stock trading stamp duty (0.3 per cent) is being charged.
India	In 2004, India introduced an STT in equity markets. It is charged at the rate of 0.125 per cent on a delivery-based buy and sell transactions and 0.025 per cent on non-delivery-based sale transactions. The rate is 0.017 per cent on F&O sale transactions. It is collected by the stock exchanges for the exchequer. The rate was reduced and also applied to commodities in 2013. Stamp duties are imposed on bonds.

Indonesia	A capital account prudential measure, serving as an implicit tax requires a one-month minimum holding period for Bank Indonesia Certificates (SBIs) of all maturities.
South Korea	Korean government considered various measures from further limits on derivative positions, a 'Tobin' tax on foreign exchange transactions, a tax on capital flows and the reintroduction of a 14 per cent withholding tax on foreign bondholders' earnings. A bank tax on foreign currency wholesale funding by maturity with a maximum cap of 50 bp – 20 bp for less than one year, 10 bp for 1–3 years maturity and 5 bp for longer than three years was applied in 2011.
Turkey	The banking and insurance transactions tax falls on all transactions of banks and insurance companies. It raises as much revenue as CIT on financial companies and about 2 per cent of total tax revenue.

Source: Web-based news items and IMF (2010);Global Review.pdf, http://www.bertelsmann-stiftung.de/cps/rde/xbcr/SID-81F700A5-4D019067/bst_engl/xcms_bst_dms_32455_32456_2.pdf, accessed in January 2011.

http://www.madhyam.org.in/admin/tender/FGF2510.pdf, accessed in January 2011

http://fs.practicallaw.com/0-504-5507, accessed in January 2011

http://www.ilo.org/public/english/bureau/inst/download/rc_confdownload/ekkehard.pdf, accessed in January 2011

http://www.ilo.org/public/english/bureau/inst/download/rc_confdownload/ekkehard.pdf, accessed in January 2011

http://www.tmf-group.com/en/Latest-News/tmf-china-news-update-new-regulations.html, accessed in January 2011

http://www.ilo.org/public/english/bureau/inst/download/rc_confdownload/ekkehard.pdf, accessed in January 2011

http://fsckorea.wordpress.com/2011/02/17/how-to-respond-to-surging-foreign-capital-inflow/, accessed in January 2011

http://www.seacen.org/GUI/pdf/publications/staff_paper/2011/sp80.pdf, accessed in January 2011

http://www.bertelsmann-stiftung.de/cps/rde/xbcr/SID-81F700A5- accessed in January 2011

4D019067/bst_engl/xcms_bst_dms_32455_32456_2.pdf, accessed in January 2011

A low tax that matches transaction fees charged would not be burdensome since the same technology has substantially reduced transaction costs. It may be easier to impose. International and cross-asset harmonization could perhaps be feasible for a simple universal tax. It can reduce complexity-driven arbitrage opportunities and help to counter the largely discretionary approach to systemic risk in Basel III.

Financial Transaction Tax (FTT) pursued by the EU is not an ideal macro-prudential instrument but belongs to a class of such measures since it can reduce short-term transactions and cross-border flows that are highly pro-cyclical. It may discourage shadow banking system since it is based on the transaction and not on the institution. Such taxes would have to fall in EMs and rise in the major financial centres where they tend not to exist.

But given resistance to a tax on transactions independent of profits made, a financial activities' tax (FAT) that falls on profits and therefore is not passed on to consumers of financial services, could be negotiated. But an FTT has the advantage that it applies in the jurisdiction where a transaction is made and potential profits earned, while a profits tax earns revenues only for the country of residence or country of source depending on tax agreements to avoid double taxation. An FTT shares taxes under dominant tax by residence clauses that favour AEs, from where the majority of portfolio investments originate.

Improving confidence in the GFA and the nature of international financial integration is the better way to reduce imbalances. In an imperfect world innovative taxes contribute to this objective.

Conclusion

From the EM perspective, areas of special concern for G20 are making the globe safer for EMs to engage with, GFA reforms to reduce inflow volatility, maintaining funds for development and alternatives for self-insurance. Improvements in financial regulation are the way to achieve most of these objectives and are where the focus should lie. Simple regulatory ratios and taxes that can be universally adopted offer the most potential.

Since India has not directly contributed to imbalances it could work towards resolutions that improve global stability such as more exchange rate flexibility for China and a long-term reduction in twin deficits for the US, without taking explicit sides in the issue. The Indian example demonstrates some flexibility in exchange rates, and gradual capital account convertibility is compatible with export growth and market development.

Asymmetric adjustment has to be resisted, however. There were pressures for EMs to allow currency appreciation to correct global imbalances and to stimulate domestic demand, while AEs were to be excused from reducing deficits (Mexico City 2012), which they had committed to in Toronto (2009) since they had to fight a prolonged slowdown. Macroeconomic policies primarily aimed at the latter were not to be regarded as currency manipulation even with depreciation as a side effect.

The massive liquidity expansion in AEs creates risk for EMs. Higher growth in EMs and near zero interest rates at home encouraged portfolio rebalancing towards EMs with reversals when persisting financial fragility created new shocks. Even if inflows help in the short-run they are unreliable and create dangerous dependencies. Controls and prudential requirements became an essential line of defence, but have a cost. Better regulations would reduce these costs. For example, position limits on commodity futures could have mitigated the commodity price bubble that began to deflate in 2013 but created inflation in EMs. AEs tend to argue that higher growth in AEs will benefit EMs but ignore the reverse. Yet, minimal regulatory changes that reduce spillovers would help EMs support global growth.

The financial reforms proposed in the G20 are in the right direction but there are delays and weaknesses. That the GFC morphed into a debt crisis shows how dangerous it is to neglect the build-up of financial risks and that prevention is much better than cure.

Countries with lax financial regulations create negative externalities for others. Simple universal rules can make them impose some minimal macro-prudential measures. Else, discretion can imply that no action is taken. Financial development is especially important for EMs. But rule-based prudential regulations on the financial sector are being applied more in EMs than in AEs.

A low uniform tax will improve financial stability in AEs, while EMs reduce imposts on their financial sectors towards global norms. This more level playing field, GFA changes and better regulations in AEs and on cross-border flows will make more market-friendly reform possible in EMs. Controls can be designed to be market friendly using developments in technology. Pure controls involve restrictions on cross-border flows by residence. Market-based controls include un-remunerated reserve requirements and taxes. For debt, pure controls must continue, but for other cross-border flows the latter set may be considered.

In general, a better balance between taxes, margins (as more OTC derivatives shift to exchanges), position limits, credit caps and loss absorbing buffers will make it possible to bring down the latter and increase credit, thus increasing stable financial intermediation. The package of universal financial reforms would differ somewhat from the current Basel III to also cover shadow banking, remove arbitrage and build in preventive incentives. Weights on different components may be adapted, on agreed principles, to the national context.

Market deepening and opening is in India's own interest. But more opening has to be calibrated and is conditional on a better GFA, better domestic macroeconomic policies and market institutions. It should, in particular, aim to strengthen regulation covering the macro-prudential and SIFI aspects and ask for work towards a valid definition of global liquidity. It should point out that regulations in crucial aspects are weaker in AEs compared to EMs. The latter do need to improve in important areas in which they lag such as in consumer protection. Participating in regional initiatives will be useful to maintain global power on an even keel; Asian groupings and bargaining power can help ensure that more reforms are actually implemented this time around.

Endnotes

[1]   This is a revised and condensed version of paper for a Ministry of Finance – ICRIER project on G20. I thank, without implicating, Parthasarathi Shome for the invitation, Kaushik Basu, Alok Sheel, Usha Titus and other participants at a Ministry of Finance presentation; J. Massey, Y.V. Reddy, H.B. Shaeffer, Shunmugam and U. Venkataraman for lively discussions on the topic; Ritika Jain for research and Reshma Aguiar for excellent secretarial assistance. The section on reserves was presented at an IEO-IMF workshop in Pondicherry University. I thank the participants, especially Dr Hans Genberg and Dr Charan Singh for useful comments.

[2]   See http://www.imf.org/external/np/exr/facts/g20map.htmfor the MAP process and http://www.imf.org/external/pubs/ft/survey/so/2012/POL071912A.htm for multilateral surveillance initiative.

[3]   The definition follows Goyal (2010). The section also draws on Goyal (2009).

[4]   The game is adapted from Goyal (2010).

[5]   Swiss banking regulators have chosen to act unilaterally on some of these criticisms. They have raised capital standards of UBS and Credit Suisse, the two big Swiss banks, to 19 per cent by 2019, with 10 per cent of this in common equity. The other 9 per cent could, at the bank's discretion, be contingent convertibles that trigger when the ratio of equity to assets reaches a predetermined value.

[6]   For example, there may be a credit-driven boom in real estate although aggregate inflation may remain low.

[7]   These comparisons are based on the cited literature and on some non-cited web-reports (but see notes to Table 2.8 for some of the web-links).

[8]   Pre-crisis regulation in the UK was principle based while it was rule based in the US. The principle-based UK FSA, set up in 2003, became a goal for the US SEC. European regulation is also principle based, but complex legislation also sets many rules while in the US more is left to regulators. US–UK tend to be investor based whereas Europe is creditor based.

[9]   Based on news reports. See http://www.ft.com/intl/cms/s/0/63a74260-f506-11e1-b120-00144feabdc0.html#axzz2M02yVSqd and http://www.ft.com/intl/cms/s/0/ebf54d1c-77c7-11e2-9e6e-00144feabdc0.html#axzz2M02yVSqd.

[10]   This together with some worsening of asset quality led to Moody's October 2011 downgrade of SBI from C- to D+ and its revised outlook on India's banking sector from

stable to negative in November. Forced public sector bank for credit growth after the Lehman crisis and the 2011-slowdown due to policy delays and sharp rise in interest rates caused the cyclical negative. But this does not negate the overall better health of Indian banks.

[11] Baba et al. (2009) explore a crisis due to these types of arrangements. European banks' foreign currency assets exceeded $30 trillion in 2008, 10 times the figure for US banks. As interbank markets dried up in 2007 they turned to US dollar money market funds (MMFs) for cheaper dollar funding. MMFs were also looking for higher returns. But they also came under stress without a floating net asset value or access to a lender of last resort. When a run on MMFs occurred in late 2008, a Treasury guarantee had to be given and swap lines opened between the Federal Reserve and European central banks to maintain dollar supply.

[12] Support to these countries can be rapid. For example, on 18 September 2008, the Federal Reserve on request increased its existing swap lines with the ECB and the Swiss National Bank (SNB) to $110 billion and $27 billion, respectively. It started new swap lines with the Bank of Japan ($60 billion), Bank of England ($40 billion) and Bank of Canada ($10 billion). On 29 September, these swap lines were at least doubled, and on 13 October the Federal Reserve was made to accommodate any demand for US dollar funding at fixed rates (Baba et. al 2009).

[13] I thank Dr Grenberg for this point.

[14] As Dr V. Y. Reddy (RBI Governor during the build-up to the global crisis) put it, whatever is the current level is the optimal size of reserves. The past value becomes the new threshold.

[15] The RBI's stated position is it only intervenes to smooth exchange rates, but this would cause an accumulation of reserves if inflows exceeded outflows.

[16] Indonesia (2010), Philippines (2009), Russia (2010), South Africa (2010), Thailand (2010), South Korea (2009–10), Turkey (2010), Brazil (2010) and Taiwan (2009) are among the countries that have taken some measures to reduce inflows.

References

Aizenman, J. 2009. *Hoarding International Reserves versus a Pigovian Tax-Cum-Subsidy Scheme: Reflections on the Deleveraging Crisis of 2008–9, and a Cost Benefit Analysis.* NBER Working Paper No. 15484.

Baba, N., R. N. McCauley and S. Ramaswamy. 2009. 'US dollar money market funds and non-US banks.' *BIS Quarterly Review*, 65–81.

Bernanke, B. S. 2005. *The Global Saving Glut and the U.S. Current Account Deficit.* Speech delivered at the Sandridge Lecture, Virginia Association of Economics, Richmond, Va., March 10. Available at: http://www.federalreserve.gov/boarddocs/speeches/2005/200503102/default.htm [Accessed in May 2009].

Bernanke, B. S., C. Bertaut, L. P. DeMarco and S. Kamin. 2011. 'International Capital Flows and the Returns to Safe Assets in the United States, 2003-2007'. Available at: http://federalreserve.gov/pubs/ifdp/2011/1014/ifdp1014.htm [Accessed in July 2011].

Bertelsmann Foundation. 2010. 'The EU Takes on Banking and Financial-services Regulation.' *The Euro Wire.* Available at: http://www.bertelsmann-stiftung.de/cps/rde/xbcr/SID-81F700A5-4D019067/bst_engl/xcms_bst_dms_32455_32456_2.pdf [Accessed in January 2011].

BIS (Bank for International Settlements). 2010a. *Group of Governors and Heads of Supervision Announces Higher Global Minimum Capital Standards.* BCBS Press Release, September 12.

BIS (Bank for International Settlements). 2010b. '*Funding Patterns And Liquidity Management of Internationally Active Banks.*' CGFS paper 39, May. http://www.bis.org/publ/cgfs39.htm [Accessed in January 2011].

BOE (Bank of England). 2009. '*The Role of Macroprudential Policy*'. Discussion Paper. Available at: http://www.bankofengland.co.uk/publications/other/financialstability/roleofmacroprudentialpolicy091121.pdf [Accessed in January 2011].

Goldstein, M. and N. Véron. 2011. 'Too Big to Fail: The Transatlantic Debate'. *Institute for International Economics,* Working paper 11–2.

Goyal, A. 2002. 'Reform Proposals from Developing Asia: Finding a Win-win Strategy'. In *Debating the Global Financial Architecture,* edited by Leslie Elliott Armijo. SUNY Press Global Politics series, under the general editorship of James Rosenau, (New York: SUNY Press).

Goyal, A. 2005. 'Asian Reserves and the Dollar: Is Gradual Adjustment Possible?'. *Global Economy Journal* 5(3): Article 3. Available at: http://www.bepress.com/gej/vol5/iss3/3 [Accessed in May 2009].

Goyal, A. 2009. 'Financial Crises: Reducing Procyclicality', *Macroeconomics and Finance in Emerging Market Economies*, 2(1): 213–23, March.

Goyal, A. 2010. 'Regulatory Structure for Financial Stability and Development'. *Economic and Political Weekly* 25 September, XLV(39): 51–61.

Goyal, A. 2014. 'Banks, Policy, and Risks: How Emerging Markets Differ'. *International Journal of Public Policy* 10(1, 2 and 3): 4–26.

G20. 2009. 'Working Group on Enhancing Sound Regulation and Strengthening Transparency (Co-Chairs: Tiff Macklem and Rakesh Mohan)'. 25 March. Available at: http://www.rbi.org.in/scripts/PublicationReportDetails.aspx?UrlPage=&ID=549 [Accessed in May 2009].

Hanson, S. G., A. K. Kashyap and J. C. Stein. 2011. 'A Macroprudential Approach to Financial Regulation'. *Journal of Economic Perspectives*, 25(1): 3–28.

IMF (International Monetary Fund). 2010. 'A Fair and Substantial Contribution by the Financial Sector, Interim Report for the G20 (April)'. Washington: International Monetary Fund.

Knutter, R. 2011. 'Blowing a Hole' in *Dodd-Frank, The American Prospect.* 18 March. Available at: http://prospect.org/cs/articles?article=blowing_a_hole_in_doddfrank [Accessed in January 2011].

Liabson, D. and Mollerstrom, J. 2010. 'Capital Flows, Consumption Booms and Asset Bubbles: A Behavioural Alternative to the Savings Glut Hypothesis'. *The Economic Journal* 120(544): 354–74.

Shin, H. S. 2011. 'Global Liquidity'. Remarks at the IMF conference on 'Macro and Growth Policies in the Wake of the Crisis'. Washington DC, 7–8 March.

Shin, H. S. and K. Shin. 2011. 'Procyclicality and Monetary Aggregates'. NBER Working Paper No. 16836. Available at: http://www.nber.org/papers/w16836.pdf [Accessed in January 2011].

Shleifer, A. and R. Vishny. 2011. 'Fire Sales in Finance and Macroeconomics'. *Journal of Economic Perspectives* 25(1): 29–48.

3 Financial Sector Reforms under G20 and the Indian Banks

Poonam Gupta

Introduction

The objective of this chapter is to assess the overall impact of the regulatory reforms of the financial sector under G20 on the Indian banking sector. The proposed reforms consist of higher liquidity and capital adequacy ratios; identification and tighter regulation of systemically important financial institutions (SIFIs) or global systemically important financial institutions; regulation of the shadow banking institutions; Over the Counter (OTC) derivatives reforms and supervisory issues. Specific recommendations, and a time frame of implementation, have so far been made for the liquidity and capital adequacy norms under Basel III, including the capital frameworks for global and domestic systematically important banks (GSIBs and DSIBs respectively), while the discussions and deliberations are still being carried out on some of the other reforms, including their applicability and time frame of implementation for developed countries and emerging markets.

This chapter focuses mainly on the liquidity and capital standards proposed under Basel III and asks how the enhanced capital and liquidity standards would affect the Indian banking sector. Since the first Basel capital accord in 1988, emphasis on capital has been an important part of bank regulation, because with a larger capital cover the banks can absorb losses with their own resources, without becoming insolvent or necessitating a bail-out with public funds. Higher capital ratios perhaps also reduce the incentives for excessive risk taking. Over the last twenty years, reflecting the growing complexity of modern banking, regulatory capital requirements have been refined and broadened to cover various types of risks and to differentiate among asset classes of different risks. Basel III, finalized by the Basel Committee on Banking Supervision (BCBS) and endorsed by the G20 at the Seoul Summit in November 2010, is a step in the same direction.

One of the main reforms under Basel III is to increase the quality and quantity of capital that the banks maintain. It requires the banks to increase the minimum level of total capital of at least 8 per cent of their risk-weighted assets at all times. It also requires the banks to build up capital buffers in good times, that can be drawn down in periods of stress, through two types of capital provisions, first, a capital conservation buffer of 2.5 per cent in the form of common equity to withstand periods of stress; and second, a countercyclical buffer of 0 to 2.5 per cent which would be imposed when, in the view of the national authorities, the credit growth is judged to be excessive and to be associated with the build-up of system-wide risk. Basel III puts greater focus on common equity, which is the highest-quality component of bank capital, in absorbing losses.

In principle, these new enhanced capital and liquidity standards would make the banks safer, with a greater ability to withstand and absorb shocks and by discouraging investment in riskier assets. However, it can also induce the banks to change their asset allocation towards the ones with low risk weight such as government securities and liquid assets and away from sectors with a high risk weight, thus reducing the availability of credit to the private sector and especially to informationally opaque medium-and small-scale borrowers.

How compliance with stricter capital requirements ultimately affects bank stability and the availability and cost of credit is an empirical question, and the empirical evidence on the effects of compliance with Basel Core Principles has been mixed. Lack of clear evidence perhaps points to the fact that compliance with higher capital requirement under Basel Core Principles by itself is not sufficient to make the banking system resilient and to avoid banking distress.

In the Indian context, a natural question to ask is whether the Indian banks are prepared to meet the higher capital and liquidity requirements and what would be the effects of meeting these requirements on the cost and availability of credit and their risk profile. To this end, the chapter first recognizes that the Indian banking sector is very different from most of the other G20 countries. It is predominantly state owned and has a mandate to make its credit available to the government and to the sectors which are considered socially useful. While the sector has been significantly liberalized after the financial crisis in 1991, but it still remains subject to several prudent regulations, including on sectoral exposures. As a result, the Indian banks in general are quite sound, as reflected in their low non-performing loans, high profitability, high liquidity and low leverage ratios. The sector has also proven to be quite resilient by withstanding the recent global crisis. In addition, as the RBI has indicated, the Indian banks are well on their way to achieve the Basel III, and the sector as a whole is likely to meet the requirements well ahead of time.

Using the bank level data from 1996–2007, we analyse the correlation between the capital adequacy ratio of the banks on one hand and several variables which measure the performance and asset allocation of banks such as the net interest margin; cost of deposit or borrowing; interest rates on loans; allocation of credit to the government and private sector; and the ratio of non-performing loans on the other. Our results show that a higher capital adequacy ratio is correlated positively with profitability, namely the return on assets and return on equity; and with the quality of assets, measured by non-performing loans as a per cent of bank advances. However, a higher capital adequacy ratio is not correlated significantly with higher interest rates on loans and deposits or with a higher credit allocation to government. So, on net the results show that increases in capital adequacy ratios have been associated with an improvement in bank-related variables.

Our overall assessment thus is that meeting the additional higher capital ratio would not significantly affect the cost or availability of bank credit and would actually make the banks healthier through a larger cushion to absorb shocks. At the same time it is important to ensure that adherence to Basel III is commensurate with the liberalization process that is underway in the Indian banks and is treated as a complement rather than a substitute for the liberalization process.

Despite this favourable assessment, and as has been established elsewhere, the fact remains that the Indian banks under-lend to the private sector. There are many possible reasons for this phenomenon, such as: high fiscal deficit; lack of collateral; incentive structure of the public sector bank managers which does not encourage lending to the private sector, priority sector lending; lack of credit registry, etc. While a high capital requirement by itself may not have a large negative effect on credit, the challenge to ensure that credit flows to the private sector and is not merely parked in government securities still remains. The latter would require addressing the above-mentioned factors, as well as the issues related to the financing needs of the government.

The rest of the chapter is organized as follows: Section 2 provides a snapshot of the regulatory reforms under consideration. Section 3 discusses the proposals under Basel III. Section 4 discusses the existing cross-country evidence on the effect of compliance with the Basel Core Principles on the resilience and health of the banks. Section 5 discusses the issues specific to the Indian financial sector and the likely impact of meeting the Basel III requirements on Indian banks; and the last section concludes.

A Snapshot of the Regulatory Reforms being Proposed[1]

The recent agenda of regulatory reforms programme, being overseen and coordinated by the Financial Stability Board (FSB) in accordance with the national authorities and international bodies such as the IMF and the World Bank, has evolved in wake of the global financial crises that started in 2007. Some of the objectives of this programme are to align the regulations of the financial sector across countries, so that different regulations do not result in regulatory arbitrage, to increase the capital requirements on the banks and to ensure that enough liquidity is maintained so as to make the financial sector safer. While some of the proposed regulations have been fleshed out, the others are still being put in place. The regulations have specific time lines of implementation and in principle recognize the need for these time lines to differ across countries. These also, in principle, allow for differences across countries in accordance with the specific conditions of developing countries. The main reforms that have been proposed by the FSB include the following:

1. The Basel III principles, put together by the Basel Committee on Banking Supervision (BCBS) and endorsed by G20 at the Seoul Summit in November, 2010, aim at strengthening the bank capital and liquidity standards. These principles require banks to hold more and better quality capital and more liquid assets; to maintain an internationally harmonized leverage ratio to constrain excessive risk taking; build-up capital buffers in good times; maintain minimum global liquidity standards and observe stronger standards for supervision, public disclosure and risk management (details are provided in the next section).

2. FSB submitted policy recommendations to the G20 Seoul Summit in November 2010 to address the moral hazard risks posed by SIFIs or systemically important financial institutions, which if at risk could cause significant disruption to the global financial system and economic activity. The recommendations envisage that the policy framework for SIFIs should combine a resolution framework and other measures to ensure that all financial institutions can be resolved safely, quickly, without destabilizing the financial system and without exposing the taxpayer to the risk of loss.

Financial institutions that are systemic in a global context should have higher loss absorbency capacity than the minimum levels agreed in Basel III and should be subject to more intensive coordinated supervision and resolution planning to reduce the probability and impact of their failure.

3. The proposed reforms with their focus on tightening regulations in the banking sector can put banks at a competitive disadvantage relative to non-bank financial sectors and result in some of the activities shifting to lightly regulated financial institutions resulting in a resurgence of shadow banking activity. Thus the FSB's reform agenda includes devising and applying regulatory safeguards for the shadow banking.

4. Another proposed area of reform is to improve OTC derivatives markets and mandatory reporting of OTC derivatives transactions to trade repositories, to enable the authorities to assess the build-up of potential vulnerabilities in the financial system. Main recommendations thus include standardization, central clearing, organized platform trading and reporting to trade repositories.

5. A successful implementation of these proposals requires that the countries have a supervisory system to ensure the implementation and enforcement of these regulations and to make sure that the risk assessments are carried out to detect problems and intervene early to reduce the impact of potential stresses. For this, the supervisors must have the mandates, sufficient independence and appropriate resources at their disposal. Efforts should be underway to improve the supervisory standards and to increase the frequency of assessments of supervisory regimes.

The FSB has been following up the implementation of these recommendations by monitoring and regularly reporting on the progress, ensuring their consistency across countries through peer reviews of risk disclosures and of mortgage underwriting practices, the reviews of deposit insurance standards and assess the macroeconomic and financial system responses that the implementation of regulatory reforms would trigger.

While the core components of the Basel III capital framework were finalized in 2011, the committee has completed several other components of the regulations between 2011–13. These included issuing the capital frameworks for globally systemically important banks (GSIB) as well as domestic systemically important banks (DSIB). It also issued final guidelines of liquidity coverage ratio (LCR) in January 2013. The progress made on different components and the expected date of implementation is provided in Table 3.1.

Table 3.1: Status of Basel III Components and Target Dates for Implementation

Core component of Basel III	Progress
Basel III capital adequacy reforms	Published in 2011; implementation from 1 January 2013
GSIB/DSIB framework	Published in 2011 and 2012; implementation 1 January 2016
Liquidity Coverage Ratio	Published in 2013; implementation from 1 January 2015
Leverage ratio	Disclosure starting in 2015 with a view to migrate to Pillar 1 in 2018
Net Stable Funding Ratio	Under review; minimum standard to be introduced in 2018

Source: BCBS, April 2013.

Bank Capital and Liquidity Standards under Basel III

Since the first Basel capital accord in 1988, the prevailing approach to bank regulation has put a lot of emphasis on capital, since with the capital buffer the banks can absorb losses with their own resources, without becoming insolvent or necessitating a bailout with public funds. Capital buffer also reduces the incentives for excessive risk taking. Over the last 20 years, reflecting the growing complexity of modern banking, regulatory capital requirements have been refined and broadened to cover various types of risks and to differentiate among asset classes with different risks.

Basel III, finalized by the BCBS and endorsed by G20 at the Seoul Summit in November 2010, is a step in the same direction. It requires banks to hold more and better quality capital and more liquid assets; maintain an internationally harmonized leverage ratio to constrain excessive risk taking; build-up capital buffers in good times; maintain minimum global liquidity standards and observe stronger standards for supervision, public disclosure and risk management.

One of the main proposals under Basel III is to increase the quality and quantity of capital that the banks maintain. It requires the banks to increase the minimum level of common equity from 2 to −4.5 per cent of their risk-weighted assets; to increase the minimum level of Tier 1 capital (Common Equity Tier 1 and Additional Tier 1) from 4 to −6 per cent of risk-weighted assets and to increase the total capital (Tier 1 Capital plus Tier 2 Capital) to at least 8 per cent of their risk-weighted assets at all times.

It also requires the banks to build-up capital buffers in good times that can be drawn down in times of stress through two types of capital provisions. First, banks would be required to hold a capital conservation buffer of 2.5 per cent in the form of common equity to withstand periods of stress and second, a countercyclical buffer of 0 to −2.5 per cent which would be imposed when, in the view of the national authorities, the credit growth is judged to be excessive and to be associated with a build-up of system-wide risk. The countercyclical buffer would have to be covered with common equity or other fully loss absorbing capital (Table 3.2).

Basel III puts greater focus on common equity, which is the highest-quality component of bank capital, in absorbing losses. The definition of common equity and other regulatory capital components has been strengthened by applying stricter criteria for eligibility and by deducting certain types of assets from common equity.[2]

Table 3.2: Capital Requirements and Buffers
(All numbers in per cent of risk-weighted assets)

	Common equity tier 1	Tier 1 capital	Total capital
Minimum	4.5	6.0	8.0
Conservation buffer	2.5		
Minimum plus conservation buffer	7.0	8.5	10.5
Countercyclical buffer range	0–2.5		

Source: BCBS (2010)

In terms of the timeline, it envisages phasing in the minimum required level for common equity and Tier 1 capital beginning in 2013 and making it effective at the beginning of 2015. This implies that the minimum common equity and Tier 1 capital will increase from the current 2 and 4 per cent levels to -3.5 and 4.5 per cent, respectively, at the beginning of 2013 and to 4.5 and 6 per cent, respectively, at the beginning of 2015. The capital conservation buffer of 2.5 per cent, comprised of common equity will be phased in progressively from 1 January 2016 and will become fully effective on 1 January 2019. A detailed timeline by when these have to be met is provided in Appendix 1. Basel III proposes some other regulations as well. In order to help contain the build-up of excessive leverage in the financial system, perhaps one of the reasons why banks in many developed countries faced distress even while meeting the Basel II requirements, a leverage ratio is proposed to be introduced as a supplementary measure to the risk-based capital requirements. New global minimum liquidity standards based on the LCR and Net Stable Funding Ratio (NSFR) are expected to be introduced as well, from 2015 and 2018, respectively. The LCR would make banks more resilient to potential short-term disruptions in their access to funding, while the NSFR would address longer-term structural liquidity mismatches in banks' balance sheets.

While in principle these new enhanced capital and liquidity standards would make the banks safer, with a greater ability to withstand and absorb shocks through enhanced capital and liquidity and by discouraging the investment in riskier assets, it can also change the allocation of credit in less desirable ways and increase the cost of credit. In order to meet the increased requirements banks would have to hold more equity, which would require them to either rely on the government to inject more capital or to raise it from the market. In either case, the demand for funds would increase and perhaps result in an increase in the cost of funds. Increased capital, with the banks' profitability largely unchanged, would also lower the return on equity. If the banks change their asset allocation towards the ones with low risk weight such as government securities and liquid assets and away from sectors with a high risk weight, this would reduce the availability of credit to the private sector and especially to informationally opaque medium and small-scale borrowers.

Basel committee members agreed to begin implementing the capital standards from 1 January 2013, which required that they translate the Basel III standard into their national laws and regulations before this date. However, progress towards this goal has been mixed. While many countries have made progress towards this, some have lagged behind. As per the April 2013 report of the BCBS, 14 countries have issued the final Basel III-based capital regulations, three have issued final rules and were expected to bring them into force by end 2013; but the remaining 13 countries have merely issued their draft regulations. This last set of countries includes nine in the European Union, Indonesia, Korea, Turkey and the United States. India is among the first set of countries which have issued the final capital regulations based on Basel III regulations.

How ultimately compliance with stricter capital requirements affects the bank's stability and the availability and cost of credit is an empirical question and this is what we turn to next.[3]

Evidence on the Effectiveness of Basel Core Principles

Empirical evidence has been mixed on the effects of compliance with Basel Core Principles (BCPs) including with the higher capital requirements. Some observers, perhaps rightly so, have argued that the recent financial crisis has demonstrated that higher capital requirements are inadequate to prevent a crisis. In fact, many of the banks which faced problems and had to be rescued during the 2007 crisis were in compliance with the minimum capital requirements, not just before but also during the crisis. The argument thus goes that a tightening of these standards further is unlikely to be a sufficient, or perhaps even a necessary condition to avoid problems of similar nature.

Earlier specific evidence on the effects of compliance with BCPs is provided by Barth, Caprio and Levine (2001, 2004 and 2006). They compiled and analysed an extensive database on banking sector laws and regulations using surveys of regulators around the world and studied the relationship between alternative regulatory strategies and bank-related outcomes. They found that the tightening of capital standards does not lead to banking sector development, improves bank efficiency, reduces corruption in lending or lowers banking system fragility. Their findings thus are a challenge to the Basel Committee's emphasis on capital requirements and official supervision.[4]

A number of other papers around the same time also used assessments of compliance with the BCPs for effective banking supervision to study the relationship between bank regulation and performance. For example, Sundararajan, Marston and Basu (2001) used a sample of 25 countries to examine the relationship between an overall index of BCP compliance and two indicators of bank soundness, non-performing loans and loan spreads. They found that the BCP compliance is not a significant determinant of these measures of soundness. On the contrary, Podpiera (2004) extended the set of countries and found that better BCP compliance lowers non-performing loans.[5]

The evidence continues to remain mixed. Beltratti and Stulz (2009) examined how differences in bank corporate governance and country-level regulatory approaches affected bank stock returns in the financial crisis. Their main findings are that the banks that are located in countries with strong capital regulation performed better. Berger and Bouwman (2009) using the data for US banks ask whether banks with higher capital ratios withstand a crisis better. They examined the effect of pre-crisis bank capital ratios on banks' ability to survive financial crises and on their competitive positions, profitability and stock returns during and after such crises. They also distinguished between small, medium and large banks. They found that capital helps banks to survive banking crises across all bank sizes. According to this study, better capitalized banks did significantly better in the early 1990s, but not in the recent crisis.

In more recent work, Demirgüç-Kunt and Detragiache (2010) study whether compliance with BCPs is associated with bank soundness, but do not find support for the hypothesis. that better compliance with Basel Core Principles results in sounder banks. Specifically, using the bank level data for over 3,000 banks in 86 countries, they found that neither the overall index of BCPs compliance nor its individual components were robustly associated with bank risk, measured by Z-scores (the number of standard deviations by which bank returns have to fall to wipe out its equity) or systemic risk, measured by a system-wide Z score.

In subsequent work, these authors along with Merrouche find that better capitalized banks experienced a smaller decline in their equity value during the 2007 crisis and that this effect was larger and robust for the larger banks. They also find that stock returns during the crisis were more sensitive to the leverage ratio than to the risk-adjusted Basel ratio and that Tier 1 capital had a more significant effect, especially for larger banks.

They interpret these results as an endorsement for the view that a stronger capital position is important during a systemic crisis, and that the current emphasis on strengthening capital requirements is therefore broadly appropriate. They also find support for the introduction of a minimum leverage ratio to supplement minimum risk-adjusted capital requirements and for greater emphasis on higher quality capital in the form of Tier 1 capital that are parts of recommendations under Basel III.

Our take on these findings is that most of this evidence is too simplistic and perhaps not sufficiently rigorous to guide the course of policy. There are many factors that have not been accounted for in these empirical analyses. For example, these studies do not distinguish between banks under different ownership structure: public, domestic private, small or regional foreign banks and larger, global foreign banks; between countries with different levels of development of their financial sectors or the prevailing macroeconomic conditions of the countries in their analyses.

These limitations notwithstanding, lack of clear evidence also points to the fact that compliance with higher capital requirement under BCP by itself is perhaps not sufficient to make the banking system resilient and to avoid banking distress. What could be the reasons for this disconnect between the compliance with BCP and perceived riskiness of banks? It could be due to the difference between the adoption of rules and actual compliance or because the banks could maintain high leverage ratios while still meeting the capital requirements or due to the macroeconomic imbalances elsewhere in the economy.

Does meeting the increased capital requirement come at a cost? For instance, does it result in higher cost of capital or reduce the availability of credit? Evidence shows that the increased capital requirement often results in the banks shifting their portfolios towards safer government securities, thus resulting in less credit to the private sector. Though not established empirically, this shift is perhaps larger in countries with a larger presence of public sector banks. The compliance can also raise the cost of credit, though there is no existing evidence on this, and since the cost of credit is affected by many other factors, including the demand and supply of credit from alternative sources, it is also difficult to establish this link empirically.

Finally, calibration of the cost-benefit analysis for several countries in G20 has been conducted by the BIS and national authorities, in partnership with the World Bank and IMF [Bank for International Settlements (BIS) 2010, BIS 2011, Macroeconomic Assessment Group (MAG) 2010]. These calculations show that the net effects of the proposed reforms are likely to be modest and mildly positive. BCBS and the MAG have assessed the transitory and long-term impacts of the new regulatory standards. These assessments show a small negative effect of the regulations on output growth during the implementation or transition period and also a small negative effect on long-run growth of output. The studies also show that these negative effects are likely to be outweighed by the positive effects of the dampened output volatility and reduced frequency and severity of financial crisis.

More specifically, MAG (2010) estimates a modest short-term negative effect on growth, amounting to 0.04 per cent reduction in growth rate for four years, followed by a recovery of growth towards the baseline. The BCBS assesses the impact of the new regulatory standards on long-term economic performance and economic fluctuations and the impact of countercyclical capital buffers on economic fluctuations. The calculations show that for each percentage point increase in the capital ratio (or liquidity regulation), there would be about a median 0.09 per cent decline in the level of steady state output, relative to the baseline. Higher capital and liquidity ratios would also have a modest effect on dampening output volatility, and the countercyclical capital buffers are likely to have a more sizeable dampening effect on output volatility.

However, just like the empirical literature, these calibrations have their limitations as well. The calibrations usually depend on a large number of underlying assumptions, and the quantitative analyses are quite sensitive to these assumptions and as such may not be a useful tool to guide policy.

Basel III and the Indian Financial Sector[6]

Indian financial sector is somewhat unique in the group of G20 countries in that a large and predominant share of banks, at nearly 70 per cent, is under government ownership, see Table 3.3. The effect of Basel III on Indian banks has to be understood in the context of the specific features of the banking sector.

Table 3.3: Number and Share of Banks in Total Assets in 2007 by Ownership Groups

Bank type	No. of banks	Share in assets (%)
State Bank of India and its associates[7]	8	23.3
Public sector banks	20	47.2
Private banks	25	21.5
Foreign banks	29	8

Source: Gupta *et al.* (2011)

On the whole, the Indian banking sector was heavily regulated until the early 1990s, with regulations taking the form of asset allocation through cash requirements, requirement to hold government securities and lending to the priority sector, interest rate ceilings, entry barriers, etc. Starting in 1991, Indian banking sector has experienced far-reaching reforms, which included the removal of controls on interest rates, reduction in reserve and liquidity ratios, entry deregulation, relaxation of credit controls and the introduction of an inter-bank money market as well as auction-based repos and reverse repos.

There have been large impacts of these liberalization measures on competition, profitability and efficiency of banks. First, the liberalization allowed for entry of new banks and an increase in the share of private banks, resulting in a decline in the degree of concentration in the banking sector, as shown in the Herfindhal Index (based on the shares in assets for all banks including foreign banks) in Figure 3.1. Second, the increased competition improved banks' efficiency as well. As has been carefully documented elsewhere, Indian banks, especially the public sector banks, have made remarkable progress in improving profitability. Starting from significantly lower operating profits and returns on assets in the early 1990s, public sector banks were broadly at par with private banks by 2007, as shown in Figure 3.2.

Figure 3.1: Herfindahl Index for the Banking Sector

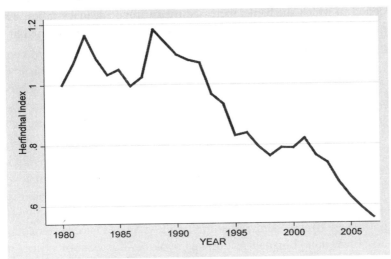

Source: Gupta *et al.* (2011)

Figure 3.2: Profitability of Public and Private Banks
(Return on Assets in per cent)

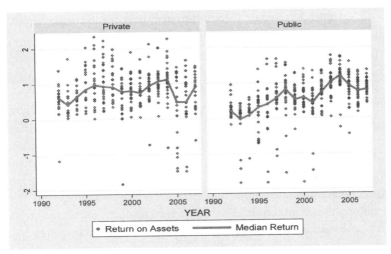

Source: Gupta *et al.* (2011)

Third, commensurate with the freeing up of interest rates, effective interest rates have declined for all types of banks. As Figures 3.3 and 3.4 show the average interest rates paid or received by the banks have declined, and the decline is more or less uniform across banks under different ownership structures. Interestingly, the decline in the cost of funds has happened in the period in which the banks increased their capital adequacy ratios. Thus, the higher capital adequacy ratios do not seem to have been attained at the expense of higher interest rates.

Figure 3.3: Average (Mean) Interest Paid (per cent of Assets)

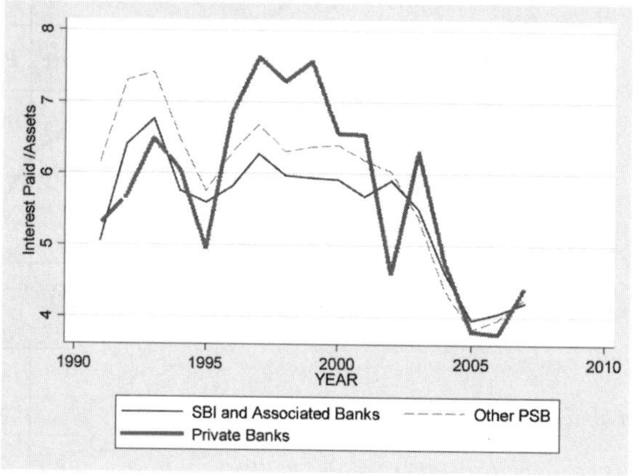

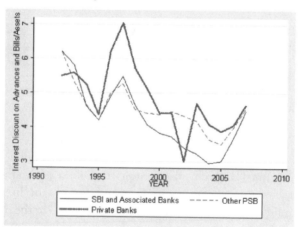

Source: Gupta *et al.* (2011)

Figure 3.4: Average (Mean) Interest Received on Advances

Source: Gupta *et al.* (2011)

Finally, reflecting better asset quality of the banks, non-performing loans and loan loss provisions have declined dramatically for public banks. These trends can also be seen in Table 3.4, in which the average profitability of public banks was much lower than that of a private bank in the early 1990s. The profitability increased for both public and private banks in subsequent years but the increase was sharper for public banks.

Table 3.4: Profitability and Efficiency Indicators for Public and Private Banks
(All variables are calculated as per cent of assets)

	1993		1995		2000		2007	
	Public	**Private**	**Public**	**Private**	**Public**	**Private**	**Public**	**Private**
Profitability (% of assets)								
Operating Profits	.44***	1.32	1.18***	2.13	1.51*	1.88	1.78	1.72
Return on Assets	-1.48***	0.49	0.11***	1.04	0.54**	0.88	0.84	0.75
Expenses (% of assets)								
Wages	2.02	2.08	1.95	1.78	1.90***	1.28	1.13	1.08
Non Wage Operating Expenses	0.87	0.92	0.91	0.82	0.70***	0.89	0.65***	1.08
Interest Paid	7.3***	6.53	5.79	6.08	6.08*	7	4.24	4.49
Provisions	2.01***	0.83	1.1	1.1	0.97	1	0.94	0.98

Note: The numbers represent simple means of variables for bank groups. The symbols *, ** and *** denote if the average of the public banks is significantly different from the average of the private banks at 10, 5, and 1 per cent levels, respectively.
Source: Gupta *et al.* (2011)

Despite this convergence in efficiency and profitability, public and private banks have remained different in one important dimension and that is the allocation of credit to the private sector and investment in government securities. Public banks lend a smaller share of their assets to the private sector and this share did not increase for many years despite the resources freed up by the formal reductions in the Cash Reserve Ratio (CRR) and the Statutory

Liquidity Ratio (SLR) post liberalization, as shown in Figure 3.5. Similarly, Figure 3.6 shows that public sector banks prefer to invest a larger share of their assets in government securities, and this share increased for public banks post liberalization for many years.[8] The preference for government securities over private credit could very well have been due to the increased capital adequacy ratios that the banks had to maintain during this period.

Figure 3.5: Credit to the Private Sector by Private and Public Banks (per cent of assets)

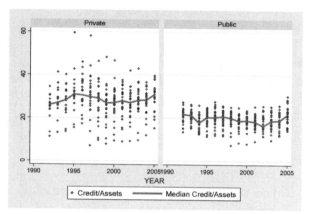

Source: Gupta *et al.* (2011)

Figure 3.6: Investment in Government and Other Approved Securities by Private and Public Banks

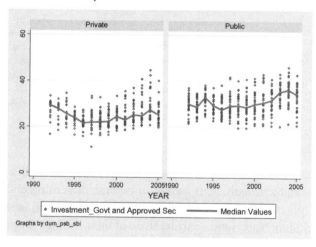

Source: Gupta *et al.* (2011)

Despite the reforms and relaxation of many regulations, Indian banks remain subject to strict but prudent regulations, as a result of which, on many standard indicators of vulnerabilities and risks, Indian banks come over very safe and strong. As shown in Figure 3.7, in a cross-country comparison, Indian banks are seen to have among the lowest loan-deposit ratio (a high loan-to-deposit ratio would indicate high leverage). Though the ratio did increase during the past decade but it still remains smaller than the average of advanced countries and that of most large emerging markets.

Figure 3.7: Loan–Deposit Ratios of Banks

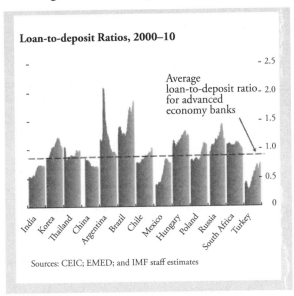

Source: IMF (2011)

An appropriate characterization of the Indian banking sector would thus be that it is owned largely by the government, is profitable and well capitalized and is considered safe due to a low leverage ratio, low exposures to volatile sectors and low non-performing loans. In addition, because of the existing capital controls, the sector is quite insulated from the build-up of large external borrowings and currency exposures, so the risk of an external shock affecting the Indian banks is low. However, partly because of its ownership and the mandate of the public banks and partly because of their desire to remain safe, banks seem to under-lend to the private sector.

Given these salient features of the Indian banking sector, the right questions to ask then are whether the Indian banks are prepared to meet the higher capital and liquidity requirements and what would be the effects of meeting these requirements on the cost and availability of credit and their risk profile. These are the questions we turn to next.

Are Indian Banks Prepared to Meet the Capital Adequacy Ratios under Basel III?

RBI's assessment is that at the aggregate level, Indian banks would be able to meet the new capital adequacy ratio rather easily. RBI provides estimates of the capital ratios of the banking system under Basel III, as shown in the Table 3.5 (as indicated in the RBI 2010), the estimates are based on the data furnished by banks in their off-site returns and are approximate.

Table 3.5: Capital Adequacy Ratios of Indian Banks under Basel III

Parameter	Under Basel III	Actual value for Indian banks as on 30 June 2010	
		Under Basel II	Under Basel III
Capital to risk-weighted assets ratio (CRAR)	10.5	14.4	11.7
Of which Tier I capital	8.5	10.0	9.0
Common equity	7.0	8.5	7.4

Source: RBI (2010), Five Frontier Issues in Indian Banking

Governor Duvvuri Subbarao cautions in RBI (2011) that while the Indian banks would be able to comfortably comply with the new capital rules in aggregate, some individual banks may fall short of meeting the requirements and may have to raise capital. Even then, since the phase-in time allowed in meeting these requirements is long enough, RBI expects that all banks would be able to make the adjustment to enhanced capital level comfortably.

Econometric Analysis of the Effect of Capital Adequacy Ratio on Credit Allocation and Cost of Financing

A quantitative effect of meeting the higher capital adequacy ratio on credit allocation and cost of financing would depend on many factors. These include how the banks meet the additional capital requirements – by raising more capital, through retained earnings, increasing their earnings or by substituting their portfolios towards assets with low risk weight and on the demand conditions in the market for credit including the demand from the government, for example, if there is less demand for funds from the government at the time that the additional capital requirements are met, then the effect on cost and availability of credit is likely to be subdued. Everything else remaining the same, increased capital requirement would increase the cost of credit.

Investment in government securities would depend on how the banks meet the additional capital requirement and on bond yields, fiscal deficit and the demand for funds from the government. In general, the investment in government securities (as a percentage of assets) is likely to increase and the credit to private sector to decrease in response to a higher risk-weighted capital cover.

To the extent that banks may have an efficiency gap and hence the potential to improve efficiency, increased capital requirements may act as a trigger to prompt the banks to improve efficiency, which may in turn also dilute the effect on the cost of credit. Quality of bank assets will likely improve as the assets are reallocated towards safer securities and as the moral hazard declines. These effects are summarized in Table 3.6 below.

Table 3.6: Expected Effect of Higher Capital Adequacy Ratio on Bank Level Variables

Bank level variables	Measured by	Determinants of effects	Net expected effect
Cost of credit	Interest on deposits, interest on bank loans	The effect would depend on how the additional capital requirement is met by the banks, the demand and supply conditions in the market for funds and improvement in efficiency.	Cost of credit would increase
Availability of credit to private sector	Credit to private sector as per cent of bank assets	The magnitude would depend on how the additional capital requirement is met by the banks and the demand and supply conditions in the market for funds	Availability of credit to private sector would decrease

Bank level variables	Measured by	Determinants of effects	Net expected effect
Investment in government securities	Investment in government securities as per cent of bank assets	It would depend on how the banks meet the additional capital requirement, bond yields, fiscal deficit and the demand from the government	Investment in government securities would increase
Efficiency	Net interest margin, operational costs	Banks may improve efficiency if there is an efficiency gap. The effect on net interest margin in addition would depend on the relative increase in the interest rates on deposits and credit.	?
Quality of bank assets	Ratio of non-performing loans to assets or advances	It would likely improve as the asset is reallocated towards safer securities and as the moral hazard declines	Quality of bank assets would improve

Source: Compiled by author.

Rather than calibrating the effect of increased capital requirements, as done in the studies conducted by the BIS, we analyse the relationship between capital adequacy ratios of the banks and impact variables using the past data for Indian banks. The data used are for scheduled commercial banks from the RBI's database on banking statistics and are available for 1996–2007, i.e., the period in which Basel II was primarily implemented. The data are available for total capital adequacy ratio and separately for Tier 1 and Tier 2 capital ratios.

Figure 3.8 shows the median values of capital adequacy ratios for private and public banks during 1997–2007. The public banks started this period with a lower capital ratio but steadily caught up with the private banks, and by 2007, the public and private banks were at par with respect to their capital ratios. These averages for total capital adequacy ratios mask important difference in the composition of total capital in Tier 1 and Tier 2 capital. Private banks hold a larger share of Tier 1 capital than public banks. Not only do the public banks hold a larger share of Tier 2 capital than private banks but they seem to have achieved their higher capital ratios primarily through an increase in their Tier 2 ratios.

Figure 3.8: Capital Adequacy Ratio of Public and Private Banks (Median Values)

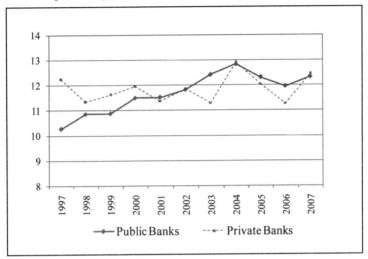

Source: Based on author's regression estimates

We regress variables to proxy the leverage of the banks, cost of financing, allocation of credit to safer securities and to the private sector, quality of assets and returns on assets or equity on the capital adequacy ratio of the banks. Though the data are available at the bank level for all ownership groups, we limit our analysis to only public banks and domestic private banks. The regressions equation is given in equation 3.1 below.

$$Y_{it} = \gamma_i \text{ Bank Dummies}_i + \alpha \text{Year dummies}_t + \lambda \text{Bank Size}_{it} + \beta \text{Capital Adequacy}_{it} + \varepsilon_{it} \quad (3.1)$$

In equation 3.1, subscript i refers to bank and t to year and Y_{it} to different dependent variables. In the regression specification we include bank fixed effects to take into account bank-specific factors, which are not otherwise explicitly controlled for and the year fixed dummies to account for the factors that vary over the years but are the same across banks, such as the demand conditions for credit. We also include bank size in the regressions. We estimate the regressions separately for public and private banks. We estimate two different specifications, one with the current value of the capital adequacy ratio and another with one year lagged values of the capital adequacy ratio. Results are in Table 3.7 for public sector banks and in Table 3.8 for private banks.

Results show that a higher capital adequacy ratio is correlated positively with the profitability measures, namely the return on assets and return on equity and with the quality of assets, measured by non-performing loans as a per cent of bank advances. However, a higher capital adequacy ratio is not associated significantly with the interest rates on loans and deposits or with the credit to bank assets ratio.[9] The results are broadly similar across private and public banks.

Table 3.7: Correlation of Capital Adequacy and the Banking Variables: Public Sector Banks

Dependent variables	(1) Credit/ Deposit	(2) Invest in govt. Sec/ assets	(3) Interest on deposit	(4) Return on advances	(5) Net interest margin	(6) Return on asset	(7) Return on equity	(8) NPL/ advances
Capital adequacy	0.26	0.13	0.00	0.02	0.05***	0.06***	1.17***	-0.47***
	[0.93]	[1.61]	[0.43]	[0.88]	[2.78]	[3.16]	[3.54]	[7.45]
Log assets	4.75	-0.31	0.37*	-0.73*	-1.9***	0.20	0.91	1.27
	[0.96]	[0.17]	[1.92]	[1.65]	[7.57]	[0.87]	[0.17]	[0.96]
Observations	244	323	323	244	244	244	244	323
R-squared	0.43	0.55	0.93	0.89	0.39	0.53	0.44	0.77
Number of banks	28	28	28	28	28	28	28	28

Source: Based on author's regression estimates Robust t statistics are in parentheses. The symbols **, *** indicate that the coefficients are significant at 10, 5 and 1 per cent levels, respectively. All variables are measures in percentage points.

Table 3.8: Correlation of Capital Adequacy and the Banking Variables: Private Banks

Dependent variables	(1) Credit/ Deposit	(2) Invest in govt. Sec/ assets	(3) Interest on deposit	(4) Return on advances	(5) Net interest margin	(6) Return on assets	(7) Return on equity	(8) NPL/ advances
Capital adequacy	-0.29	0.04	-0.01	-0.02	0.03**	0.07**	1.32*	0.00
	[1.50]	[1.07]	[1.31]	[0.76]	[2.07]	[2.01]	[1.85]	[0.02]
Log assets	-3.00	-1.78	-0.17	-0.42	0.10	1.39***	26.0***	-0.52
	[0.46]	[1.26]	[0.32]	[0.86]	[0.53]	[3.74]	[3.98]	[0.81]

	(1)	(2)	(3)	(4)	(5)	(6)	(7)	(8)
Dependent variables	Credit/ Deposit	Invest in govt. Sec/ assets	Interest on deposit	Return on advances	Net interest margin	Return on assets	Return on equity	NPL/ advances
Observations	178	239	239	178	178	178	178	239
R-squared	0.45	0.36	0.76	0.859	0.17	0.49	0.53	0.47
Number of banks	22	22	22	22	22	22	22	22

Source: Based on author's regression estimates Robust t statistics are in parentheses. The symbols *, **, *** indicate that the coefficients are significant at 10, 5 and 1 per cent levels, respectively. All variables are measured in percentage points.

Interpolating from these results it seems that meeting the additional higher capital ratio would not significantly affect the cost or availability of bank credit and would actually make the banks healthier through a larger cushion to absorb shocks. Similar results are obtained with lagged capital adequacy.

It is difficult to estimate the macro effects of these regulations on GDP growth, investment and capital flows. These would depend not just on the net bank level effects, which are likely to be modest, but also on how these bank level effects interact with the macro conditions at home and globally, such as the business cycle, global liquidity conditions, fiscal deficit, monetary policy conditions, etc. As the exercises done by the BIS show, the design of such an exercise would also be very sensitive to the specific assumptions made in the model.

Cross-country Progress in Adhering to Basel III Regulations, with Specific Reference to India and the Issues that May Need Attention

In a recent RBI working paper, Prakash and Ranjan (2012) discuss the progress made by the G20 countries in meeting Basel III regulations. Their main findings are that even though there is variation across countries, the G20 countries in general are adhering well to the norms. India in general fares well and is somewhere in the middle in terms of the progress it is making with respect to the regulations as well the performance of its banking sector. On the performance indicators, the authors compare the banking sectors across several indicators of capital, liquidity and profitability and find that the performance of the G20 countries has either stayed the course or has improved after the adoption of Basel III regulations.

More importantly, on capital adequacy most countries studied in the chapter, including India, are more than meeting the capital norms set out under Basel III. For example, many countries in G20 – Canada, Germany, Indonesia, Japan, South Africa, the US and the UK increased their capital adequacy ratios between 2009 and 2011. Overall the ratio ranged between 11.1 and 18.2 per cent, well above the level of 8 per cent prescribed under Basel III. Tier 1 capital also exceeded the norm of 50 per cent of the total capital. The ratios for India were 13.5 for total capital and 9.3 for Tier 1 capital in 2011 Q1. Similarly, the banks maintained comfortable liquidity positions. Prakash and Ranjan report that the countries such as Germany, Korea and Brazil maintained more than 100 per cent of their short-term liabilities as liquid assets. Indian banks as well had comfortable liquidity position, bolstered by the investment by banks in liquid government securities under SLR requirements.

There are some regulatory issues related to financial sector in G20 that may need more discussion, especially from the point of view of the developing countries. It has been recognized and emphasized that care would need to be exercised to strike an appropriate balance between prudent liquidity requirements and the risk of excessively constraining credit growth. The proposed risk-weighting rules can act as a disincentive for banks to lend to small and medium enterprises. In developing countries where the capital markets are not very deep or liquid, the banks' ability to raise the liquidity buffers is also likely to be limited. Thus, there should be adequate scope to adapt the reform initiatives to local circumstances.

As has been written elsewhere, the cost of capital remains high in India, while it remaining an under-banked country. Complying with higher capital adequacy and maintaining higher liquidity is likely to put further strain on the cost of operations of the banking and result in higher lending costs. The banks may also scale back their lending operations in order to meet the capital requirements. In either case, the cost of fund is likely to increase. One way to get efficiency gains while complying with Basel III would be to open up the banking sector, encourage a healthy mix of public sector banks, private banks as well as foreign banks, bring down the states' pre-emption of loanable funds and allow technology to play a larger role, especially in the public sector banks. All of these measures are likely to bring down the cost of credit and make credit more accessible to various factions of society.

From the Indian perspective, the current regulations also lack full clarity on how the SLR holdings of government securities would be treated in calculating the leverage and liquidity ratios. RBI (2011) cautions that in India, and perhaps also in other developing countries where the financial sector is rather small and undeveloped, more clarity is needed on the variables that would be used to calibrate the countercyclical capital buffer. In the same context, operation of countercyclical buffers would require better understanding and development of business cycle models, and the developing countries may lack the technical skills to develop these models.

Critics point out, perhaps rightly so, that adherence to Basel II did not stop the occurrence of the current crisis, and thus it is not evident whether the enhanced regulations would be effective this time. While the regulations to limit leverage are a step in the right , so would perhaps be a sectoral approach to credit to complement this. What is also important is to detect bubble formation early enough so that timely actions can be taken ahead of time.

None of the Indian banks are likely to cross the bar to be identified as GSIB. Even if the largest banks such as the SBI or the ICICI meet the size criterion at some time in the future, they are unlikely to qualify as 'systematically important' given their primarily domestic orientation. Thus the regulations pertaining to the GSIBs are unlikely to affect the Indian banking sector. On the contrary, to the extent that there are foreign banks present in India and the central bank plans to open up more space for foreign banks going forward, stricter regulatory oversight, accounting and transparency requirement and higher capital standards would make the operation of foreign banks safer in India and elsewhere. Finally, what is also important is to ensure that adherence to Basel III is commensurate with the liberalization process that is underway in Indian banks and is treated as a complement rather than a substitute for it.

The regulatory strictness has resulted in regulatory arbitrage, whereby certain financial activities have shifted to arenas which do not face these regulations. Hence the extent of Shadow Banking has increased across countries which have imposed stricter financial regulation measures. The size of shadow banking has reached a record $67 trillion in 2011, according to a report by the FSB, a regulatory task force for the world's group of 20 economies. US has the biggest shadow banking system, followed by the Eurozone and the United Kingdom.

The existence of shadow banking defeats the very purpose for which the regulation had been strengthened and has led to calls for regulations of the shadow banking activities as well.

In keeping with the international trends, the RBI has sought to tighten norms to regulate shadow banking as per the recommendations of the Usha Thorat Committee. The committee has recommended increasing Tier 1capital and increasing the risk-weight on the assets of Non Bank Finance Companies(NBFCs), the purveyors of shadow banking.

The RBI has been using the macroprudential measures to contain the risks in the banking sector and to smooth out the 'boom' phase of the boom-bust cycle in sectoral bank credit. The components of macroprudential policies have included countercyclical capital and provisioning regulations and risk-weights on specific sectors.[10] For example, during what the RBI describes as an expansionary phase, from 2004–08, it tightened the prudential norms on credit to the sectors such as commercial real estate. These indeed helped moderate the flow of credit to the specific sectors. The RBI cautions that the countercyclical buffer advocated under Basel III and which is based in the credit/GDP metric might not be very easy to implement in emerging markets, due to the difficulty of separating out structural and cyclical components of the credit. Rather, a sectoral approach might be better to dampen the credit growth to sectors which are more prone to the boom–bust cycles. As indeed the experience in India, noted above, shows.

Conclusion

The chapter discussed and assessed the overall impact of the regulatory reforms of the financial sector under G20 on the Indian banking sector and discussed the progress that India has made. Focusing mainly on the liquidity and capital standards proposed under Basel III, it asked how the enhanced standards would affect the Indian banking sector.

Basel III requires the banks to increase the minimum level of total capital to at least 8 per cent of their risk-weighted assets at all times and build-up capital buffers to be drawn down in periods of stress through a capital conservation buffer and a countercyclical buffer, all three requirements adding up to 13 per cent of risk-weighted assets. Basel III also puts greater focus on common equity, which is the highest-quality component of bank capital in absorbing losses.

In principle these new enhanced capital and liquidity standards would make the banks safer, with a greater ability to withstand and absorb shocks and by discouraging investment in riskier assets. However, it can also induce the banks to change their asset allocation towards the ones with low risk weight such as government securities and liquid assets and away from sectors with a high risk weight, thus reducing the availability of credit to the private sector and especially to informationally opaque medium and small-scale borrowers. The empirical evidence has been mixed on the effects of compliance with BCPs and high capital requirements, pointing to the fact that these by themselves are perhaps not sufficient to make the banking system resilient and to avoid banking distress.

Our overall assessment is that complying with the Basel III requirements would not significantly affect the cost or availability of bank credit and would actually make the Indian banks healthier through a larger cushion to absorb shocks. What is perhaps most pertinent is that the reforms under G20 are not seen as a substitute for the country's own reforms agenda in the financial sector comprising ownership issues, opening up of the sector for entry, consolidation, entry of foreign banks, etc. Rather the adherence to Basel III should be treated as a complement to the domestic reforms road map.

Finally, as has been established elsewhere, the Indian banks are seen to under-lend to the private sector due to reasons such as the high fiscal deficit; lack of collateral; incentive structure of the public sector bank managers which does not encourage lending to the private sector; priority sector lending; lack of credit registry, etc. While a high capital requirement by itself may not have a large negative effect on credit the challenge to ensure that the credit flows to the private sector and is not merely parked in government securities would remain and would require addressing the above-mentioned factors.

Appendices

Appendix 3.1: Basel III Phase-in Arrangements (All dates are as of 1 January)

	Phases	2013	2014	2015	2016	2017	2018	2019
Capital	Leverage Ratio	3.5%	Parallel run 1 Jan 2013 – 1 Jan 2017 Disclosure starts 1 Jan 2015				Migration to Pillar 1	
	Minimum Common Equity Capital Ratio		4.0%	4.5%				4.5%
	Capital Conservation Buffer				0.625%	1.25%	1.875%	2.5%
	Minimum common equity plus capital conservation buffer	3.50%	4.00%	4.50%	5.125%	5.75%	6.375%	7.0%
	Phase-in of deductions from CET1*		20%	40%	60%	80%	100%	100%
	Minimum Tier 1 Capital		5.5%	6.0%				6.0%
	Minimum Total Capital	4.5%	8.0%					8.0%
	Minimum Total Capital plus conservation buffer		8.0%		8.625%	9.25%	9.875%	10.5%
	Capital instruments that no longer qualify as non-core Tier 1 capital or Tier 2 capital		Phased out over 10 year horizon beginning 2013					
Liquidity	Liquidity coverage ratio – minimum requirement			60%	70%	80%	90%	100%
	Net stable funding ratio						Introduce minimum standard	

*   Including amounts exceeding the limit for deferred tax assets (DTAs), mortgage servicing rights (MSRs) and financials. -------transition periods

Appendix 3.2: Basel Committee on Banking Supervision Reforms – Basel III Strengthens Microprudential Regulation and Supervision, and Adds a Macroprudential Overlay that Includes Capital Buffers

	Capital					Liquidity
	Pillar 1			Pillar 2	Pillar 3	Global liquidity standard and supervisory monitoring
	Capital	Risk coverage	Containing leverage	Risk management and supervision	Market discipline	
All banks	**Quality and level of capital** Greater focus on common equity. The minimum will be raised to 4.5% of risk-weighted assets, after deductions. **Capital loss absorption at the point of non-viability** Contractual terms of capital instruments will include a clause that allows – at the discretion of the relevant authority – write-off or conversion to common shares if the bank is judged to be non-viable. This principle increases the contribution of the private sector to resolving future banking crises and thereby reduces moral hazard. **Capital conservation buffer** Comprising common equity of 2.5% of risk-weighted assets, bringing the total common equity standard to 7%. Constraint	**Securitizations** Strengthens the capital treatment for certain complex securitizations. Requires banks to conduct more rigorous credit analyses of externally rated securitization exposures. **Trading book** Significantly higher capital for trading and derivatives activities, as well as complex securitizations held in the trading book. Introduction of a stressed value-at-risk framework to help mitigate procyclical-ity. A capital charge for incremental risk that estimates the default and migration risks of unsecuritized credit products and takes liquid-ity into account **Counterparty credit risk** Substantial strengthening of the counter-party credit risk framework.	**Leverage ratio** A non-risk-based lever-age ratio that includes off-balance sheet exposures will serve as a backstop to the risk-based capital requirement. Also helps contain system wide build-up of leverage.	**Supplemental Pillar 2 requirements** Address firm-wide govern-ance and risk management; capturing the risk of off-balance sheet exposures and securitization activities; managing risk concen-trations; providing incentives for banks to better manage risk and returns over the long term; sound compensa-tion practices; valuation practices; stress testing; accounting standards for financial instruments; corporate governance; and supervisory colleges.	**Revised Pillar 3 disclosures requirements** The requirements introduced relate to securitization exposures and sponsorship of off-balance sheet vehicles. Enhanced disclosures on the detail of the components of regulatory capital and their recon-ciliation to the reported accounts will be required, including a compre-hensive explanation of how a bank calculates its regulatory capital ratios.	**Liquidity coverage ratio** The liquidity coverage ratio (LCR) will require banks to have sufficient high quality liquid assets to withstand a 30-day stressed funding scenario that is specified by supervisors. **Net stable funding ratio** The net stable funding ratio (NSFR) is a longer-term structural ratio designed to address liquidity mismatches. It covers the entire balance sheet and provides incentives for banks to use stable sources of funding. **Principles for Sound Liquidity Risk** Management and Supervision The Committee's 2008 guidance Principles for Sound Liquidity Risk Management and Supervision takes account of lessons learned during the crisis and is based on a fundamental review of sound practices for managing liquidity risk in banking organizations.

Capital					Liquidity
Pillar 1			Pillar 2	Pillar 3	Global liquidity standard and supervisory monitoring
Capital	Risk coverage	Containing leverage	Risk management and supervision	Market discipline	
All banks — on a bank's discretionary distributions will be imposed when banks fall into the buffer range. **Countercyclical buffer** Imposed within a range of 0-2.5% comprising common equity, when authorities judge credit growth is resulting in an unacceptable build-up of systematic risk	Includes: more stringent requirements for measuring exposure; capital incentives for banks to use central counterparties for derivatives; and higher capital for inter-financial sector exposures. **Bank exposures to central counterparties (CCPs)** The Committee has proposed that trade exposures to a qualifying CCP will receive a 2% risk weight and default fund exposures to a qualifying CCP will be capital-ized according to a risk-based method that consistently and simply estimates risk arising from such default fund				**Supervisory monitoring** The liquidity framework includes a common set of monitoring metrics to assist supervisors in identifying and analysing liquidity risk trends at both the bank and system-wide level.
SIFIs — In addition to meeting the Basel III requirements, global SIFIs must have higher loss absorbency capacity to reflect the greater risks that they pose to the financial system. The Committee has developed a methodology that includes both quantitative indicators and qualitative elements to identify global SIBs. The additional loss absorbency requirements are to be met with a progressive Common Equity Tier 1 (CET1) capital requirement ranging from 1% to 2.5%, depending on a bank's systemic importance. For banks facing the highest SIB surcharge, an additional loss absorbency of 1 % could be applied as a disincentive to increase materially their global systemic importance in the future. A consultative document was published in cooperation with the FSB, which is coordinating the overall set of measures to reduce the moral hazard posed by global SIFIs					

Endnotes

[1]   This section draws on various reports published by the FSB and other sources as provided in the references.

[2]   For more details including on risk weights, definition of common equity, Tier 1 and Tier 2 capital etc. see BCBS (2010).

[3]   For a more detailed literature survey see Detragiache and Demirguc-kunt (2010).

[4]   Though many of the studies look at the overall compliance with the BCPs and not just with the capital adequacy ratios but to the extent that the compliance across principles is highly correlated, it does not matter.

[5]   Das *et al.* (2005) relate bank soundness to a broader concept of regulatory governance, which encompasses compliance with the BCPs as well as compliance with standards and codes for monetary and financial policies. They found that better regulatory governance is associated with sounder banks, particularly in countries with better institutions.

[6]   Discussion on the Indian financial sector draws on Gupta, Kochhar and Panth (2011).

[7]   In 2008, Bank of Saurashtra was merged with the State Bank of India (SBI) and in 2010 the State Banks of Indore was merged with the SBI. There are now five associated banks besides the SBI in the group.

[8]   We do not show the data for 2006 and 2007 in the charts when fiscal deficit declined substantially in these years and credit to private sector by public banks increased.

[9]   Similar results are obtained if we take the cost of funds rather than just interest on deposits in column 3 or if we use gross non-performing assets rather than net non-performing assets in the last column.

[10] See address by Deputy Governor Anand Sinha (2011).

References

Bank for International Settlement. 2010. 'Assessing the macroeconomic impact of the transition to stronger capital and liquidity requirements'. December.

Bank for International Settlement. 2010. 'Basel III: A global regulatory framework for more resilient banks and banking systems'. December.

Bank for International Settlement. 2011. 'BASEL III: Long-term impact on economic performance and fluctuations'. BIS Working Papers No. 338. February 2011

Barth, James R., Caprio Jr., Gerard and Levine, Ross. 2001. 'The Regulation and Supervision of Banks Around the World: A new Database'. In *Integrating Emerging Market Countries into the Global Financial System, Brookings – Wharton Papers in Financial Services* edited by Litan, R.E. and Herring, R.J., 183–240. Washington: Brookings Institution Press.

Barth, James R., Caprio Jr., Gerard and Levine, Ross. 2004. 'Bank Regulation and Supervision: What Works Best?' *J. Finan. Intermediation* 13(2): 205–248.

Barth, James R., Caprio Jr., Gerard and Levine, Ross. 2006. *Rethinking Bank Supervision and Regulation: Until Angels Govern.* Cambridge: Cambridge University Press.

Basel Committee on Banking Supervision. 2010. 'An Assessment of the Long-Term Impact of Stronger Capital and Liquidity Requirements (LEI Report)'.

Basel Committee on Banking Supervision. 2011. 'Basel III: A global regulatory framework for more resilient banks and banking systems'. June.

Basel Committee on Banking Supervision. 2012. 'Report to G20 Finance and Central Bank Governors on monitoring implementation of Basel III regulatory reform'. June

Berger, N. Allen and Bouwman Christa H.S. 2009. 'Bank Capital, Survival, and Performance around Financial Crises'. Working Papers/Financial Instituions Center, Wharton School, University of Pennsylvania.

Betratti, Andrea and Rene' M. Stulz. 2009. 'Why Did Some Banks Perform Better During the Credit Crisis? A Cross-Country Study of the Impact of Governance and Regulation'. Fischer College of Business Working Paper 2009–12. Columbus: Ohio State University.

Cosimano, Thomas F. and Dalia S. Hakura. 'Bank Behavior in Response to Basel III: A Cross-Country Analysis'. IMF Working Paper.

Cosimano, T. F. and B. McDonald. 1998. 'What's Different Among Banks?' *Journal of Monetary Economics* 41: 57–70.

Demirgüç-Kunt, Asli and Detragiache, Enrica and Ouarda Merrouche. 2010. 'Bank Capital: Lessons from the Financial Crisis'. IMF Working paper, WP/10/286.

Demirgüç-Kunt, Asli and Detragiache, Enrica. 2010. 'Basel Core Principles and Bank Risk: Does Compliance Matter?', *Asli Demirgüç-Kunt and Enrica Detragiache* WP/10/81.

Elliott, D. J. 2009. 'Quantifying the Effects on Lending of Increased Capital Requirements'. *Brookings Briefing Paper.* Washington, D.C.: Brookings Institution.

Financial Stability Forum. 2008. 'Report of the Financial Stability Forum on Enhancing Market and Institutional Resilience'. April.

Financial Stability Forum. 2010. 'Progress of Financial Regulatory Reforms'. November.

Flannery, M. J. and K. P. Rangan. 2008. 'What caused the Bank Capital Build-up of the 1990's'. *Review of Finance* 12: 391–429.

G20. 2009. 'Declaration on Strengthening the Financial System'. London, London Summit, 2 April 2009.

G20. 2011. Communiqué. Meeting of Finance Ministers and Central Bank Governors, Paris, 18–19 February.

G20. 2011. Communiqué. Meeting of Finance Ministers and Central Bank Governors, Washington D.C., 14–15 April.

Gupta, Poonam, Kalpana Kochhar and Sanjaya Panth. 2011. 'Bank Ownership and the Effects of Financial Liberalization: Evidence from India'. IMF Working paper; WP/11/50; March.

International Monetary Fund. 2011. 'Global Financial Stability Report, Durable Financial Stability, Getting There from Here'. April.

Mohanty, Deepak. 2011. 'Lessons for Monetary Policy from the Global Financial Crisis: An Emerging Market Perspective'. Paper presented by Mr Deepak Mohanty, Executive Director of the Reserve Bank of India, at the Central Banks Conference of the Bank of Israel, Jerusalem, 1 April 2011.

Iorgova S., Kışınbay T., Le Leslé V., Melo F., Ötker-Robe İ., Pazarbasioglu C., Podpiera J., Sacasa N. and Santos A.2010. 'Impact of Regulatory Reforms on Large and Complex

Financial Institutions'. IMF Staff Position Note No. 2010/16 Washington D.C.: International Monetary Fund.

Podpiera, R.. 2004. 'Does Compliance with Basel Core Principles Bring any Measurable Benefits?' IMF Working Paper 04/204. Washington D.C.: International Monetary Fund.

Prakash, Apupam and Rajiv Ranjan. 2012. 'Benchmarking Indian Regulatory Practices to the G20 Financial Reforms Agenda'. RBI Working Paper, 03/2012.

Reserve Bank of India. 'Financial stability Report, 2010'. Reserve Bank of India; December; Mumbai; India.

Reserve Bank of India. 2010. 'Discussion Paper-Presence of foreign banks in India'. New Delhi: Reserve Bank of India.

Reserve Bank of India. 2010. 'Five Frontier Issues in Indian Banking'. Speech by Governor Duvvuri Subbarao. Inaugural address by Dr Duvvuri Subbarao, Governor, Reserve Bank of India at 'BANCON 2010' in Mumbai on December 3, 2010. Reserve Bank of India. 2011. 'Frontier Issues on the Global Agenda Emerging Economy Perspective'. Speech by Duvvuri Subbarao. Commemorative oration by Dr Duvvuri Subbarao, Governor of the Reserve Bank of India, at the 60th anniversary celebrations of the Central Bank of Sri Lanka, Colombo, 29 March 2011.

Rose, Norton. 2010. 'An Introduction to Basel III-Its Consequences for lending'. Available at: http://www.nortonrosefulbright.com/knowledge/publications/2010/pub31077/an-introduction-to-basel-iii-its-consequences-for-lendings.

Sinha, Anand. 2011. 'Macroprudential Policies: Indian Experience'. Address at Eleventh Annual International Seminar on Policy challenges for the Financial Sector. Washington D.C., 1–3 June.

Slovik, Patrick and Boris Cournede. 2011. 'Macroeconomic Impact of Basel III'. OECD Economics Department Working Papers, No. 844. Paris: Organization for Economic Cooperation and Development Publishing.

Subbarao, Duvvuri. 2010. 'Five Frontier Issues in Indian Banking'. Inaugural Address at 'BANCON 2010', Mumbai.

Viñals, Jose, Jonathan Fiechter, Ceyla Pazarbasioglu, Laura Kodres, Aditya Narain and Marina Moretti. 2010. 'Shaping the New Financial System'. *IMF Staff Position Note* 10/15.

———— ❖ ————

Section 3
Global Macroeconomic Coordination and Reforming International Financial Institutions

———— ❖ ————

4 The G20MAP, Sustaining Global Economic Growth and Global Imbalances: India's Role in Supporting Cooperation among Global Macroeconomic Policymakers

David Vines

Introduction

The challenges global macroeconomic policymakers facing today are like the challenges faced by John Maynard Keynes and his colleagues at the Bretton Woods conference in 1944. The Bretton Woods system was built with the memories of the 1930s in mind and was designed to enable countries to grow rather than to fall into depression in the way they did after World War I. We face a similar challenge now, in ensuring that growth returns to a sustainable level, after the onset of the Great Recession in 2008. This is an international problem, and as in 1944, a solution to this problem requires global cooperation. The G20 Mutual Assessment Process (MAP) is the platform on which this cooperation can be developed. And there is a role for India in helping to bring about such cooperation.

At the time of the G20 Summit in Cannes in November 2011, the global economy found itself in a dangerous phase, with a recovery which was weakening and with intensifying risks of financial instability. As a result of these dangers, G20 Leaders endorsed policy actions by members designed to ensure progress towards strong, sustainable and balanced growth.[1] These policy actions are discussed in this chapter. Although it was initially written in the run-up to that Summit, the analysis remains relevant today. Some of what is discussed below is presented in more detail in Adam et al. (2012) and in Temin and Vines (2013).

The chapter is structured as follows: Section 2 presents a detailed discussion of the G20MAP; Section 3 considers the nature of the cooperation which emerged in the Bretton Woods system – it does this in order to provide a background to the later discussion of the international cooperation which is now needed; Section 4 describes why international coordination of policies ceased to be practised in the international monetary system that emerged after the collapse of the Bretton Woods framework and it describes the role of 'Bretton Woods II' within that system; Sections 5 and 6 discuss needs for cooperation which have re-emerged in the world economy and discusses the risks to this cooperation which come from the needs of East Asia, Europe and the US; Section 7 considers how the required global cooperation might be brought about and Section 8 concludes the discussion.

The Cooperative Framework Established in the G20MAP

The Origins of the G20MAP: Cooperation Arising out of Crisis

The Global Financial Crisis of 2008–09 caused the largest downturn in global economic activity[2] since the IMF was established in 1944. The initial policy response to the crisis effect at the G20 Summit in London in April 2009 displayed a remarkable degree of international cooperation. The macroeconomic policies agreed at that summit played a significant part in preventing the financial crisis from turning into another Great Depression. This was cooperation of a kind which would have been admired by those who had gathered at Bretton Woods.

Recovery from that crisis has been underway since late 2009 but has continued at a slow pace. This recovery has created a need for macroeconomic cooperation of a rather different kind from the policies agreed in London in April 2009. At that time the task was to stimulate the world economy on a broad front to prevent global collapse. This was something about which – it now seems–was relatively easy to achieve agreement. Now the task is, instead,to sustain global growth and – in part – to bring this about through international rebalancing. But it is now widely questioned whether this objective will be achievable in the way that is necessary.

At the Pittsburgh G20 Summit in September 2009, global leaders pledged cooperation and initiated a Framework for Strong, Sustainable, and Balanced Growth (which is referred to in the following as the Framework).[3] That Framework was concerned with achieving financial stability and environmental sustainability and with raising the living standards of those in developing countries (G24, 2011 and Qureshi 2011). But we will concentrate only on cooperation in relation to macroeconomic policies.

The backbone of this collaborative activity has been the creation of a multilateral process through which G20 leaders (i) identified a set of macroeconomic objectives for the world economy, (ii) agreed at a set of macroeconomic policies which would be needed to achieve these objectives, and (iii) committed themselves to a mutual assessment of their progress towards meeting their objectives. This mutual assessment of progress has become known as the G20 Mutual Assessment Process or G20MAP.

Since Pittsburgh, the G20MAP has gone through a number of stages.[4] The IMF was to provide technical analysis to support the G20MAP. As noted above, the Framework is about macroeconomic outcomes; but it is also about achieving financial stability, with environmental issues and with the raising of living standards in developing countries. A wider range of concerns is being assisted by technical inputs from a range of international institutions far beyond the IMF, including the Bank for International Settlements (BIS), the WTO, the World Bank and other international institutions. I concentrate here on inputs by the IMF into this process. Subsequently, the IMF's role in the process was fleshed out. First, the Fund would evaluate how members' macroeconomic policies should fit together. It would also assess whether, collectively, countries are likely to achieve the G20's goals.[5] Since then, three further crucial decisions have been taken about the Fund's role. First, it would investigate the policies of a particular set of countries, rather than just concentrating broadly on the world or regions. Second, which particular countries would be examined would depend upon the imbalances that have become evident between countries. Finally, the way in which this decision was actually taken would depend on a set of indicators. By early May 2011, these decisions led to three important outcomes.

First, at the Paris meeting of G20 finance ministers and central bank governors, in February 2011 a communiqué was issued, which agreed on a set of indicators to allow policymakers 'to focus ... on those persistently large imbalances which require policy actions'. Second, at the Washington meeting of G20 finance ministers and central bank governors in April 2011 the approach for analysing these indicators was specified. Third, an agreement was made to analyse, in depth, the policies of seven countries: the US, China, Japan, Germany, India, the UK and France.

The analysis which was carried out to reach this list was not revealed. But the list reflected the range of indicators which had been selected. A moment's thought will suggest why India was selected – given its large public deficit. The role of indicators in the G20MAP was as a selection device for further, in-depth analysis of what policy adjustments are necessary for a good global outcome.

The analysis was to produce recommendations for policy in time for the G20 Summit in Cannes, held during 3–4 November 2011. The recommendations were published, as intended, in the run-up to the Summit and the policy conclusions were summarized in the IMF's Factsheet on the G20MAP available on the IMF's website.

The G20MAP and Global Surveillance

The IMF has needed to ensure that the policy analysis of the US, China, Japan, Germany, India, the UK and France is carried out in a fearless and objective manner. IMF officials have been required to integrate the policies which the countries put forward into alternative global scenarios. The aim is to consider their global outcomes and to check if:

1. adjustment takes place – because China (and East Asia) adjusts, and Germany (and Europe) and the US adjust, and growth is maintained; and

2. adjustment does not take place and there is inadequate global growth.

IMF has to ensure that global analysis is also done in a manner not subject to political compromise.

The in-depth analysis has led to difficult issues since these countries have seemed likely to continue to adopt policies which may not contribute to a satisfactory global outcome. This is particularly true for China, Germany and the US, the cases for which are discussed below.

IMF's previous multilateral surveillance process (MSP), which operated from 2004 to 2007, was heralded at the time as going beyond the Fund's process of bilateral surveillance. Nevertheless, it did not do this adequately. A report of the IMF's Independent Evaluation Office (IMF 2006) noted that as a result of its country-by-country orientation, the IMF's multilateral surveillance had not sufficiently explored options to deal with policy spillovers in a global context. Mervyn King, Governor of the Bank of England, elaborated on this theme in speeches in New Delhi and Melbourne (King 2006a,b), making it clear that a more effective regime of multilateral surveillance would require that: (1) countries make clearer commitments about their objectives for macroeconomic policies (i.e., fiscal, monetary and financial); (2) the Fund's Article IV process and the World Economic Outlook focus more transparently on cases when these policy commitments and the countries' policy actions are not globally consistent; (3) that this process also transparently demonstrates the negative spillover effects that come from such a lack of consistency and (4) this process proposes a set of policy actions which would reduce such negative spillovers.

But this earlier process of multilateral surveillance was overshadowed by a bilateral disagreement between the US and China. For some years, the US had been worried that the Chinese exchange rate was giving rise to global imbalances. And the Chinese have been worried that the US fiscal position was also causing imbalances.[6]

The governance structure of the IMF ensured that it made no criticism of, or exercise any sanction on, the US as a result of its large current account deficit. The US can veto any decision taken by the Executive Board, and the threat of such a veto, even if it is only implicit, circumscribes what the Fund can do.

The Fund was also unable to exert any discipline on China, as a result of its undervalued exchange rate. China has no veto, but since the US had effectively threatened to use its veto against criticism or sanction of the US, this prevented the US from mobilizing criticism of China or bringing any sanction against China. It became necessary to prevent a bilateral conflict from breaking out between the US and China and to prevent these two countries from subverting the MSP.

The G20MAP, Global Macroeconomic Policymaking and Global Economic Governance

The G20MAP has been a response to the governance difficulties outlined above. There are four aspects of this response.

First, indicative indicators to signal the existence of needs for policy action have been helpful. As a matter of intellectual content, the indicators' work has been of little significance in determining what policies are required. This is because, as explained below, whether imbalances are good or bad depends on the macroeconomic circumstances, and a decision about what policies are needed requires a detailed analysis of economic structure. Engaging non-economists in a discussion on indicators has, however, been useful that allowed them to learn about the causes of global growth and imbalances. It led to disagreements about the interstices of indicator measurement, rather than about something more fundamental. And, crucially, it created space for detailed analysis on global macroeconomic management. It has become possible for the IMF to study policies needed for global recovery, how these policies fit with the need to deliver global rebalancing and how this might be managed. Such study is crucial if the needs for cooperation described in this chapter are to be satisfied. The G20MAP has provided such a framework for the first time.

Second, the G20MAP reports directly to G20 leaders in contrast to the MSP which reported to the IMF's Executive Board which effectively blocked any significant discussion on adjustment outcomes under pressure from countries most likely to be affected. It will be harder to carry out such a blocking operation with the leaders themselves engaged in the process of hammering out a satisfactory outcome.

Third, the G20MAP has made it more difficult for the US and China to block a satisfactory outcome for another reason. The disagreement between them has been located within the context of a larger group of players, all of whom are engaged in the G20MAP. Using words which Keynes initially used at Bretton Woods, this has given the US and China 'a perpetual reminder that they belong to the whole world'. The prospect of a wider deal, or deals, within the G20 has enabled other countries to put other issues on the table. And it locked these countries into a wish for a settlement.[7] Further, it became possible for these countries to push the US and China towards a settlement.

Finally, the separation of the technical analysis and the decisions about policy analysis that has been achieved in the G20MAP has been crucial. It has enabled the experienced and high-quality staff of two of the IMF's key departments –Research and Strategy, Policy and Review – to be charged with working on the technical analysis. And this separation means that the analysis can be carried out free from political interference. Political judgments need to be exercised when working out the necessary policy responses. It has been possible to ensure that the necessity for these political judgments neither compromise the technical analysis nor prevent it from 'speaking freely'. The separation is thus likely to improve the transparency of the G20MAP and to increase its credibility and acceptability. The IMF's analysis has been openly published. It can then be made clear to outside observers whether the leaders of G20 countries manage to face, in the policy-decision stage, the challenges which the IMF's analysis has produced.

This kind of process has effectively given IMF officials the task of transparently pointing the heads of state of G20 governments towards the kind of policy adjustments needed to move the world towards a globally cooperative outcome. Such a process might well, over time, help to lock IMF officials and policymakers and officials from the G20 countries into a situation in which they together seek adjustment with growth.

India's Role

It appears that India is well placed to help lead the G20MAP in such a process. There are two reasons for this.

First, India has no particular macroeconomic interest at stake in the G20MAP. Its pressing imbalance concerns the fiscal deficit. Resolving this imbalance without endangering the growth process is needed for domestic policy reasons. There is no apparent clash between India's domestic objectives and the objectives of the G20MAP. This gives India a certain freedom to act.

Second, India has an advantage which is conferred by its international political position. India has been the Co-Chair of the G20 Working Group which is charged with studying these problems. In addition, an Indian Minister of Finance has been Vice Chair of the G24 and became Chair in 2012. That group may also be able to exercise some influence on the G20MAP.

As a result, there are two crucial roles which India might play.

First, India might help to ensure that the G20MAP leads to a separation between analysis and political decision-making as discussed above. India was able to use its influence during 2012 to ensure that this separation was embedded in the G20MAP process, and that the results of the IMF's analysis continue to be published in the future.

Second, India might push for the establishment of a disinterested committee of global leaders – a group which includes economists but which also has a broader membership – to comment on the way in which the G20 deal with the G20MAP. Its aim would be to comment publicly on the political decisions which are made at G20 Summits, and, in particular, to comment on the extent to which these decisions actually respect the IMF's analysis. It could comment on the extent to which the decisions reflect the challenges posed by the IMF's analysis. Such a group of qualified outsiders would question whether G20 policymakers really had responded in an appropriate manner. The knowledge that there would be such an outside committee charged with commenting on the policy outcomes might well be important in pushing G20 policymakers in a helpful direction. In doing this, such a group might significantly increase the transparency and credibility of the G20MAP.

The second suggestion grows out of a proposal made by Montek Singh Ahluwalia earlier in the summer of 2010. This suggestion was aired at a conference organized by ICRIER, CEPII and BRUEGEL in New Delhi on 1 and 17 September 2010, with the title 'International Cooperation in Times of Global Crisis: Views from G20 Countries'. At that meeting, Ahluwalia argued that up until then, the G20MAP had been too secretive and too non-transparent. He called for the establishment of a disinterested committee of global leaders to oversee the G20MAP, both to increase its transparency and credibility and to ensure that its work was not excessively held back by political constraints. What has been done so far has responded to the second of Ahluwalia's concerns in an important way, in that the G20MAP has been separated into two stages: the analysis stage, to be carried out by the IMF and the policy-decision stage, to be carried out by the G20 leaders. This committee would be building on what the IMF has achieved and would be seen to make a constructive contribution to the political decision stage of the global policy process.

Cooperation in the Bretton Woods System

In order to analyse international cooperation in today's macroeconomic policymaking it is useful to first understand the nature of cooperation in the Bretton Woods system. That system was designed to enable countries to promote high levels of employment and output by means of domestic macroeconomic policies, policies which, at that time, were mainly fiscal. It was hoped that such policies would ensure that slumps in growth could be avoided. They would thereby prevent the re-emergence of anything like the Great Depression of the 1930s. Each region would aim for full employment of its resources, and each would use its own macroeconomic policy, which at that time consisted mainly of fiscal policy, in the pursuit of that objective (Williamson 1983 and Moggridge, 1976).

But such policies would be put at risk if some countries needed to import more at full employment than they were able to pay for by means of their exports. Those meeting at Bretton Woods were not prepared to return to a Gold Standard system. In that system adjustment in such countries could only happen by gold flowing out, leading to a reduction of demand and deflation, something which had happened to the UK after it returned to the gold standard in an uncompetitive position in 1925. Instead, the IMF was to oversee a global system of pegged-but-adjustable exchange rates. Exchange-rate pegs would be adjusted if there was a 'fundamental disequilibrium' – precisely whenever the real exchange rate was not at a level that would ensure that exports could equal imports at full employment. That kind of test was designed, with memory of the 1930s in mind, to prevent countries having to undergo a long period of deflation if they were uncompetitive. A country with longer-term balance of payments difficulties would be declared to be in 'fundamental disequilibrium' and would be expected to devalue its currency by an appropriate amount after consulting with the Fund and obtaining the required approval. Similarly, a country with an excessively large and sustained balance of payments surplus would be expected to appreciate its currency (Vines, 2003, House, Vines and Corden, 2008 and Vines, 2008), and such appreciations were to be required.

This setup was central to the Bretton Woods structure. While profoundly shaped by Keynes' *General Theory*, this setup was far from those that were fully articulated in the Bretton Woods agreements. It was only set out in the book by James Meade (1951) and the paper by Trevor Swan (1955). However, as Vines (2003) and Temin and Vines (2013) argue, Keynes recognized that this framework was essential to an understanding of the Bretton Woods system.[8]

Underpinning our understanding of this structure is a view of adjustment in which macroeconomic policy instruments need to be deployed to simultaneously achieve not only internal balance – in other words full employment of resources without excess demand pressures – but also a sustainable external balance – an outcome in which exports are sufficiently competitive to meet full-employment import demand, along with interest payments abroad, after allowing for capital inflows. The resources of the IMF were to be made available in the short run to forestall the use of more distortionary (trade restricting) measures in the safeguarding of external balance. But to achieve adjustment required a combination of expenditure switching policies (exchange rate change) and expenditure changing policies (the management of internal demand).

Crucially, the 'fixed-but-adjustable' exchange rate regime underpinning the Bretton Woods system embodied a built-in incentive for 'beggar-thy-neighbour' policies. Each country was faced with the implicit (and easier) policy choice of pursuing competitive devaluation as a means for achieving internal balance, even when it did not have a balance of payments problem, rather than pursuing full employment by means of a sufficient increase in domestic demand. This would involve countries 'stealing jobs' from other countries. 'Beggar-thy-neighbour' policies adopted by some countries would impose on other countries the problem that they could only achieve external balance by means of a policy of austerity leading to unemployed resources. To prevent such devaluations only countries in 'fundamental disequilibrium' would be allowed to engage in currency depreciation. As discussed below, this kind of difficulty remains something which is important in today's world.

In this system, adjustment was also to be required of surplus countries: a country with an excessively large and sustained balance of payments surplus would be expected to appreciate its currency. The 'scarce currency clause' contained in the original Bretton Woods agreements was included precisely to ensure that adjustment pressure was brought to bear on surplus countries as well as on deficit countries. By the 1960s, Germany and Japan were running large trade surpluses but were unwilling to appreciate their currencies. This clearly created tensions in the system.

It is thus simple to see why cooperation was important for the Bretton Woods system. It enabled adjustment by deficit countries, it was designed to enforce adjustment on surplus countries and it was designed to prevent 'beggar-thy-neighbour' currency depreciations.

The Bretton Woods system provided an international monetary framework which underpinned the 'golden age' of economic growth, a period lasting from 1945 until 1971. This was the most remarkable period of economic expansion that the world had ever known, in which growth was even more rapid than that which had been experienced in the late Victorian era. During this time, the motor of global growth was a process of economic catch-up, first by Europe and then by Japan.[9] The Bretton Woods system appears to have played a significant part in ensuring that this catch-up was possible.[10]

The Global Non-system: From Bretton Woods to the Great Moderation

The Bretton Woods system survived only for as long as controls on international capital flows remained sufficiently effective as to allow countries to fix their exchange rates and pursue internal balance through domestic fiscal and monetary instruments. Substantial imbalances emerged in the global economy in the wake of US involvement in Vietnam, which led to the US becoming the major deficit country; in addition Germany and Japan were unwilling to revalue their exchange rates in the way which the system required. Ultimately, the rapid growth of international capital flows throughout the 1960s led to a massive speculative attack on the US dollar and to a collapse in the Bretton Woods system in 1971 (Corden, 1993). This led to the abandonment of a fixed exchange rate system and ushered in a 'non-system' of floating exchange rates.

The Reasons for a Global Non-system

The end of the Bretton Woods system marked the end of any serious attempt to bring about international cooperation about macroeconomic policy, for reasons which we will now explain.

The pursuit of internal balance remained important as an objective of macroeconomic policy. Increasingly, this was done through monetary policy, and there was a brief experiment with monetarism at the time of high inflation in the 1970s. But by early 1990s macroeconomic policies had become focussed on an inflation-targeting system, pursued through the use of monetary policy. The basic idea of this was simple – when inflation rises above target, the interest rate would be increased in order to discourage demand in the economy and discipline the rate of inflation and vice versa if inflation was low. Such an approach to policy explicitly focuses on the control of inflation. But it also requires the central bank to influence the level of spending in the economy to keep the economy close to full employment. As time went on, in the 1990s and early 2000s, with inflation under control, it became the task of the central bank to cut interest rates to stimulate spending and counter unemployment and also to raise interest rates when demand became too high. Monetary policy became devoted to the pursuit of internal balance.

The behaviour of floating exchange rates became central to such a use of monetary policy to ensure internal balance. If demand is low and the interest rate is cut to promote employment, part of the desired stimulus will be brought about by the depreciation in the exchange rate that follows a reduction in the interest rate, because the depreciation will cause an increase in exports and reduction in imports. Such a perspective on adjustment – articulated using the Mundell–Fleming model, which was put forward at the IMF in the 1960s (Fleming, 1962; Mundell, 1963) emphasized how, with floating exchange rates, monetary policy can engineer movements in the exchange rate which will help to bring about the changes in demand that are required. Thus, while the pursuit of internal balance remained central to this policy system it now relied importantly on external effects as part of the process of achieving this objective.

But external balance ceased to be a policy objective. It was thought that there was no longer any need to use policy to pursue external balance, precisely because of the operation of floating exchange rates. Increasingly, the world was characterized by a high degree of capital mobility with the result that countries were able to borrow internationally for considerable periods of time. In such a world, if exchange rates are floating, the exchange rates will adjust to enable a country to repay what it borrows. Of course such an outcome requires that the private sector is able to repay what it borrows – both nationally and internationally. But, in principle, all that is necessary as a matter of active policy in normal times is appropriate movements of interest rates and the operation of disciplined fiscal policies to ensure that government budget deficits are balanced over the longer term.

Crucially, this policy system did not require international cooperation in the making of macroeconomic policies.[11] In each country monetary policymakers would set interest rates to ensure full employment of resources in that country. And floating exchange rates would move as part of the process of ensuring full employment in each country. External balance was no longer an objective of policy, since, at least over the longer term, external balance would be ensured by the floating rate regime. Max Corden once described such a set-up as an 'international monetary non-system', where the term 'non-system' was a term of praise (Cordon, 1994).

Of course policy outcomes in home and foreign countries remained jointly determined – since countries were interconnected. Think of what happened in this period in the US and Europe. In the US policymakers set the interest rate to ensure a full employment outcome, so as to reach internal balance. In Europe, policymakers set the interest rate to ensure a full employment there too. But open international capital markets meant that the two interest rates needed to end up being similar; movements in the exchange rate ensured that the outcomes were consistent with the level of world interest rates that was established. If European policymakers needed to set a higher interest rate than that in the US to achieve internal balance in Europe – as happened after German re-unification in the 1990s – then capital flowed out of the US and into Europe, causing the European exchange rate to appreciate relative to the dollar, making Europe less competitive. Such exchange rate movements only ceased when the appreciated exchange rate in Europe reduced demand in Europe and stimulated demand in the US enough to ensure that the interest rate which European policymakers wished to set was similar to that set in the US.

These policies were accompanied by more deregulated domestic financial systems and by a belief that fiscal policy should not be adjusted on a discretionary basis in any attempts to control the economy. Such light-touch policy framework was very different from the interventionist framework of the Keynesian era and the international cooperation that underpinned the Bretton Woods system. The global non-system appeared to be doing very well, right up until the recent Global Financial Crisis. In his paper called 'The State of Macro' published in 2008, Olivier Blanchard argued that things were going well in macroeconomic theory (Blanchard, 2008). The same appeared to be true with macroeconomic policy.

The Global Non-system and Macroeconomic Policy in East Asia

From the 1980s onwards the international order became more complex with the rise of East Asia. But in 1997 the Asian miracle turned into the Asian financial crisis. The expansion of credit in the run-up to that crisis was based on an underpricing of risk which bore some similarity to what happened in the period preceding the global crisis of 2008. In the East Asian case this underpricing was underpinned by a system of fixed exchange rates. But after that crisis, growth in East Asia returned, at a spectacular rate, led by China (Corbett and Vines, 1999a, b; Corbett, Irwin and Vines, 1999 and International Monetary Fund, 2003).

The exchange rate regime between East Asia and the rest of the world remained one of very nearly fixed exchange rates – a system which became known as Bretton Woods II (Dooley, et al. 2004a,b). This influenced the international monetary system which emerged in the period of the Great Moderation that followed the East Asian crisis. Relations between the advanced countries – principally in the US and Europe – but also Japan, Canada, Australia and some other countries – followed a path similar to that described earlier. But relations between the advanced world and East Asia were carried out in a different manner.

Nevertheless, the outcome was still one in which international cooperation was not needed. To see this, I now describe what happened between East Asia and the advanced world after the East Asian Crisis. Households and firms in East Asia saved a great deal, and, after the East Asian crisis, investment was reduced for many years as a result of the uncertainty which the crisis had created. This had implications for relations between China and the US. Rapid growth in China required a depreciated real exchange rate to enable China to run a current account surplus, so as to keep demand high and offset the gap between savings and investment within the country. It also required that people in the US continue to spend, so that global demand remained high enough for the global economy to continue to expand. Such a high level of spending in the rest of the world was assured in the period of the dot-com boom. But after the dot-com crash it required a reduction in US real interest rates (brought about by the Greenspan put), to ensure that global demand remained high. At that time it became necessary to ensure that domestic demand in the US remained high enough, even after running a deficit with East Asian countries and in particular with China. As a result what was observed in the period after the East Asian crisis was an outcome in which China (and other East Asian countries) pursued depreciated real exchange rates, and the US and other advanced countries held domestic interest rates at historically low levels. The result was a trade surplus in China and the rest of East Asia – and a deficit in the US. This describes the origin of global imbalances in the early years of the twenty-first century (Adam and Vines, 2009).

But throughout the period of the Great Moderation, as long as governments and private agents remained inter-temporally solvent, there was no constraint imposed on this system by the need to ensure a current account balance. All that was necessary as a matter of policy was to ensure that exchange rates in China and other emerging market economies moved in the way required to bring about growth in those regions and that interest rates in the US and other advanced countries moved so as to bring about growth there too. Global imbalances between East Asia and advanced countries were not a problem (Blanchard and Ferretti, 2011).

As a result, Bretton Woods II also came to be a system which did not require international cooperation of macroeconomic policies. In each country, policymakers set his or her instrument with the objective of ensuring full employment of resources in that country; East Asia – and particularly China – set the real exchange rate to promote full employment in their countries, and interest rates in the rest of the world were set with the objective of ensuring full employment and growth in the rest of the world. The global imbalances which emerged were simply a reflection of a loan from East Asia to advanced countries. Although exchange rates between East Asia and the rest of the world were not floating, providing that the exchange rate between emerging market economies and the rest of the world was adjusted in the way described, this was not an obstacle to the independent setting of policies. No coordination was necessary. And in such a world, global imbalances did not constitute a problem.

The Global Non-system and Macroeconomic Policy within Europe

The collapse of the Bretton Woods system and crisis of the 1970s which followed led to much disquiet in Europe about the volatility of exchange rates which had emerged in the decade post-1971 and, it was believed, posed a threat to the free market in trade which was emerging within Europe and which became the Single European Market. Policy in Europe thus turned to the reconstruction within Europe of a system of pegged but adjustable exchange rates and the European Monetary System or EMS was established in the 1980s. This set Europe on the path towards European monetary union (EMU) which was finally established with the creation of the Euro in 1999 (Temin and Vines, 2013).

Until 2009, it appeared that the establishment of the Euro had been successful. Many Member States enjoyed the benefits of belonging to a currency union, notably the high growth rates which resulted. The area appeared to be cushioned against economic shocks, and disruptions due to intra-European exchange rate realignments appeared to be a thing of the past.

Macroeconomic policy for Europe as a whole consisted of two parts – here we consider policy for Eurozone as a whole and put countries outside this zone to one side. The European Central Bank (ECB) managed monetary policy for the Eurozone to ensure a satisfactory rate of growth of demand for the region as a hole. The Stability and Growth Pact (SGP) was put in place in 1997 to bring about fiscal discipline, so as to provide a commitment by EMU countries 'to respect the medium-term budgetary objective of positions close to balance or in surplus'. This policy was designed to allow Eurozone countries to deal with normal cyclical fluctuations while keeping their government deficit below a reference value of 3 per cent of GDP. The approach to fiscal policy embodied within the SGP meant that fiscal policy was assigned the task of ensuring a satisfactory outcome for the level of public debt. But, beyond this, fiscal policy was assigned no other macroeconomic responsibility – the kind of position that it had come to occupy in other advanced countries.

For the Eurozone, it was thought that cooperation with other countries was not necessary in the setting of macroeconomic policies for the world as a whole. The part which Europe played in the global economy was understood in the way discussed previously. This relied on the ability of the Euro to float against the dollar, in the way discussed there; in such a floating rate system each region would set its own monetary policy in relation to its own objectives.

There were wide divergences in growth rates within the Eurozone, which set the stage for the Eurozone crisis which we discuss subsequently. But until 2009 these had not created a global problem.

The Need for Cooperation in the Current World

The Great Moderation came to an abrupt end in 2008, leading to the most rapid decline in economic activity since the Great Depression (Eichengreen and O'Rourke, 2012). The task of global macroeconomic policy since then has become that of safeguarding and sustaining the world's recovery from that crisis. It is this task which now requires cooperation.

Immediately after the crisis, governments acted worldwide to stimulate aggregate demand. Monetary policy became immediately expansionary and interest rates were cut to the zero bound. Fiscal policy also became expansionary, through increases in public expenditure, by the cutting of tax rates, and, in particular, by allowing tax receipts to fall as output fell, rather than raising tax rates in order to offset the effect of falling tax revenues.

The G20 Summit in London in April 2009 brought together countries with a similar purpose where all of them agreed to act in this way.

Resolving the resulting policy conflict now requires cooperation of a rather different kind from what was required from global policymakers in the immediate aftermath of the financial crisis, when the requirement was simply to stimulate demand. The demands on macroeconomic policy are large.[12] The fact that global interest rates have been at their zero bound has made it impossible for policymakers in the US and Europe to meet their policy objectives through the use of monetary policy. Furthermore, the size of the public sector deficit has led to fiscal discipline and austerity in many countries.

In response to this policy problem, the US Federal Reserve and the Bank of England have been relying on quantitative easing (QE), and the ECB has been doing something similar. Such a policy involves a central bank buying longer dated government bonds with newly created money, so as to lower the long-term interest rate and thereby stimulate demand. Nevertheless, global aggregate demand remains inadequate.

The QE policy has the effect of pushing down the exchange rate in the country which is pursuing it. Achieving a satisfactory level of aggregate demand output in each of the key regions is in danger of conflicting with the objective of doing this in the other region. Each region is attempting to depreciate its real exchange rate and recover in part through export-led growth, at the expense of the other. This is in danger of creating the beggar thy neighbour devaluations that policymakers at Bretton Woods were keen to avoid.

At the same time, the low levels of East Asian exchange rates have enabled a high level of output growth to be preserved by East Asia, by means of continued export growth.[13] This, of course, is continuing to lead to a reduction in demand and output in the US and also to a reduction of demand in Europe.

It is not possible to draw a clear outcome, until we are told how this policy conflict will be resolved.

The global challenge is becoming more significant as time passes. In both the US and Europe, financial markets and policymakers are focussed on reducing public deficits and debt. In Europe, as discussed below, the EMU crisis has led to urgent fiscal cuts in the GIIPS (Greece, Italy, Ireland, Portugal and Spain) but insufficient compensating rise of spending in Germany, so that – all other things being equal – Europe also has an interest in seeking export-led growth, taking demand away from the rest of the world. Finally, and crucially, in East Asia, domestic demand is expanding only gradually, due to the slow speed of adjustment within in China, so that export expansion remains important there too.

To ensure a return towards a satisfactory global rate of growth requires that demand grows fast enough at the world level to compensate for the effects of fiscal consolidation, for the effects the crisis in Europe and for gradual adjustment in China and East Asia. In the absence of this cooperation the policy moves contemplated will lead to an outcome which does not ensure sufficient growth but instead leads to stagnation.

We can summarize the situation as a prisoner's dilemma, in which there are two possible outcomes.

A cooperative solution in which there is a sufficient increase in spending within countries in all regions of US, Europe and East Asia, including sufficient fiscal expansion. This solution would enable the world to move towards meeting all three growth objectives, that is, to make a move towards internal balance in all three regions.

A non-cooperative outcome in which there is insufficient increase in spending coupled with continuing fiscal retrenchment and in which all regions attempt to grow through the pursuit of rapid export growth. This creates the prospect of conflict as all regions attempt to grow through exporting.

This second case is one in which a global adding-up problem is manifest. In these circumstances we can expect beggar-thy-neighbour currency depreciations in deficit countries as each region attempts to obtain export-led growth by means of currency depreciation. At present the UK has attempted to pursue this strategy – acting as a single small open economy. Recently Japan – a much larger economy – has begun to act in the same way. We can expect significant conflict if two major regions of the world – both Europe and the United States – pursue this option while at the same time demand does not expand sufficiently rapidly in China and East Asia. Other countries are likely to suffer from this, in experiencing a too-low level of interest rates and a level of competitiveness vis-a-vis the dollar and the Euro which it is difficult to sustain.

The IMF's *World Economic Outlook* warned in June 2010 against an outcome of this kind. But subsequent exercises have suggested that this outcome continues to be likely.

What is at the heart of this problem? The world is caught in a pincer movement. On the one hand, aggregate demand is low in advanced countries, both because they are deleveraging after the financial crises, so that private sector spending is abnormally low, and because fiscal spending is being curtailed in the face of rising levels of public sector debt. On the other hand China is continuing with a slow speed of adjustment. Germany is forcing a speedy and unprecedented degree of austerity adjustment on the peripheral countries in Europe but is not ensuring a correspondingly rapid expansion of demand at home. Instead, it continues to use its competitive position to ensure that it grows rapidly by means of an export surplus. This explains why many in Europe are keen to see the Euro fall against the dollar.

This bad global outcome must therefore be seen as a necessary consequence of fiscal constraints in many countries of the deliberate slow-adjustment choices being made by the Chinese authorities and of the policies of Germany. The world needs cooperation to ensure that the recovery is sustained through moderation in fiscal austerity, through a more rapid adjustment in China and the rest of East Asia and a more rapid expansion in Germany. Only if that happens it will be possible for fiscal consolidation in advanced countries to proceed without aggravating unemployment.

Issues which Influence the Need for Global Cooperation

Moderating the Speed of Fiscal Consolidation

Immediately after the financial crisis, governments acted world-wide to keep up aggregate demand. Effectively, the public sector supplied assets which were acquired by the household sector as it increased its saving and held by the financial sector as it has deleveraged out of its holdings of risky assets. As a result the public sector debt increased rapidly in many countries.

In the medium run, this fiscal position must be reversed. But timing is crucial. Both in the US and in Europe fiscal policymakers have been under pressure from markets to cut the deficit, and in the US it has been forced on the Administration by a failure by Congress to agree on fiscal policy, leading to the fiscal sequester. Such fiscal contractions are making it more difficult to achieve growth in demand, the objective discussed in this chapter.

The planned fiscal reductions in Europe are large (Institute for Fiscal Studies 2011). In the UK, the plan is for a reduction in demand of 1.4 per cent a year, over five years, i.e., a total of 7 per cent of GDP. In Ireland, Greece, Portugal and Spain, the planned consolidations are respectively, 6, 10, 8 and 4 per cent over the same period. In Germany, the numbers are much smaller, but still significant. In the US, the stimulus package is being withdrawn and the effects of the fiscal sequester are large.

In the long run, there is a risk that sufficient fiscal correction does not happen and that a sustained global recovery might be jeopardized through continuing fiscal laxity. A continuation of sustained fiscal deficit is likely eventually to cause interest rates to rise and to subvert the global recovery. If that situation is accompanied by a fear of longer-term fiscal insolvency, such a position may, ultimately, lead to a fiscal crisis. What is needed is a coherent strategy of long-term deficit reduction, so as to stabilize the ratio of public debt to GDP, and to beg into bring it down (Altschuler and Bosworth, 2010).

The argument for delay in fiscal consolidation is that once the growth in private sector demand has recovered, fiscal consolidation can be matched by lower interest rates, preventing the consolidation from causing growth to falter. But at a time of a zero bound, each tightening of the fiscal position will lead to a further reduction in output and to further loss in tax revenues. It is quite possible that in the short term, fiscal consolidation can lead to such a large fall in output the consolidation actually causes the ratio of public debt to output to rise (Blanchard and Leigh, 2013).

A delay in fiscal consolidation in the US will require an end to the process of fiscal sequestration. There is every likelihood that growth in domestic demand remains low. And there is a risk that the US will come to rely on further depreciation of the dollar to sustain demand and growth.

Increasing the Speed of Adjustment in East Asia and Reducing Global Imbalances

One important way of sustaining global demand is through a reduction in global imbalances through a reduction in the size of East Asian exports relative to imports. Even if international capital mobility means that global imbalances are not a problem themselves, a reduction in East Asian surpluses will lead to an increase in global aggregate demand and lessen the policy conflict described above.

Optimism has been expressed by some scholars about the possibility of expanding demand in East Asia, particularly in relation to China. Lau (2010) contains an argument suggesting that the turn around in the Chinese current account surplus which happened in 2008–09, as global world trade collapsed, might be the harbinger of a longer run structural change. However, the recent surge on the Chinese current account surplus suggests that this view might be over-optimistic.

The distinctive feature of the 15 years since the East Asian crisis has been the transformation of the Asian export-led recovery strategy, which was used in the aftermath of the crisis, into a longer-lasting export-led growth strategy. Undervalued exchange rates and rapidly growing exports meant that sustained external demand growth allowed these economies, and especially China, to solve the development challenge of generating sufficient productive employment to absorb a vast quantity of surplus labour in the agricultural sector.

Such a policy encouraged a build-up of reserves for use in the future – a public-sector strategy of self-insurance against future crises (Eichengreen, 2004; Portes 2009). This explains what happened for the first few years after the Asian crisis, but it is not a satisfactory medium-run story. High gross savings rates in Asia, particularly in China, have continued to reflect slow-changing structural and demographic characteristics, including relatively weak social security and pension systems (Prasad, 2009; Wei and Zhang, 2009). Third, domestic investment rates in countries other than China remained substantially below their pre-crisis levels much more than a decade after the crisis, partly because of underdeveloped financial markets (Caballero *et al.*, 2008; Mendoza *et al.*, 2007). Finally – and most importantly – an aspect of the 'Bretton Woods II' strategy argument, which we discussed above, was that several major developing and emerging market countries, in particular China, deliberately pursued an export-led growth strategy so as to sell their products into existing global markets, using best-practice global technology, partly introduced through foreign direct investment, without having to build domestic markets.[14]

Yu Yongding (2009) is cautious about the extent to which the required correction is taking place. He notes that at present savings in China are high and domestic demand low, partly because of the high level of profits, both in the old state enterprises and in the rapidly growing private sector. These profits are not being distributed to the household sector in a way which could stimulate the required increase in consumption, but are instead being used to fund investment. In addition, he notes, a large fraction of the Chinese fiscal stimulus has also been used to finance large increases in public infrastructure investment, rather than to finance increases in consumption. He argues that this adjustment process in China is not sustainable. In due course the extra investment will create extra capacity to produce output. If that capacity is to be fully utilized, then exports must remain high and must continue to grow.

Yu Yongding (2012) adds a further argument. For a variety of reasons there are incentives in many regions to attract high levels of FDI, which compete with domestic investment for finance, and which thereby crowd out domestic investment. If savings remain high, this means that exports must be high and growing if demand for domestic output is to grow at the required rate. There is – of course – a solution to Yu's problems in the form of a more rapid increase in real wages, and such real wage increases are happening in China. These increases tend to encourage domestic consumption. But there is a real worry as to how quickly such adjustment in factor prices and in production technology will actually happen in China.

The longer this takes, the longer will Chinese policymakers need to seek an outlet for their growing production through exports – pushing the world back towards an outcome with global imbalances. It appears that for domestic political reasons, China may not be in a position to ensure the rapid recovery in consumption and the demand-driven appreciation of the renminbi, that this would entail.

Yiping Huang and Bijan Wang (2010) present a complementary argument, focusing on costs, rather than on demand. They argue that a key determining factor of China's imbalances are the repressed costs and prices of a number of factors of production, not just labour. They identify heavily distorted markets for all of labour, capital, land, resources and the environment. They note that these repressed factor prices are, in effect, implicit subsidies for producers, investors and exporters. Such subsidies boost growth but, at the same time, lift investment and exports. They note that previous policy efforts to resolve imbalances have focused mainly on administrative measures, which – they argue – are not and have not been sustainable. They suggest that a more fundamental solution to the imbalance problem will require more market-oriented reforms of the markets for factors of production, with the liberalization of prices for all of labour, capital, land and resources.

These explanations are complementary, because a sustainable rebalancing will require both an increase in domestic consumption and an increase in domestic costs relative to those abroad. These arguments suggest that any rebalancing will be slow, however much it is in the interests of policymakers to move in this direction. Blanchard and Milesi-Ferretti (2010) produced simulations of such gradual adjustment, using the IMF's global economic model. They suggest that adjustment will be so sluggish that Chinese net exports will continue to subtract nearly 1 per cent of world GDP from the level of demand facing other countries. Similar suggestions have been expressed in the IMF's *World Economic Outlook for 2013*.

Thus in East Asia, particularly in China, there appear to be circumstances which are holding back the growth of domestic demand and dampening the adjustment of relative prices. This means that East Asia continues to have an interest in sustaining demand through means of an export surplus. The more this can be moderated, the more this will contribute to a solution of the global policy problem.

Moderating Austerity within Europe and Reducing Global Imbalances

There were wide divergences in growth rates within the Eurozone during its first ten years. Capital flowed into the periphery of the GIIPS that experienced a boom. Countries of the North, led by Germany, grew much more slowly. Partly as a result of this difference, there were also wide divergences in inflation rates; these were higher in the GIIPS countries and lower in the North. That led to serious divergences in the competitiveness levels and in balance of payments positions of the Eurozone economies.

This was not meant to happen. Within a monetary union, wages and prices in each country need to be set in the knowledge that a country needs to remain sufficiently competitive, relative to the other members of the union. How this was meant to work was made very clear by Otmar Issing, a prominent member of the Bundesbank in the 1980s and of the ECB in the 1990s. Issing's view stressed the need for wage and price setters throughout the monetary union to be aware of the need for discipline – of the need to be competitive, and to cut costs, so as to ensure that the firms for which they worked were competitive in their local market and in the European and global marketplace (Issing, 2002).

Nevertheless, until 2009, the divergences appeared to be manageable. It was thought that SGP for fiscal policy, coupled with an awareness of inter-

European competitive positions, would be sufficient to ensure the necessary discipline for wages and prices over the longer term.

The collapse within the GIIPS which has taken place since 2010 in Europe has shown just how wrong these beliefs were. Indeed the European policy framework, which was described above, has made things worse. The divergence of inflation rates led to a divergence of real interest rates – with lower real interest rates in the European periphery encouraging the boom there which magnified inflation and led to a further worsening of the competitiveness gap. This difficulty has become known as the Walters critique of a monetary union (Allsopp and Vines, 2007, 2010 and Temin and Vines, 2013). This should have been counteracted by fiscal policy. But the single-minded focus of the SGP on budgetary positions prevented this – indeed fiscal revenues were abnormally high in the periphery (even allowing for cyclical correction) which pointed policymakers away from taking any corrective action. Only after the crisis arrived causing government revenues to collapse was the argument for fiscal tightening strongly presented.

Countries within the GIIPS are now suffering from their uncompetitive position. Since 2011, they have been dealing with very high-risk premia, on account of fears of sovereign default, fears that the Eurozone will collapse and interrelated fears of collapse of the banking system.

Macroeconomic adjustment to these difficulties is hard. The constraints of a common currency area lead to an inability to correct competitiveness within the monetary union through exchange rate adjustment. They thereby prevent a recovery from crisis of the kind engineered by the countries of East Asia after the 1997 crisis. The result has been both unemployment and crisis in the GIIPS. Currency risk has emerged as a result of a belief that external deficits will need to be corrected to enable recovery to take place, although these deficits had been happily tolerated during the earlier period of rapid growth. Sovereign risk has emerged for related reasons. Policymakers in these crisis countries have been unable to sustain internal demand in the face of their external deficits. Indeed austerity has been imposed as a response to these risks.

The European response to the crisis – austerity – has been based on the assumption that fiscal profligacy has been the villain and this continues to be the case. This may have been so in Greece and even in Italy. But it was not the case in the other crisis countries. What kind of solution within Europe appears to be necessary?

As explained in our discussion of the Bretton Woods system, adjustment requires both expenditure changing policies – which in the absence of monetary policy will require changes in fiscal policy – and expenditure switching policies – to be brought about by changes in relative competitiveness. As in the Bretton Woods system, adjustment will require changes in policies in both the deficit country and the surplus country – i.e., in both the GIIPS and in Germany (Temin and Vines, 2013).

It is clear that costs and prices need to fall in the GIIPS and this is already happening. But they also need to rise in Germany relative to what would otherwise have happened, to ensure that the whole of the adjustment is not forced on the GIIPS. The adjustment in expenditure policies has already happened in Spain to a very great degree; what is needed for adjustment is more flexible fiscal policies in Germany. Of course such adjustments are made more difficult by the zero bound which means that the monetary policy of the ECB cannot sustain an adequate level of demand for the Eurozone as a whole, something which puts additional demands on German fiscal policy. The necessary changes in fiscal policy require a loosening of the requirements of the SGP, both for GIIPS countries and for Germany as well.

This adjustment solution must not be derailed by risk premia during the course of adjustment. This is something which has so far been assured by the action of the ECB, the promise of Mario Draghi, the President of the ECB to do whatever it takes to save the Euro. In particular, through its programme of Outright Monetary Transactions, it stands ready to buy the bonds of GIIPS governments and to thereby depress these risk premia.

These aspects of a solution must all go together. A move towards a higher level of activity within Europe can be achieved. The crisis countries also need to be reassured that Germany will not push for austerity so severe that they will not be able to adjust and grow again. It appears at the time of writing that write downs of debt of the some of the members of the GIIPS will be necessary for this to be possible. But given the adjustment pressures which are being imposed on the GIIPS, at the core what is required is an increase in demand in Germany and so a move towards a higher level of activity in Germany and an increase in inflation in Germany to bring about higher costs within Germany relative to those in the GIIPS countries. This would enable Germany to rebalance away from its very large current account surplus. Rebalancing, through a reduction in Germany's current account surplus is part of what is needed in Europe, precisely because the GIIPS countries are being required to rebalance.

It is possible that monetary policymakers in Europe will seek to use the effects of the ECB's Outright Monetary Transactions on interest rates in the GIIPS as a way of encouraging a fall in the Euro and so encouraging recovery in Europe as a whole. This would involve seeking to promoting European growth at the expense of growth in the rest of the world. This is a risk which we have seen in all regions of the world. This should be prevented by policy cooperation at present.

The Role of the G20MAP and India

The analysis in the IMF's World Economic Outlook for Spring 2013 has suggested that the global recovery continues to be slow. This chapter has suggested reasons as to why this might have come about as a result of pressures for fiscal consolidation and pressures by too many countries to pursue export-led growth at once. This is not an adequate response to a global shortage of demand; it creates a global adding-up problem.

The G20MAP has been underway for three years now, with the aim of avoiding such a problem. At a number of G20 Summits, most recently at the Los Cabos Summit in June 2012 G20 Leaders have committed to adopting policy measures to strengthen demand and support global growth. Officials working for the G20MAP have carried out a detailed analysis of the policies of seven particular countries identified as having large imbalances, and the IMF has carried out detailed analyses of how macroeconomic policies will fit together for the world as a whole (IMF, 2013). Country leaders have already been given the task of collectively agreeing a set of policies which will bring about adjustment-with-growth outcome of the kind described in the previous section – rather than a low-growth outcome. The overall analysis has pointed towards the existence of cooperative policies which might move the world towards a more expansionary outcome (Faruqee and Srinivasan, 2012; IMF, 2013).

It is now the task of the G20MAP to deliver on the promises which have been made.

How might India help to ensure that the G20MAP leads to a good outcome for the world? It is clearly important for India to carry out policies which lead to a satisfactory domestic outcomes. But beyond this there are things which India could do to help improve the overall global outcome. In an earlier section of the chapter two proposals were made.

The first suggestion raised previously in the chapter concerned the need to ensure that the detailed analyses carried out by the IMF were conducted in a way free from political influence and that the results are made public. Both these things have happened. However, pressures may be brought to bear to prevent this in the future, and India should see its role as helping to ensure that such pressures are resisted.

The second suggestion raised was that comment on G20 decisions at summits might be sought from a body of internationally respected economists and other leaders, drawn from a number of countries. These economists might be invited to comment, both on the way in which the global decisions about policy come to be made and on the way in which these decisions do or do not properly respond to the challenges posed by the IMF's detailed analysis. The availability of such outside commentary might assist G20 leaders in their deliberations. As noted above, this suggestion follows up on and develops a proposal which was made by Montek Singh Ahluwalia at a conference organized by ICRIER, CEPII and BRUEGEL in New Delhi in September 2010.

It is possible that as the world comes to operate the G20MAP, the international policymaking community might learn something from the way in which inflation targeting regimes were constructed in many G20 countries over the past 20 years. In such regimes, central banks came to exercise their policies in remarkably successful ways, which have been largely free from political interference. Lessons have been learned about the usefulness of transparency about accountability and about credibility in the construction and operation of these regimes. Of course the construction of the G20MAP is a much more difficult and ambitious task than the construction of national inflation targeting regimes because it is global and because it explicitly involves the need for global cooperation. Nevertheless, the lessons from the constructions of those national regimes might be helpful in the creation of any longer-lasting G20MAP.

Cooperation needs to build on shared information. But it also requires shared analysis. It is clear that at present different views about the need for fiscal consolidation are at the heart of the difficulty ensuring cooperative action. There are also conflicting views about the extent to which adjustments need to be made in the surplus countries. To reach agreement on these issues will involve process of trust. This depends partly on building a process of shared information and analysis in the way described above. It also depends on a shared process of working together, which the G20MAP has brought about.

The experience of the G20MAP might turn out to be important for global institution design. We may end up with an international community of policymakers and officials – both in the G20 nations and at the IMF – who are committed to resolving global macroeconomic problems and to sustaining global growth. If this works, the G20MAP will institutionalize a new shared responsibility for managing the global macroeconomy.

Conclusion

In 1944, at Bretton Woods, Keynes saw a need for global support of good policies in individual countries and a need for a global coordination of policies. This was a rules-based system and one in which there was a mutual assessment of national policies. Now, in the face of our present problems, we need something similar. The late Tomaso Padoa Schioppa very recently restated the benefits which might result from the re-creation of such a rule-based global monetary system, to replace the present non-system (Padoa Schioppa, 2010).

There will of course be differences in details between then and now. But, as in the Bretton Woods system, there will need to be a multilateral regime, in which there is a set of rules shared by countries that countries agree to follow. Allowances will need to be made for countries to act with discretion, where necessary, and not to follow strictly prescribed rules. There will need to be a formal process of policy-assessment, carried out within the G20MAP and managed by the IMF. Finally, there will need to be a multilateral process of decisionmaking about policies, a process which ensures that the rules are followed, and/or ensures that, when they are not followed, this is for cogent reasons which are publicly visible.

This is a demanding agenda. But such an agenda appears to be necessary if global policymakers are to ensure that the recovery from the global financial crisis really is sustained.

Endnotes

[1] See International Monetary Fund (2011) for a discussion on the IMF's role in the G20 process.

[2] See Eichengreen and Irwin (2009).

[3] See IMF (2011).

[4] These stages are set out in IMF (2011).

[5] International Monetary Fund interchangeably has been referred as the 'IMF' or the 'Fund'.

[6] It is worth noting that this disagreement is similar to that which occurred between the United Kingdom and the United States at Bretton Woods; see Temin and Vines (2013).

[7] Putting other issues on the table might involve introducing issues of cooperation about financial policies, climate-change policies and development. We do not discuss such wider issues in this chapter. But Brown (2011) discusses how a deal which includes this wider set of issues might be brought about.

[8] Keynes initially favoured protection as a means of bringing about external adjustment and was only converted to the use of exchange rate adjustment in the run-up to the Bretton Woods conference. See Temin and Vines (2013).

[9] Such a process of convergence is, of course, what is happening in emerging markets at present.

[10] In this system, the IMF was helped by the World Bank and by the General Agreement on Tariffs and Trade (GATT). The latter was designed to supplement the Bretton Woods system by encouraging the growth of international trade. The GATT's role in promoting the liberalization of trade restrictions supplemented the Fund's role in promoting the liberalization of exchange restrictions on current account transactions. A series of GATT 'rounds' brought about tariff reductions, which helped to create markets for exports as countries expanded. With high employment, balance-of-payments deficits dealt with as described above and with many countries growing by exporting, there were clear incentives for most countries to support trade liberalization. That, in turn, made exports and imports more sensitive to exchange-rate levels and so made balance of payments adjustment easier to achieve by exchange-rate adjustments. These linkages between different aspects of the overall post-war policy framework are difficult to pin down empirically. As a result, there is still some disagreement as to how quantitatively important the Bretton Woods system was in sustaining the golden age of growth. But there is no disagreement that its effect was large (Matthews et al., 1982; Matthews and Bowen, 1988; Temin, 2002 and the papers in Eichengreen, 1995 and Eichengreen, 2007).

[11] Initially, in the inflationary period of early 1980s, it was thought that cooperation would be necessary and difficult to achieve (Oudiz and Sachs, 1984). At that time, economists worried that countries with a high rate of inflation would seek to raise interest rates and appreciate their exchange rates so as to dampen inflation by cheapening imports. At the same time, the inflation would be exported to other countries whose imports would become more expensive. But these fears proved overblown. It was gradually realized that in successful inflation-targeting regimes such policy conflicts would be temporary. And concerns about them subsided, as inflationary pressures disappeared, and advanced countries grew steadily during the 1990s and early 2000s.

[12] The policy challenges are discussed in Blanchard et al. (2013) and in the papers referred to in that note.

[13] The real exchange rate has appreciated significantly in China, but the very rapid technical advance in China, coupled with low wages, means that the exchange rate in China remains undervalued. The fact that the Chinese trade balance has improved is partly a feature of the low output in the US and Europe and the consequential low level of demand for East Asian goods in the US and Europe.

[14] Aizenman et al.(2004) among others have shown that contrary to the textbook model of capital allocation, the growth record of developing countries that are net exporters of savings is consistently superior to those that are net importers.

References

Adam, Christopher and David Vines. 2009. 'Remarking Macroeconomic Policy after the Global Financial Crisis: A Balance Sheet Approach'. *Oxford Review of Economics Policy,* 25 (4), 507–52 December.

Allsopp, Christopher and David Vines. 2007b. 'Fiscal Policy, Labour Markets, and the Difficulties of Intercountry Adjustment Within EMU'. In *The Travails of the Eurozone,* edited by David Cobham. London: Palgrave Macmillan.

Allsopp, Christopher and David Vines. 2010. 'Fiscal policy, intercountry adjustment, and the real exchange rate within Europe'. In *The Euro: The First Decade,* edited by Buti, M. S., Deroose, V. Gaspar and J. Nogueira Martins. Cambridge: Cambridge University Press. Also available as European Economy. Economic Papers. No 344. October 2008. Available at: http://ec.europa.eu/economy_finance/publications/publication_summary13256_en.htm [Accessed in October 2013].

Altshuler, Rosanne and Barry Bosworth. 2010. 'Fiscal Consolidation in America: the Policy Options'. Paper presented at a Macro Economy Research Conference on Fiscal Policy in the Post-Crisis World, held at the Hotel Okura, Tokyo, 16 November.

Blanchard, Olivier J. 2008. 'The State of Macro'. NBER Working Paper No.14259.

Blanchard, Olivier J., Giovanni Dell'Ariccia and Paolo Mauro. 2010. 'Rethinking Macroeconomic Policy.' IMF Staff Position Note, February, SPN/10/03. Available at: http://www.imf.org/external/pubs/ft/spn/2010/spn1003.pdf [Accessed in October 2013].

Blanchard, Olivier J., Giovanni Dell' Ariccia and Paolo Mauro. 2013. 'Rethinking Macro Policy II: Getting Granular'. IMF Staff Discussion Note No. 13/03. Available at: http://www.imf.org/external/pubs/ft/sdn/2013/sdn1303.pdf [Accessed in October 2013].

Blanchard, Olivier J. and Daniel Leigh. 2013. 'Fiscal consolidation: At what speed?', VoxEU. Available at: http://www.voxeu.org/article/fiscal-consolidation-what-speed [Accessed in October 2013].

Blanchard Olivier J. and Gian Maria Milesi Ferretti. 2010. 'Global Imbalances – in Midstream?'. IMF Research Department.

Blanchard Olivier J. and Milesi Ferretti. 2011. 'Why should current account imbalances be reduced?'. IMF Staff Note.

Brown, Gordon. 2010. *Beyond the Crash: Overcoming the First Crisis of Globalisation.* London: Simon and Schuster.

Caballero, Ricardo J., Emmanuel Farhi and Pierre-Olivier Gourinchas. 2008. 'An equilibrium model of "global imbalances" and low interest rates'. *American Economic Review* 98(1); 358–93.

Corbett, Jenny and David Vines. 1999a. 'Asian Currency and Financial Crises: Lessons from Vulnerability, Crisis, and Collapse'. *World Economy,* 22 (2): 155–77.

Corbett, Jenny and David Vines. 1999b. 'The Asian Financial Crisis: Lessons from the Collapse of Financial Systems, Currencies, and Macroeconomic Policy'. In *The Asian Financial Crisis: Causes, Contagion and Consequences,* edited by Agenor, M. Miller, David Vines, and Axel Weber. Cambridge: Cambridge University Press.

Corbett Jenny, Gregor Irwin and David Vines. 1999. 'From Asian Miracle to Asian Crisis: Why Vulnerability, Why Collapse?'. *In Capital Flows and the International Financial System*, edited by David Gruen and Luke Gower. Sydney: Reserve Bank of Australia.

Corden, W. Max 1993. 'Why Did the Bretton Woods System Break Down'. In *A Retrospective on the Bretton Woods System*, edited by Bordo, M. and Barry Eichengreen. Chicago: The University of Chicago Press.

Corden, W. M. 1994. *Economic Policy, Exchange Rates, and the International System*. Oxford: Oxford University Press.

Dooley, Michael P., David Folkerts-Landau and Peter Garber. 2004a. 'The Revised Bretton Woods System'. *International Journal of Finance and Economics*, 9: 307–13.

Dooley, Michael P., David Folkerts-Landau and Peter Garber. 2004b. 'Direct Investment, Rising Real Wages and the Absorption of Excess Labor in the Periphery.' NBER Working Paper no. 10626.

Eichengreen, Barry. (ed.) 1995. *Europe's Postwar Growth*. New York: Cambridge University Press.

Eichengreen, Barry. 2004. 'The Dollar and the New Bretton Woods System'. Henry Thornton Lecture delivered at the Cass School of Business, London, 15 December.

Eichengreen, Barry. 2007. *The European Economy since 1945: Coordinated Capitalism and Beyond*. Princeton: Princeton University Press.

Eichengreen, Barry and Kevin O'Rourke. 2012. 'A tale of two depressions redux, VoxEU'. Available at: http://www.voxeu.org/article/tale-two-depressions-redux [Accessed in October 2013

Faruqee, Hamid and Krishna Srinivasan. 2012. 'The G-20 mutual assessment process – a perspective from IMF staff'. *Oxford Review of Economic Policy* 28(3): 493–11.

Fleming, J. Marcus. 1962. 'Domestic Financial Policy under Fixed and Floating Exchange Rates'. IMF Staff Papers 9: 369–79.

G24. 2011. 'Issues for Discussion'. G24 Technical Group Meeting, Pretoria, South Africa, 17-18 March 2011. Available at: http://www.g24.org/in0311.pdf [Accessed in October 2013].

House, Brett, David Vines and W. Max Corden 2008. 'The International Monetary Fund'. *New Palgrave Dictionary of Economics* London: Macmillan.

International Monetary Fund. 2003. 'The IMF and Recent Capital Account Crises: Indonesia, Korea, Brazil'. Report of the Independent Evaluation Office of the IMF.Washington, DC: International Monetary Fund. Available at: http://www.imf.org/external/np/ieo/2003/cac/pdf/main.pdf [Accessed in October 2013].

International Monetary Fund. 2006. 'Evaluation Report: Multilateral Surveillance'. Report by the Independent Evaluation Office, Washington: D.C. Available at: http://www.ieo-imf.org/ieo/files/completedevaluations/09012006report.pdf [Accessed in October 2013].

International Monetary Fund. 2011. 'Review of the IMF's Involvement in the G20 Mutual Assessment Process'. Available at: http://www.imf.org/external/np/pp/eng/2011/051311.pdf [Accessed in October 2013].

International Monetary Fund. 2013. 'The G-20 Mutual Assessment Process (MAP)'. *International Monetary Fund Factsheet*. Available at: http://www.imf.org/external/np/exr/facts/g20map.htm [Accessed in October 2013].

Institute for Fiscal Studies. 2011. 'How does the UK's planned fiscal consolidation compare?'. Available at: http://www.ifs.org.uk/publications/5693 [Accessed in October 2013].

Issing, O. 2002. 'On Macroeconomic Policy Coordination in EMU'. *Journal of Common Market Studies* 40(2): 345–58.

Keynes, John Maynard. 1919. *The Economic Consequences of the Peace*. London: Macmillan.

King, Mervyn. 2006a. 'Reform of the International Monetary Fund'. Speech given to the Indian Council for Research on International Economic Relations (ICRIER) in New Delhi, India, on 20 February.

King, Mervyn. 2006b. 'Through the Looking Glass: Reform of the International Institutions', Inaugural International Distinguished Lecture, Melbourne Centre for Financial Studies, Australia, 21 December. Available at: www.bankofengland.co.uk. [Accessed in October 2013].

Lau, Lawrence J. 2010. 'Some Myths about the Chinese Economy', paper presented to the Hong Kong Monetary Authority Annual International Conference on the Chinese Economy.

Matthews, R. C. O. and A. Bowen. 1988. 'Keynesian and Other Explanations of Postwar Macroeconomic Trends'. In *Keynes and Economic Policy*, edited by W. A. Eltis and P. J. N. Sinclair. London: NEDO.

Matthews, R. C. O., C. H. Feinstein and J. C. Odling-Smee. 1982. *British Economic Growth 1956–73*. Oxford: Clarendon Press.

Meade, James Edward. 1951. 'The Theory of International Economic Policy, Vol. 1'. *The Balance of Payments*. London and New York: Oxford University Press.

Mendoza, Enrique G., Vincenzo Quadrini, and José-Victor Ríos-Rull. 2007. 'Financial integration, financial deepness, and global imbalances'. CEPR Discussion Paper no. 6149.

Moggridge, Donald Edward. 1976. *Keynes*. London: Fontana.

Mundell, Robert A. 1963. 'Capital Mobility and Stabilization Policy under Fixed and Flexible Exchange Rates'. *Canadian Journal of Economics and Political Science* 24: 1345–57.

Oudiz, Gilles and Jeffrey Sachs. 1984. 'Macroeconomic Policy Coordination among the Industrial Economies'. Brookings Papers on Economic Activity 1:1–64.

Padoa-Schioppa, Tommaso. 2010. Keynote Speech at the ICRIER-CEPII-BRUEGEL Conference on 'International Cooperation in Times of Global Crisis: Views from G20 Countries'. Held in New Delhi, on 16–17 September 2010.

Portes, Richard. 2009. 'Global Imbalances'. Mimeo. London: London Business School.

Prasad, Eswar S. 2009. 'Rebalancing Growth in Asia'. NBER Working Paper No. 15169.

Qureshi, Zia. 2011. 'G20 MAP: Growth, Rebalancing, and Development'. Presentation to a G24 Meeting Pretoria, 17 March 2011. Available at: http://www.g24.org/zqu0311.pdf [Accessed in October 2013].

Regling, Klaus and Max Watson. 2010. *A Preliminary Report on The Sources of Ireland's Banking Crisis*. Dublin: Government Publications Office.

Temin, Peter. 2002. 'The Golden Age of European Growth Reconsidered'. *European Review of Economic History* 6(01): 3–22.

Temin, Peter and David Vines. 2013. *The Leaderless Economy: Why the World Economics System Fell Apart and How to Fix It*. Princeton. Princeton University Press.

Vines, David. 2003. 'John Maynard Keynes 1937–1946: the Creation of International Macroeconomics'. *Economic Journal* 113(448): F338–61.

Vines, David. 2008. 'James Meade'. *New Palgrave Dictionary of Economics*. Revised Edition. London: Macmillan.

Williamson, John 1983. 'Keynes and the International Economic Order'. In *Keynes and the Modern World*, edited by Worswick, David and JamesTrevithick. Cambridge: Cambridge University Press.

Yiping, Huang and Bijun Wang. 2010. 'Cost Distortions and Structural Imbalances in China'. *China & World Economy* 18(4): 1–171.

Yu Yongding. 2009. 'China's Responses to the Global Financial Crisis', Richard Snape, Lecture, Productivity Commission, Melbourne. Available at: http://www.eastasiaforum.org/wp-content/uploads/2010/01/2009-Snape-Lecture.pdf [Accessed in October 2013].

Yu Yongding. 2012. 'Rebalancing the Chinese Economy'. *Oxford Review of Economic Policy*, 28(3): 551–68.

5 Reform of International Financial Institutions

T. N. Srinivasan[1]

Introduction

The perceptions that the performance of International Financial Institutions (IFIs) was unsatisfactory and unless reformed they will become completely dysfunctional are widespread. These perceptions were accentuated by the belief that the IFIs failed to recognize that the growing vulnerabilities in the domestic financial systems of major financial centers could result in a global financial crisis of major proportions and failed to warn the authorities in those centers of the need for effective, coordinated and timely action by them.

The perceptions led to several proposals for reforms of IFIs, including in particular from the 'independent evaluation' offices in the IFIs themselves, IMF (2011a,b,c), Independent Evaluation Office (IEO) (2011a), the Zedillo Commission (Zedillo 2009), Committee on Foreign Relations of United States Senate (CRFUSS 2010) and leaders of G20. Governors of major Central Banks argued (Banque de France 2011) that the rising Global Current Account Imbalances threatened the stability of the global financial system. Scholarly contributions to the analytics of the global financial crisis include the papers in the Journal of Economic Perspectives (Fall 2010 and Winter 2011) and books by Rajan (2010), Reinhart and Rogoff (2009) and Shiller (2008). Many of the problems of the IFIs pre-date the global financial crisis, while the recent analyses focus on the implications of the crisis for IFI reforms.

The purpose of this chapter is to explore and sort out the IFI reform issues. Section 2 is on the declarations of the G20 leaders on IFI reforms, their responses to the financial crisis and the record of the fulfillments of their commitments. Section 3 analyses proposals for reforms of IFIs. Section 4 is on the issues discussed by India's Prime Minster at the summits. Section

5 is on the analytical literature on reforms meant to reduce the probability of a repetition of a severe global financial crisis in the future. Section 6 is on some important aspects of IFI reforms such as distribution of membership quotas, international coordination of crisis response and Global Financial Architecture. Section 7 concludes.

Declarations at G20 Summits

Founding of G20

The Group of 20 is a global policy forum of 20 largest economies.[2] It originated in September 1997 out of G22, an ad hoc group of 22 countries formed to coordinate a collective response to the 1997 Asian Financial Crisis and reincarnated as G20, a permanent forum that would meet regularly. The hitherto unchanged membership was chosen by G7 (Canada, France, Italy, Japan, the UK and the US). Geo-political considerations, rather than systemic significance from the perspective of the global economic-financial system, appear to have led to the choice of membership.[3] Whether legitimate or not, once formed, the G20 has designated itself as the premier forum for international economic cooperation at its second summit at Pittsburgh, USA in 2009 and reaffirmed it at the third in Toronto, Canada.

G20 Summit Declarations: A Brief Overview[4]

Each G20 meeting is attended by the heads of government of the member countries and for this reason is termed a 'summit'. Until the end of 2012 seven summits have been held, from the first in Washington D.C in November 2008 to the seventh at Los Cabos, Mexico, in June 2012. The eighth is scheduled to be held in St. Petersburg, Russia in September 2013. At the end of each summit the G20 leaders issue a declaration containing their assessment of the economic situation, their proposed actions and commitments. What follows is a description of some of the major topics, actions and commitments of the G20 leaders (hereafter 'The leaders') in various summits.

At their first summit in November 2008 at the onset of the global financial crisis, the topic was on Financial Markets and the Global Economy. The leaders emphasized 'our cooperation and work together to restore global growth and achieve needed reforms in the World's financial systems' and to 'lay the foundation for reform to help to ensure a that a global crisis... does not happen again' (paragraphs 1–2).

Commitments and Actions on Stabilizing the Global Financial System including Reform of IFIs

At each of the subsequent summits also the stability of the global financial system was discussed. The leaders agreed on the common principles for the reform of financial markets which included reforming the IMF and the World Bank so that they 'can more adequately reflect changing economic weights in the world economy in order to increase their legitimacy and effectiveness...'. A plan on high priority actions was also announced (paragraphs 9–10 of Washington Summit). Significant progress has been made on many of these since 2008.

At London, UK in April 2009, the leaders reported progress on their decision to establish a new Financial Stability Board (FSB) with a strengthened mandate (paragraphs 15–16) and agreed on concrete steps to increase the resources of the IMF, to support a general Special Drawing Right (SDR) allocation, committed to implementing the package of IMF quota and voice reforms (paragraphs 17–20).

At Pittsburgh the leaders launched a framework 'to generate strong, sustainable and balanced growth' (paragraph 13) designated the 'the G20 as the premier forum for our international economic cooperation' (paragraph 19), committed to a shift in IMF quota share to dynamic emerging markets and developing countries of at least 5 per cent from over-represented countries to under-represented countries using the current quota formula (paragraph 20).

The Toronto Summit in June 2010 saw the reiteration of the frameworks for Strong, Sustainable and Balanced Growth; Financial Sector Reform; Enhancing the Legitimacy, Credibility and Effectiveness of the IFIs and Further Supporting the Needs of the Most Vulnerable. While modestly claiming in paragraph 3 that 'our efforts to date have borne good results', the leaders soberly recognized in paragraph 4 that serious challenges that remain.

At Seoul, the leaders claimed to have delivered core elements of the new financial regulatory framework to transform the global financial system, endorsed the new bank capital and liquidity framework, reaffirmed that tax payers should not bear the costs of resolution and committed once again to national-level implementation of the policy recommendations prepared by the FSB in consultation with the IMF on increasing supervisory intensity and effectiveness (paragraphs 24–33).

The Seoul declaration includes three Annexes, one on Seoul Development Consensus for Shared Growth, another on a Multi-Year Action Plan on

Development and a third on an Anti-Corruption Action Plan. A supporting document on Policy Commitments by G20 Members is also appended.

At Cannes, France, in 2011 the leaders committed to reinvigorate economic growth, further structural reforms, make international financial system more representative, stable and resilient, develop the regulation and oversight of shadow banking, address commodity price volatility and promote agricultural development, strengthen multilateral system, address challenges of development and reform global governance for the twenty-first century.

At the Los Cabos, Mexico summit the leaders reaffirmed their commitment to promote growth and jobs (paragraph 2) by implementing a structural reform agenda (paragraph 5) and announced an action plan for that purpose (paragraph 7) to pursue financial inclusion and stand by the Doha Development agenda, to work towards concluding the Doha Round (paragraph 30) and in promoting Development to focus on Food Security, infrastructure and inclusive green growth. The leaders announced an Accountability Framework (paragraph 19) for reporting on progress in implementing their policy commitments. The Euro area leaders among them committed to take all measure to strengthen the integrity and stability of their area (paragraphs 6, 11).

The tasks to which the leaders committed themselves in their first Washington Summit 2008 are yet to be accomplished almost five years later in full measure. The leaders in effect admitted this fact in paragraph 12 of their Cannes declaration of 2011 and reiterated that they will implement their commitments and pursue the reform of the financial system.

Of course, the global economy seems to be on a path of recovery, albeit slow and halting, from the depth of the global recession, and the as yet unresolved Euro Zone uncertainties from 2011 on.[5] Although several factors that have been associated with and could have contributed to the crisis have been identified, there is no consensus on whether some or all played a causal role, and if they did, their relative contribution to the probability of occurrence of the crisis, let alone its spread as well as severity once it occurred. Significant progress has been made in addressing the weaknesses in the domestic and global financial system that in retrospect seemed to have played a major role, including in particular those that enabled the problems from the collapse of the bubble in housing prices in the US to spread to the US financial sector and then to the financial sectors around the globe. Significant progress had also been made in addressing possible regulatory failures in domestic financial systems. Yet some of the major tasks remain to be completed including fiscal consolidation in the US and some countries in the Euro area and India, bringing down global imbalances to sustainable levels, and concluding the Doha Round with an ambitious and balanced outcome.

Problematic Aspects of Summit Declarations: Some Examples

Toronto Declaration

Understandably with their limited time at the summits the leaders cannot examine the issues they discuss in adequate depth. The declarations are replete with clichés and their language more often than not reflects linguistic bridges between incompatible positions. They include too many commitments by the leaders to be credible. For example, at the Toronto summit the leaders established a Working Group to make recommendations on how G20 could continue to make practical and valuable international efforts to combat corruption (paragraph 40), committed to a green recovery (left unexplained) and to sustainable growth (paragraph 41); encouraged continued and full implementation of country-specific strategies and time frames based on national circumstances for the rationalization and phase out over the medium term of inefficient fossil fuel subsidies (paragraphs 42–43) and established a Working Group on Development and mandating it to elaborate a development agenda and multi-year action plans to be adopted at the Seoul Summit a year later. The last task alone cannot be meaningfully completed in a year!

The Toronto Declaration highlighted the dire consequences that would follow if there were no coordinated policy response by G20. This evaluation has little credibility in the absence of essential details of any concrete action that each member will undertake as part of coordinated actions of G20 and their monitoring of the actions credibly.

On Financial Sector Reform (paragraphs 8 to 23), the discussions are mostly of a stock-taking of various actions that had been previously agreed. A general statement stating that global action is important to minimize regulatory arbitrage, promote a level playing field and foster widespread application of the principles of propriety, integrity and transparency has little operational content besides sounding banal.

Seoul Declaration

The declaration included three Annexes, respectively on the Seoul Development Consensus on Shared Growth, a Multi-year Action Plan on Development, an Anti-corruption Action Plan and a supporting document on Policy Commitments by G20.

The Development Consensus is disappointing in its tiresome repetition of the largely rhetorical Millennium Development Goals (MDG) and failure in recognizing that the members of the UN General Assembly did not commit to take needed actions and provide resources for achieving their MDG. The Consensus seems to be driven less by the intrinsic moral goal of enabling the poor wherever they are to climb out of their poverty permanently and more by the at best instrumental role developing countries (at least some) could play as potential 'new drivers of aggregate demand and more enduring sources of global growth'. The six Development Principles are unexceptionable but banal.

The Action Plan to enhance the effectiveness and the reach of knowledge sharing is cliché-ridden with familiar phrases such as 'North-South, South-South and Triangular Co-operation' and banal ones such as 'the adoption and adaptation of the most relevant and effective development solutions' etc. The Anti-corruption Action Plan is not even an action plan but a list of nine items of the G20 Agenda on Combating Corruption! Very few of the policy commitments at Seoul seem credible holding leaders accountable for their delivery. The fiscal consolidation commitments of the US or India do not seem credible. In particular, the fiscal problems of Eurozone members are inextricably tied to their commitment to a single currency of Euro. The credibility and sustainability of the Eurozone as a Currency Union in the absence of a fiscal, let alone a political, union is being repeatedly and severely tested by the markets.[6]

The G20 leaders could still do a great service if they were to focus on those objectives on which progress is crucially dependent on their coordinated action and where sufficient analytical knowledge on what could be done already exists. For example, the leaders, appropriately mention knowledge that does exist particularly in the IMF and the MDBs. If they had looked at the available research at IMF, World Bank and ADB, they would not have been as sanguine as they appear to be about available knowledge.[7]

Independent Evaluation of IMF and the World Bank Group, Proposals for Reform from the Committee on Foreign Relations of the US Senate and Non-governmental Organizations

Evaluation of Performance of IMF by IEO and the World Bank Group by Independent Evaluation Group (IEG)

The report of the IEO (2011a) is indeed a hard hitting evaluation of the IMF's failures in the run-up to the financial crisis of 2008. The report claims, using pop-psych jargon, that the IMF's ability to identify correctly the mounting risks was hindered by a high degree of group-think, intellectual capture and a general mind-set that a major financial crisis in large advanced economies was unlikely. The report notes that weak internal governance, lack of incentives to work across units and to raise contrarian views played an important role.

Political constraints appear cryptically in the executive summary. The report recommends that IMF should create an environment that encourages candor and considers dissent. IEG (2010) on the World Bank Group raises similar concerns as IEO (2011a). However, it has relatively few critical things to say on the contrasting responses of different members of the World Bank Group to the Financial Crisis. All ex-post evaluations including the IEO's (and IEG's) suffer from the unavoidable fact of 20–20 vision of the past in their recommendations. What is needed is an ex-ante counterfactual analysis of what might happen in the future if their recommendations are accepted. There is no evidence in the report of the IEO or the IEG having done any counterfactual analysis. As an internal group staffed mostly by employees of IMF and the World Bank it is arguable whether they would do serious counterfactual analyses.

Staff Report of the Foreign Relations Committee of the US Senate

The report of Committee on Foreign Relations the United States Senate (CFRUSS, 2010) came to four key conclusions and made in all 50 recommendations for eight different organizations including the Obama administration on what each should do. The recommendations were followed by a detailed and thoughtful discussion of their rationale.

Report of the Zedillo Commission

Among the reports of non-governmental groups that reported on IFI reforms that of the Zedillo (2009) Commission appointed by the President of the World Bank and the IMF's consultation with civil society are important. The commission made five main recommendations that are claimed to have 'a unifying logic' and also that they are 'mutually-reinforcing and interdependent – they will only have their effect if they are adopted and implemented as a single package' (Zedillo 2009, xiv). These covered voice and participation of members of World Bank in its decision-making process, restructuring of its governance structure, reform of the process of selection of the President of the Bank, strengthen the accountability of the Bank's management and increasing the lending capability and resources of the Bank.

In the strong words of the Commission, only National leaders, at the level of heads of states can break the gridlock on reform of the World Bank Groups and neither the Governors of the World Bank Group nor the Group's current Board of EDs will act on their own without clear directives from heads of their governments.

However, the analytical underpinning for some of the recommendation does not seem to be well articulated. For example, the very first recommendation for enhancing voice and participation by members is not based on any deep notion on what voice, participation fairness and equity should mean in the World Bank Group whose members are national governments, many of which would not qualify as participatory democracies in domestic governance, In recommending that the special majority needed for amending articles of agreement be reduced to 80 per cent for 85 per cent, a recommendation that would affect only one member and that too in events of very low frequency, the Commission did not examine the deeper issues of a trade-off between the incentives for encouraging nations to join and for retaining them once they join.

The Commission's long discussion on quotas for membership of the World Bank and the historical linkage between shareholding the World Bank and IMF quotas seems overblown and pointless without a careful analysis of the mandates of both and purposes served by quotas in each. The Commission did not seem to have considered in depth and evaluated ways of separating voice-related considerations from those of access to resources at the two institutions.

Report on the Civil Society Consultations (Fourth Pillar) of the IMF

The IMF initiated a process to consult Civil Society on IMF governance. It constituted the last and fourth pillar of its process of gathering inputs on its performance.

Civil Society was defined as consisting of all individuals and organizations that are not government. For obvious reasons no random sample from the Civil Society could be chosen for canvassing their views. The findings of the report based on a non-random sample of respondents represent only the self-reported views of a self-selected set of respondents who participated in the video consultation, made written submissions and submitted papers. No participant appears to be from China except for one from the SAR of Hong Kong. In all the report made 16 recommendations. Its key messages of accountability, transparency and legitimacy are mostly sensible.

India's Positions on Financial Crisis, Protectionism and the Doha Round at G20 Summits

India and China are two important emerging market members of G20. The most authoritative statements on India's positions are the statements of Prime Minster Dr Manmohan Singh at the G20 Summits. The international reputation of Dr Singh's economic expertise was recognized by the other leaders. The views of Dr Singh on the financial crisis, development and developing countries were respected by the other leaders as he headed the Government of India, a developing country, which along with China experienced the effect of the global financial crisis for a relatively short period of time and recovered quickly and was growing rapidly.

India's Position on Resort to Protectionism and Concluding Doha: Dr Singh at the G20 summits and Indian negotiators on Doha

The leaders including Dr Singh voiced a strong commitment to avoid the temptation to use protectionist responses to the financial crisis in the trade policy of their countries and expressed a strong desire to bring the Doha Round of Multilateral Negotiations to a conclusion promptly with an 'ambitious and balanced outcome'. However, India's positions at the formal and informal ministerial meetings of the WTO on the Doha modalities do not seem to have changed since the December 2008 WTO Ministerial in which disagreement between India and US precluded progress towards a prompt conclusion of the round. There is a clear conflict between what Dr Singh said at various summits on Doha and India's negotiating position on Doha that mirrors ambivalence on liberalization of foreign trade, investment and capital controls in India's domestic political economy.

Trade and Investment Measures by G20 since 2008

From available official reports (WTO 2011) each of the G20 members have taken various trade and investment measures that appear to be in conflict with the declarations of the leaders at all the summits. Among all such measures taken by G20 members since 2008 two of the most undesirable are Anti-Dumping measures or ADMs and Export Restrictions (ERs). Extremely distortionary ADMs have no economic rationale behind them particularly since non-distortionary Most Favoured Nation (MFN) safeguard measures and options to raise applied tariffs closer to bound levels are available. Unfortunately, India, the EU and the US are prominent users of ADMs in recent years. ERs including complete bans on exports are often used purely from domestic political considerations. Again India uses both.

The fiscal positions of India (and the US) for example, have been unsustainable for a fairly long time. Possible contributing factors are volatility of commodity prices and the possibility of political instability of some region. But these are not new phenomena and can therefore be ruled out with the absence of domestic political consensus as the dominant cause for failure to consolidate the fisc. The longer time future is not reassuring not just because of uncertainties about fiscal correctons being undertaken and the continued adherence of G20 to the pledge not to retreat into investment protection, but far more ominously about the global economy.

Trade and Investment Measures Undertaken by India since 2008

To protect domestic consumers of producers from rises in domestic prices India has often used ERs including export bans. First on ADMs, India is clearly a disproportionate user. The data on ERs in the WTO report also show that both India and G20 as a whole have been increasing their use of ERs. The pledge of G20 together and India as its member not to use protectionist measures has been clearly violated and in particular the use of ADMs is quite disturbing.

Dr Singh on Non-trade Issues Including IFI Reforms

Dr Singh's statements exemplify his expertise as an economist and also his implicit economic framework. At the Washington summit Dr Singh noted the spread of the financial crisis, 'which a year ago seemed to be *localized* to one part of the financial system in the US' had since 'exploded into a *systemic crisis*, spreading through the highly interconnected financial markets of industrialized countries, and has had its effects on other markets also' (emphasis added).

Dr Singh noted that the financial crisis 'has choked normal credit channels, triggered a worldwide collapse in stock markets... the real economy is clearly affected' and forecast that the global recession 'will hit the export performance of developing countries and the choking of credit, combined with elevated risk perception will lead to lower capital flows and reduced levels of foreign direct investment. The combined effect will be to slow down economic growth'. Most of what Dr Singh forecast about the effects of global recession on emerging markets indeed came about.

On India, Dr Singh noted 'After growing close to 9 per cent per year for four years, our growth rate is expected to slow down... Much of India's growth is internally driven... we can maintain a strong pace of growth in the coming years, but many developing countries will be hit harder. Slowing down of growth in developing countries will push millions of people back into poverty, with adverse effects on nutrition, health and education levels. These are not transient impacts but will impact a whole generation'.

Dr Singh spoke at length on the coordinated global responses to the crisis and distinguished between immediate and long-term priorities, between engaging in short-term fiscal stimulus and long-term fiscal consolidation. For addressing the likely downturn in the private investment in developing countries, Dr Singh called for expanding infrastructure investment for its immediate countercyclical effect of demand stimulation and also for its longer-term effects of facilitating an early return to faster growth and as a signal for reviving private investment.

On the new financial architecture, Dr Singh said that 'the IMF is the logical body to perform the task of multilateral surveillance' but noted that 'over the years the Fund has become marginal to the task of policy analysis and consultations on macroeconomic imbalances and related policies in major countries' and asked for recommendations on governance reform that would enable the fund to perform the role of macroeconomic policy coordination.

On the eve of the London summit, Dr Singh made several remarks on what remained to be done to address the global slowdown and speed up recovery. Interestingly, he touched on the need for explaining to the public the rationale for rescue and bail-out of large banks. He viewed this as a political task to be handled by each national government, but the G20 can help by sending a clear message that the problem affects many industrialized countries and has to be tackled to bring about economic revival and reduce unemployment and also in convincing the public that reviving banks is important not just for the banks' shareholders, but for the economy, employment and for global prosperity generally.

He said India recognized the importance of fiscal sustainability and mentioned the intention to return to a fiscally sustainable path after 2010. Finally, Dr Singh turned to longer-term reform of global financial system and emphasized the need for stronger regulation and improved supervision of the financial system and urged the G20 to endorse the proposals to be developed by the Financial Stability Forum and the Basel Committee on

Bank Supervision for aligning national regulations with new global standards to expand the perimeter of regulatory coverage.

At the Pittsburgh summit Dr Singh reiterated what he had said at the previous two summits. At the Toronto Summit, in his brief remarks Dr Singh was clear on how to protect growth in the face of the then emerging nervousness in the markets about debt sustainability, especially in some Eurozone countries. Although currently unsustainable levels of debt would call for fiscal contraction, under the prevailing circumstances of fragile recovery and weak private demand in industrialized countries, he argued that if many industrialized countries followed contractionary policies simultaneously, a double-dip recession could follow thereby inducing very negative effects on developing countries.

At the Seoul summit, Dr Singh remarked on how swift responses of G20 managed to avoid what could have been a precipitous collapse of the World Economy. Yet, he pointed out that high unemployment in industrialized countries threatens a revival of protectionist sentiment. Moreover, uncertainty about the prospects of industrialized countries affects the investment and medium-term growth prospects of emerging market countries.

Dr Singh endorsed the Seoul Development Consensus and the associated Multi-Year Action Plans. He once again urged the industrialized countries to lend their support to ensure the satisfactory conclusion of the Doha Round and in confronting the resurgence of protectionist sentiment while commending the fact that actual protectionist action has been more limited.

Analytical Framework for Distinguishing Causal from Associated Factors underlying Global Financial Crisis and for Devising Responses and Solutions

Micro-behavioural Foundations for Holding Money and Nominal Assets

The global financial crisis originated in the collapse of what turned out to have been a bubble in the prices of real assets, namely, houses and also commercial real estate in the US. The crisis then spread to the financial sector and the entire economy in the US first and then to the global financial system and economy. It is moot whether, had the build-up in real estate prices before the collapse been understood early enough by policymakers to have been a bubble; then they could have taken steps to prevent it from continuing and ease the prices towards their fundamental values. Mishkin (2011) asks several questions about the aftermath of collapse of the bubble developed into a global financial crisis. An entirely satisfactory answer to these questions has not as yet emerged in part because to answer them one needs a well-specified analytical model that integrates the financial and real sectors. As yet, there is no model which most analysts would deem as the most appropriate.

In building such a model in which a purely financial crisis could have an impact on the real economy, one has to provide micro-behavioural foundations for current and future nominal prices of commodities, real assets and real returns to influence current and future micro decisions of vectors of production, consumption, investment and net factor accumulation. The classic contingent commodity model of Arrow and Debreu is a purely real barter model of real (i.e., relative) prices, real assets and real returns.

For the classical economists with their quantity theory of money, money is simply a veil with all equilibrium nominal prices varying in the same proportion as the exogenously set quantity of nominal money varies, with all equilibrium real magnitudes and relative prices determined independently of the nominal prices.

A micro-behavioural foundation for a monetary economy has to imply a real opportunity cost for holding or spending money and monetary assets in equilibrium. There are various ways of achieving this. Baumol (1952) and Tobin (1956) in their models with no exogenous uncertainty postulate that the real cost of a transaction such as sale (purchase) of a real commodity or asset by paying (receiving) money in exchange is lower than that of the same transaction through barter, that is, by paying (receiving) some other commodity in exchange. In this model a demand for money is for saving real costs of transaction. This ensures that in equilibrium a real price (opportunity cost) for money arises and along with an additional market clearance condition, namely that the stock of money available is at least as large as the aggregate transactions demand for money.

Other models such as the various so-called 'cash-in-advance' do not even attempt a rudimentary micro-foundation and in an ad-hoc manner simply assume that transactions can take place only in cash and the stock of money one has limits the transactions in real commodities that one can undertake. Thus, an additional nominal constraint based on cash-on-hand arises over and above the usual real budget constraint that expenditures cannot exceed resources available from endowments such as commodities and factors supplied to the market and incomes from asset holdings. Thus with a behavioural foundation such as Tobin (1956) and Baumol (1952) or with ad-hoc cash in advance assumptions, an additional constraint relating to holding of cash arises. This means that in the first order conditions of consumer welfare optimization, a shadow price per rupee of cash emerges for cash holdings. This price is the real cost of money for that consumer.

If one analysed an analogous social planner's welfare maximization problem subject to an aggregate resource and a cash constraint expressing that aggregate cash requirements for transactions do not exceed cash available, one would again get an aggregate real cost of money. Under suitable conditions, the solution of the planner's social welfare maximization could be decentralized as competitive market equilibrium with the associated public tax/subsidy and transfer interventions in the form of lump sum income transfer across consumers. In this decentralized competitive equilibrium model with money, though it is not the Arrow Debreu model, their result that a competitive equilibrium is a Pareto Optimum holds.

Dynamic Stochastic General Equilibrium Model (DSGE)

In the models of general equilibrium business cycle theory of the Dynamic Stochastic General Equilibrium (DSGE) genre, there is no financial sector with private institutions involved in the supply of credit, public regulations relating to their behaviour and no financial intermediation. They are not of much use for analysing a financial crisis (Ohanian, 2010).

Aggregate Macroeconomic Models

Issues of financial stability have always been part of the macroeconomic curriculum in the US and European Universities, though they have often been presented as mainly of historical interest or primarily of relevance to emerging markets (Woodford, 2010). Financial instability is viewed as a pathology no longer present in the developed world but not yet eradicated in the emerging markets of the developing world. The fact that the crisis originated in and had such a disruptive consequence in the US with its well-developed and deep financial system came as a surprise and brought home that even in economies like the US, significant disruption of financial intermediation remains a possibility (ibid). Woodford not only discusses why neither standard macroeconomic models that abstract from financial intermediation nor traditional models of the bank lending channel are adequate as a basis for understanding the recent crisis and sketches, the basic elements of an approach that allows financial intermediation and credit frictions to be integrated into macroeconomic models in a straightforward way. Woodford cites research based on some version of his approach. But his approach remains to be tested adequately empirically allowing for context specificities. For example, two DSGE models for India by Anand *et al.* (2010) and Gabriel *et al.* (2010) do not incorporate the fact that in the Indian economy a large share of savings and investment do not involve financial intermediation.

Cabellero (2010) views the current core of macroeconomics as the DSGE model and recognizes its logical coherence and the precision of its analytical conclusions. But he argues that the profession of macroeconomists has become so mesmerized by the internal logic (of DSGE) that it has begun to confuse the precision (of DSGE) about its own world with the precision it has about the real world and 'the root cause of the poor state of affairs lies in a fundamental tension in academic macroeconomics between the complexity of its subject and the micro-theory-like precision to which we aspire'.

A far more serious problem is the attribution of expected outcomes in a model to the real world. For example, in trade policy discussions, outcomes (e.g., gain in social welfare) from a policy (e.g., trade liberalization) that a model with one set of assumptions (e.g., absence of any domestic or external distortions) delivers are often attributed to a world in which the assumptions do not hold (e.g., a world full of distortions). Then disappointment that the attributed outcomes from the model are not seen in the real world is to be expected.

Alternative Perceptions of the Origins of and Contributory Factors to the Financial Crisis and the Associated Policy Reforms

Mishkin (2011) divides the financial crisis of 2007–09 into two phases, the first and more limited one from August 2007 to August 2008 affecting a relatively small segment of the US financial system, namely, sub-prime residential mortgages. In mid-September, 'the crisis entered a far more virulent phase. In rapid succession the investment bank Lehman Brothers entered bankruptcy on September 15, 2008; the insurance firm AIG collapsed on September 10, 2008; and there was a run on the Reserve Primary Fund, a money market fund, on the same day; and the highly publicized [political] struggle to pass the Troubled Asset Relief Program (TARP) began'.

Mishkin asks why 'something that appeared in mid-2008 to be a significant but fairly mild financial disruption transformed into a full-fledged global financial crisis? What caused this transformation? Did the government responses to the global financial crisis help avoid a worldwide depression (the leaders of G20 answer this question in the affirmative with no caveats whatsoever)? What challenges do these government interventions raise for the world financial system and the economy going forward?'. These questions are appropriate and relevant.

In his answers, Mishkin basically focussed on the credit channel and explains how a financial crisis widens the spread between interest rates on Baa Corporate and treasury bonds. He supports his claims about the credit channel with data on credit-spreads, bank-lending and net issuance of asset-based securities. He then discusses the various policy interventions including unconventional monetary policy tools. Mishkin's view is that 'Conclusions about the effectiveness of policy should begin by considering the counterfactual – that is, what would have been the likely course of events be without the policy interventions'. He finds that 'Some parts of the government intervention were less helpful than others. But taken as a whole, I believe the government actions helped to prevent a far deeper recession and even possibly a depression'. He offers two key lessons: 'first, the global financial system is far more interconnected than was previously recognized and excessive risk-taking that threatened the collapse of the world financial system was far more pervasive than almost anyone realized and second, extraordinary actions by central banks and governments have [arguably] contained this global financial crisis, but successfully unwinding these policies will prove to be a challenging task'. Both lessons are appropriate. Mishkin's perception and conclusion about the crisis are so widely shared as to be deemed as conventional.

Reinhart (2011), with his different and provocative perspective, argues that the crash of 1929 and the attendant deep economic contraction were widely viewed then as excesses of speculation and competition, and the economics profession came around to the view that 'cartelization of industry could promote growth, restriction on financial firms and transactions in the financial sector were a preferred way to dampen volatility, flexible exchange rates were destabilizing It took decades for economists to revise this perspective…'.

In Reinhart's view the conventional narrative of events since 2008 [such as Mishkin's (2011)] makes an error similar to the misreading of and prescriptions that followed the 1929 crash, namely, 'that the global economy was hit by a "perfect storm" of disruptive forces in late 2008…key financial authorities in yellow slickers – a sort of Corps of Financial Engineers (CFE)

– fought the elements [the "perfect storm"] and made decisions about which flood waters to divert, which leaves to reinforce, and which sluice gates to open'.

In his perspective – the CFE consisting of President Geithner of New York Federal Reserve, Chairman Bernanke of Federal Reserve Board and Treasury Secretary Paulson – 'inserted the government into the resolution of the Investment Bank Bear Stearns in March 2008 [because they mis-] interpreted the death throes of the mid-sized investment bank as a problem of systemic importance and, with an ill considered intervention protected the creditors of Bear Stearns and raised the expectation of future bail outs. When the same CFE failed to intervene in September 2008 when Lehman Brothers entered bankruptcy the resulting market seizure was in part a counter – reaction to the early Bear Stearns intervention'

For Reinhart the right question is not 'Why not Save Lehman?' but 'Why Save Bear Sterns?' He focuses 'on a course not taken in March 2008 of prompt recognition of economic losses' and on why the path of recognizing losses and forced mark downs might not have been taken in March 2008 and describes the biases inherent in crisis management that make similar mistakes likely in the future.

Global Imbalances and Exchange-rate Flexibility

Global imbalances, meaning persistent increases in surpluses in the current account in some of the emerging market countries [e.g., China] and current account deficits in industrialized countries [e.g., US] in recent years have attracted the attention of policy makers. Since the onset of the financial crisis, the rhetoric has escalated with charges of currency manipulation, potential outbreak of competitive currency devaluations and currency wars as a response to the decline in export demand have been bandied about.

The G20 and also the economic profession seems focussed too much on a single policy instrument, namely the exchange rate, while from an economic perspective, current account deficit or surplus is influenced in addition by other policies including fiscal and monetary policies. The apparent unanimity of views of G20 on exchange rates, capital controls, etc. do not seem to be based on any deep analysis. The fact that IMF now views the use of capital controls could be appropriate in some contexts is of limited significance. Put another way – ruling out *a priori*, the use of one instrument of policy, namely capital controls, without establishing that control-free capital flows is a dominant policy strategy independent of contexts is inappropriate anyway. As long as the uses of capital controls are not dominated strategies, it is obvious that their use would be in a portfolio of usable contingent policy choices. The papers of IMF (2011d) on a conceptual framework for the use of capital controls with its explicit reference to context specificities and of Ostry et al. (2011) on tools to use to manage capital flows are timely and useful.

In addressing global imbalances, if exchange-rate policy changes are the only ones to be used or if only one set of countries adjust, the welfare cost for individual countries and for the world as a whole would be higher as compared to using all available policy instruments including exchange rates, fiscal and monetary policies and all countries participated in the adjustment towards a lower imbalance.

Perspectives of Three Central Bank Governors, on the Role of Global Imbalances in the Financial Crisis

Rising global imbalances have been viewed as having fuelled and contributed to the financial crisis. The views on the crisis of Governors of three important central banks, Bernanke of the Federal Reserve (Fed) of US in which the financial crisis originated and Mervyn King of Bank of England (BOE), UK which was one of the developed countries that was most affected by it and Subbarao of Reserve Bank India (RBI), which was indeed impacted by the crisis, though briefly and not severely, are of interest. The three and Governors from central banks around the world had expressed their views on global imbalances (Financial Stability Review, February 2011).

Bernanke's (2011) paper is analytically the most interesting. He explicitly disavows having provided a causal mechanism by which foreign capital flows contributed to the financial crisis: 'To be clear in no way do our findings assign the ultimate causality for the housing boom and bust to factors outside the United States. Domestic factors… were the primary sources of the boom and bust and the associated financial crisis. However, an examination of how changes in the pattern of International Capital Flows affected yields on US assets is important for understanding the origins and dynamics of the crisis'.

His analytical framework is a generalization of the Global Savings Glut Hypothesis (GSGH) of Bernanke (2005) that 'increased capital flows to the United States from countries in which *desired saving* greatly exceeded desired investment were an important reason that US longer-term interest rates during this period were lower than expected'. In short, the generalized GSGH is advanced by Bernanke as an explanation of the downward pressure on US asset yields exerted by capital inflows from GSGH countries and also from others in which portfolio preferences shifted. Financial innovation in transforming risky and poor quality products into securities that were rated as AAA by rating agencies played its part in expanding the supply of seemingly safe US assets. The crisis revealed the many weaknesses in this house of cards.

Bernanke provides empirical support to generalized GSGH as an explanatory hypothesis for the onset of the crisis. However, no microbehavioural foundation is offered for the shifts in inter-temporal and risk preferences of households and investors that led to aggregate or macrosavings glut. A large part of the capital flows resulted from choices of public authorities whose non-transparent objectives and actions are not adequately allowed for in GSGH. Whether founded on solid rock of microbehavioural foundations or quick sands of conventional macroeconomic thinking, undoubtedly conventional and non-conventional policies adopted by the US Fed have been influenced by his framework.

Governor King's (2011) paper is also analytically interesting and is complementary to Bernanke's (2011). King's claim that global imbalances contributed to the crisis and rebalancing is the key to recovery is in contrast to Bernanke's claim that they in no way contributed in a build-up and bursting of the US housing bubble in which the crisis originated. Secondly, for policy makers, King's 'key message is that in today's highly interconnected global economy, a top priority for national policy makers must be to find ways to rebalance global demand, that it is important to ensure both the level of world demand and that it is sufficient for the world recovery to continue...'. King suggests two principles, first to focus discussion on the path of real spending that is sustainable and second to consider many potential policy measures going beyond the single issue of exchange rates. He pleads for a 'grand bargain' among major players in the world economy that constitutes a compromise on the path of economic adjustment without resort to protectionism and uses all logical measures including exchange-rate adjustments for implementing the rebalancing part of the grand bargain.

King recognizes that while the natural forum to strike the grand bargain is the G20 the failure of the G20's framework for strong and sustainable and balanced growth rules it out. He cryptically suggests that if we cannot achieve cooperation voluntarily then a more rules-based automatic system needs to be considered to restore global demand and to maintain future global economic financial stability.

Finally, King's analytical foundations are the well-understood problems of uninternalized externalities and collective action. In his words 'Global imbalances are a reflection of today's decentralized international monetary and financial system. All the main players around the world are rationally pursuing their own self-interests. But the financial crisis has revealed that what makes sense for each player individually does not always make sense in aggregate. These actions had collective consequences. The main lesson from the crisis is the need to find better ways of ensuring the right collective outcome'. The classic issue of externalities of self-interested actions is one that G20 should have understood and should have collectively addressed. But from the evidence thus far, the prospects of the G20 doing so do not appear high.

Subbarao (2011) agrees with King that global imbalances were major contributors to the financial crisis and with Bernanke that the 'global savings' glut as having exerted downward pressure on global interest rates. Unlike the other two, he mentions explicitly (i) the accumulation of foreign exchange reserves by public authorities; (ii) their conservative norms for investment as having crowed out private demand for the same and (iii) their 'abetting' the underpricing of risk in the US markets on the presumption that the current account deficit of the US will be financed on a sustainable basis by the foreign reserves controlled by the rest of the world's public authorities. Another factor that only he mentions is that the status of the US dollar as the dominant global reserve currency, in combination with the global savings glut-induced global imbalances fuelled the asset price bubble. The final element of what he terms as the casual chain is another effect of the absence of any effective alternative to the US dollar as a global reserve currency. Every element of Subbarao's causal chain calls for analytical and empirical justification that, unlike Bernanke and King, Subbarao does not offer.

Subbarao points out that India is not a contributor to the persistent accumulation of global imbalances or their propagation; India's growth process has not been dependent on external finance and in the demand structure for its output (i.e., GDP) foreign (i.e., export) demand accounts for a relatively small share; India does not target a particular level of current account surplus or deficit, nor does it pursue an explicit policy of reserve accumulation and the exchange rate of the rupee is essentially market determined.

The excess of investment over savings is a measure of current account deficits (CD). Subbarao's Chart 3 suggests that CD had remained positive in absolute value except for the five years 2001–01 to 2004–05 of the twenty-nine-year period of 1980–81 to 2009–10. But the chart also shows an increasing phase for CD during 1980–81 to 1990–91, steeply declining phase in 1996–97- and 2004–05 and a steeply increasing phase subsequently. It is unlikely that this particular pattern is pure coincidence and had nothing to do with policy as Subbarao argues.

An alternative interpretation, though not necessarily causal but consistent with the observed pattern, starts from the break in the 1980s from the fiscal conservatism of the previous three decades in India's fiscal policy into a phase of fiscal profligacy financed by domestic and external borrowing, particularly from non-concessionary private capital markets. The increasing phase during 1980–81 to 1990–91 of CD in absolute value is consistent with fiscal profligacy. The fiscal and balance payments crisis of 1990–91 and the post-crisis reform with fiscal consolidation as a major item are consistent with a CD that fluctuated without a trend during 1992–93 to 2000. The emergence of a steeply declining phase thereafter until 2004–05, followed by a steeply increasing phase is consistent with the post-1991 fiscal consolidation efforts losing steam after 1996–97, attempts to resuscitate it thereafter through the enactment of Fiscal Responsibility and Budget Management Acts at the Centre and States and the rise in FDI and portfolio flows.

The validity of Subbarao's statements on exchange-rate policy cannot be inferred from the ex-post data presented. His view that the thrust of the exchange-rate policy has been to contain undue volatility, particularly that arising from volatile capital flows, leaves open the questions around what path of the exchange rate would the volatility be contained (presumably, around a market-driven flexible exchange-rate path), how volatility is to be measured and how the norms within which it is to be contained were defined and set.

Subbarao argues that the variations in reserves are an offshoot of the exchange-rate policy of containing volatility. If this were so, it would be very unusual that variations observed over a decade are all positive, that is, of net increases in reserves. His characterizations of parts of the stock of foreign exchange reserves as 'borrowed funds' and 'qualitatively different' from reserves accumulated through trade and current account surpluses are puzzling. From the perspective of the use of reserves, there is no and cannot be a distinction between components of the stock of reserves.

Subbarao's description of India's policy approach to capital flows suggests a somewhat nuanced view of the use of capital controls that goes beyond maintaining financial and macroeconomic stability. He suggests that an ex-ante framework for managing capital inflows is preferable to a framework of letting the inflows to be free of any capital controls and restrictions and dealing the consequences of free inflows ex-post. The experience with ex-ante controls that are not price based in India does not give one great confidence in being able to achieve the desired social objectives through ex-ante controls and avoid the likely economic distortions as well as their manifestations the political economy of India (Srinivasan, 2011).

IMF Framework for Analysis of Global Financial Stability and Management of Capital Inflows

IMF (2011a) is a very useful periodic report assessing key risks and vulnerabilities to global financial stability and challenges in sustaining it. The key risks are macroeconomics risks, emerging market risks, credit risks and market and liquidity risks in the context of relevant monetary and financial conditions and the appetite for risk. Although there is no explicit framework of analysis in the report, the report's analytical description is adequate to identify the transmission mechanisms through which various risks could destabilize the financial system and also how policy responses and through what mechanism could mute, if not neutralize, the threats to stability.

IMF (2011b and 2011c) deals with managing capital inflows. The first is on tools to use and the second on a framework for IMF to help countries manage large capital inflows. IMF (2001c) lays out a set of six key principles and lessons emerging from its research that could serve as the foundation on which the national authorities can base their policies. The six principles are based on a review of stylized facts and country-specific experiences.

Reform of International Financial Institutions

Structural Aspects of Inter-state Organizations

The G20, IFIs, MDBs and more generally the UN family of institutions are inter-state institutions. At any point of time, the representative of the regime in power in a country voices its position on any issue and articulates what it is or its not willing to commit at that time. In the IFIs and the WTO membership is nearly universal with their membership criteria requiring only that the regimes aspiring to be their members abide by their articles of agreement. In the WTO an aspiring member has to also agree to abide by any other requirements that each of the existing members require of it at the same time of its application for membership.

Structural features of IFIs have many implications. The most obvious is that requiring 'One Member One Vote' in analogy with 'One Citizen One Vote' in a society for decision making has no satisfactory foundation in moral and political philosophy.

Second, being the head of government, no G20 leader will commit to an action if the action would involve significant political risk and opposition at home. Nor could he or she necessarily commit any future government to continue with whatever action he or she has committed to taking. Domestic political opposition to fiscal consolidation measures that impose austerity and which are widely seen as distributionally unfair can be expected. Surprisingly, in the G20 summits, leaders made no reference to the domestic political economy constraints that they faced in implementing their commitments.

The ongoing Eurozone crisis arose from the response some of its members who faced a stark choice between drastic fiscal consolidation through imposition of austerity measures and default on external debt, devaluation of the domestic currency and exiting the currency union represented by the Euro. Given this stark choice some chose not to default but to adopt severe austerity and stay in the Eurozone. The apparent willingness of other Eurozone members not to bail out members facing this stark choice illustrates the seriousness of the domestic and regional political economy considerations.

The failure of the leaders to keep their commitments on concluding the Doha negotiations is the lack of strong domestic political support for doing so in their countries. The apparent disconnect on issues discussed and commitments made by leaders at their summits and the substantial differences among politicians in their home countries on the very same issues, and particularly about the feasibility let alone desirability of some of the commitments made by the leaders, are realities that cannot be ignored.

The demand from non-state actors such as NGOs and civil society organizations to be heard at IFIs have elicited varying responses across institutions. Some IFIs and WTO have given the status of observers to NGOs and civil society organizations. The appellate body of WTO's Dispute Settlement Mechanism accepts amicus briefs. The IMF took the initiative to consult civil society on issues of IFI Reforms.

Certainly many national and multinational NGOs and civil society organizations provide basic public services for the poor and vulnerable within and across countries and means for the voice of the poor and vulnerable to be heard on issues and policies that are of concern to them. There are others which are open or thinly veiled lobbies of special interest groups. In established constitutional democracie, a well-functioning and accessible process exists for any NGO to articulate its aspirations and seek support. For such an NGO to be given an opportunity to be heard at the IFI process also is undesirable for many reasons. However, if the domestic process of choosing a government is not democratic the problem becomes worse.

Put in another and more general way, the basic issue is the reality that there is no global government or global legislature or global judiciary that are parts of and functioning under a global constitution. Had such global institutions existed the problem of voice and participation of non-state actors in IFI would not have arisen. Attempting to circumvent this reality through a process of giving voice to NGOs, some of which could be of questionable legitimacy, is of limited value.

Role of Quotas and their Distribution in the IMF and World Bank[8]

The role of Quotas in the IMF (and the World Bank)

Mikesell (1994) correctly points out that:

> the use of a single Fund quota to serve three purposes was both illogical and unnecessary, and this was frequently pointed out during the [Bretton Woods] conference. There could well have been one quota based on say, foreign trade and export variability to govern drawing rights [on Fund's resources], a second quota based on reserves and balance of payments history to govern contribution to the Fund [i.e. capacity to contribute] and a third quota based on economic and political importance to determine voting rights [i.e. voice and participation]. All three quotas could have been adjusted at, say, five-year intervals in accordance with formulas that might be revised every decade or so [to reflect shifting economic and political realities] (pp. 36–38).

The quota is also a signal of the incentives for seeking membership and importantly for existing members to remain. Unfortunately, the discussions in G20 summits on quotas and their distribution across countries etc. do not even question the logic (or more precisely, the illogic) of a single quota and focus more on voice and participation and less on how the quotas ought to be determined.

The setting of the same quota of each member for the Fund and the Bank was a historical accident. It had no logical foundation and was imposed by Harry Dexter White of the US. Mikesell's statement that

'White and his staff used an arbitrarily determined procedure to produce the recommended quotas and then tried to keep the formula from the delegates' is telling. Despite these dubious origins of the Bretton Woods formula of quota determination, it has lived on in revised forms in mandated review of quotas every five years or so. The G20 should insist on a thorough reexamination of single identical quota for membership in both and explore the possibilities for more than one quota for each.

Proposals for the Revision of the Quota Formula of 2008 for IMF and the World Bank

The major concerns with the formula are first the use of the same quota for the IMF and the World Bank and second, the weights in the formulas for GDP (weighted average of GDP at market and PPP exchange rates), openness, economic variability and international reserves.

There is no reason to continue the use of an identical formula for setting common quota any longer. Replacing it by one or more quotas for the Bank and IMF would require a careful consideration of the mandates of the two institutions and how the quotas would serve the fulfillment of the mandates as well as interests of their members in each.

A distinction should be made (Mikesell, 1994) among the purposes served by quotas: capacity of a member to contribute resources, its access to resources and its voice in the decision-making processes. Currently the membership quotas determine voice and participation and access to resources in the IMF. But access to Bank's lending is independent of membership quotas. At least three different quotas for each institution reflecting the three purposes should be considered.

The heterogeneity in capacities, needs and other dimensions across IMF countries is admittedly large. It would seem that a formula with the same weights for each variable for all countries does not make sense. It would be impractical of course to use country-specific formulae for calculation of quotas. However, it is in principle possible and desirable to devise separate formulas for each of a few groups of countries within a typology of countries.

Mandates of IFIs

In six decades of operation, both World Bank and the IMF have invented new roles following changes in the world economy and shifting fads in development economics. The Bank is now a group of institutions, with a huge staff and a bewildering range of activities, including the promotion of interfaith dialogue! The IMF has essentially become an agency for sovereign debt collection and an implicit credit rating agency and lender for structural adjustment and poverty reduction. Shutting down both and starting all over again is not an option.

Any reform of the IFI has to include reform of their current mandates. Addressing strictly domestic constraints that require domestic policy actions should not be among the mandates of IFIs. Similarly, those that have been added over time without any well-thought-out rationale have to be removed. The mandate of the IMF should be just two: maintaining the stability of the global financial system and providing advice to its members on macroeconomic policies.

Since IMF cannot serve the two roles effectively while also involving itself as now deeply into poverty reduction (e.g. its Poverty Reduction and Growth Promotion (PRGP) facility) structural adjustment and growth issues, these issues should not be part of IMF's mandate. The IMF should have the requisite analytical and research capacity in house to anticipate and evaluate potential threats to stability to the financial system from both exogenous and endogenous (policy) shocks. Through its surveillance mechanism the IMF not only should be able to provide timely advice to member countries on their policies and needed changes, but it must also have the assurance that any advice tendered that is based on careful analysis and mutual consultations with country authorities will be seriously considered and implemented by them. However, IMF's capacity for proper and effective surveillance has proved to be very limited.

The current mandate of the World Bank is development, which is a multifaceted concept. Considerations that would have to be taken into account in devising a set of quota formulas for the World Bank is far more complex than in the case of IMF. On one issue, there is less room for debate: the aspirations of all developing countries are to become developed and stay developed as soon as feasible. This means that once a member achieves its aspiration within a reasonable time horizon, the World Bank and MDBs would have no further roles to play in that member as a donor. Actively working for reaching the development goals at the earliest possible date and shut down should be the objective of the World Bank and other MDBs.

The Bank should cease to lend to middle income countries and those who have (or could have) adequate access to private capital, such as most Latin American countries, China and India. It should operate only in those few countries which lack technical and financial resources but have a leadership credibly committed to development.

India on the one hand is still accessing resources of the World Bank after 60 years of planned development, and on the other, its experience has contributed to the formulation of Bank's policies and development. India is in an eminent position to prepare and submit a thoughtful analytical paper on the World Bank's role on development.

International Coordination in Response to the Crisis: Fiscal Stimulus

Why Coordinate?

The G20 leaders have emphasized on policy coordination. For example, if effects of fiscal stimulus of individual countries are interdependent in large part because of externalities from one country's fiscal stimulus on another country's economy, then coordinated choices of fiscal stimuli (or fiscal contraction by some countries) would maximize the beneficial impact on the global economy. It is likely that many countries are only weakly connected with the rest of the world and for others the direction of dependence is mostly one way (i.e., the actions of the rest of the world affect them far more intense relative to what their action would be on the rest of the world). It would not be surprising if coordination among a few systemically important countries would have significant benefits but even these are likely to be modest.

Global Financial Architecture

Financial Sector Reforms

The actions of leaders on national financial sector reforms as part of the reform of global financial architecture were appropriate, needed and generally well designed. A couple of issues need attention: the heterogeneity of formal and informal financial institutions and public ownership of banks. For example, in India, about a third of gross domestic savings and capital formation do not involve any formal financial intermediation at all. Also, a large share of the assets of the Indian banking system are in public sector banks which makes closing of failing banks virtually impossible and also their recapitalization using public resources inevitable.

The focus of G20 on developed country financial systems was understandable given the virus of the financial crisis originated in the US and then spread to infect the rest of the world. But for thinking about reforms of the global financial system a much broader perspective is needed.

Dominance of the US Dollar as a Reserve Currency

Subbarao (2011) alleged that the fact that many countries choose the US dollar as their reserve currency induced the US to be less stringent on its regulations of domestic financial institutions and also to backload fiscal consolidation and adjustment than would be desirable. There is no evidence in support of the allegation. The decision to use the US dollar as its reserve currency is not forced on any country by the US but a voluntary one on its own.

Conclusion

This chapter explored the issues of reform of IFIs. The reform was seen not only as necessary and essential, but also as urgent by analysts, media and civil society and above all policy makers, after the onset of the 2008–09 global financial crisis. These groups had become dissatisfied with the perceived inadequacies of performance of IFIs prior to the crisis and were convinced that unless reformed IFIs would soon become ineffective and irrelevant. Independent evaluations within the IMF and the World Bank had also come up with critical reports on their performance during the run up to the crisis. Many proposals for needed reform have also been advanced by analysts, policy makers and also the independent evaluators.

The most important group of policy makers at the highest level is the group of heads of governments of 20 countries designated as G20. The second section of the chapter is on the declarations of G20 group of policy makers at their five summits, particularly their commitments.[9] It examines whether all their commitments have been delivered and to what extent their fulfilled commitments have contributed to the amelioration of the impact of the crisis and to reducing the chances of occurrence of a future financial crisis similar to the current one. It concludes that the record of fulfillment of their commitments by the leaders of G20 is mixed. The commitments to engage in a coordinated fiscal stimulus to mitigate the output loss and the rise in unemployment have been fulfilled.

The third section is on independent evaluation of the IMF and World Bank and proposals for their reforms by the Committee on Foreign Relation of the US Senate and non-governmental organizations. Briefly, IEO (2011a) on IMF's performance during the run-up to the financial crises was very critical and identified several systemic failures. The non-official groups focussed on the issues of distribution of voice and participants of members and identified the need for reforms of the structure of decision making in the IMF and the World Bank.

The fourth section is on India's positions on financial crisis, protectionism and Doha Rounds at G20 summits. India was supportive of the decisions with respect to both the leaders. Dr Singh in his personal capacity as a well-known economist provided economic rationale for many of the decisions of the G20 leaders including their commitments not to take protectionist measures in response to the crises and also to conclude the Doha round of multilateral negotiations promptly.

The fifth section focuses on an analytical framework for distinguishing causal from associated factors underlying the global financial crisis and for deriving responses and solutions. It also discusses the necessity of a counter factual analysis of future implications of alternative policies. The academic literature on aggregate models and policy recommendations based on them as well as views of Governors of Central Banks are discussed. The specific issues of causes and consequences of growing global current account imbalances including their being a contributory factor to the global financial crises are also discussed. The recent formulation by the IMF of its framework for managing capital inflows is also covered.

The discussion concludes that a behaviourally based and integrated model of the financial and real sectors of the economy does not exist. However, the suggested causes of the financial crises such as failures of the regulatory system and proposed policies for correcting them seem plausible, but in the absence of the needed model, one cannot be definitive about their efficacy.

The sixth and final section on structural aspects of inter-state organizations discusses the political origins without any convincing economic rationale of the identical membership quotas of each member in the IMF and the World Bank. It also explores alternatives for the current quota system that would better reflect the many purposes served by a quota. The related question of reform of the mandates of IFIs and the capacity of the IFIs to serve them cost effectively and efficiently is also explored. The importance of building in-house analytical and research capacities is emphasized. The issue of coordination of actions of the G20 is analysed.

Endnotes

[1] This is a revised and considerably shortened version of a draft completed when the author was Yong Pung Howe Chair Professor at LKY School of Public Policy, National University of Singapore during 2011. I would like to thank Partho Shome, Ajay Shah, Ashima Goyal and participants at my seminar at the Indian Council for Research on International Economic Relations (ICRIER) and at the Department of Economic Affairs for their comments. I

thank Azad Singh Bali, PhD. student at the Lee Kuan Yew (LKY) School of Public Policy, National University of Singapore for his research assistance. I thank Krishan Kumar of ICRIER, V.N. Ramaswamy, formerly of ICRIER, Diana Ng formerly at LKY School and H. S. Sudha at the Institute of Financial Management and Research at Chennai for their administrative assistance.

[2] It includes EU and its members, namely France, Germany and the UK individually. The developing members vary substantially their populations, economic sizes, state of development and per capita real incomes.

[3] This paragraph draws heavily from The G20 (Group of 20) http://www.brookings.edu/~/media/Files/Programs/Global/backgrounders/G20_backgrounder.pdf [Accessed in May 2011].

[4] The paragraph numbers in this section and in the rest of the chapter are of the declarations of the relevant summit. The summit declarations can be accessed from http://www.g20.utoronto.ca/summits/index.html.

[5] The draft completed in June 2011 does not cover in any detail global economic developments from July 2011 on including the Cannes, France and Los Cabos, Mexico summits of 2011 and 2012, respectively. In particular the as yet (1 June, 2013) not fully resolved Euro Zone crisis is not discussed elaborately.

[6] This basic issue has not been resolved as of April 2013 after several partial resolutions of crises through the imposition of severe and unpopular austerity in Cyprus, Greece, Ireland and Spain.

[7] I was one of the members, the other being Francesco Giavazzi of MIT, of the three-member team headed by Professor Mishkin of Columbia University that evaluated IMFs research. Its report was discussed by the Executive Board of IMF in 1999. Surprisingly the subsequent evaluation of IMFs research was 12 years later (IEO, 2011b). In 2010, I chaired a team that evaluated the research at the Asian Development Research Institute done at (ADBI) in Tokyo. Professor Angus Deaton of Princeton University headed the team that evaluated World Banks Research. The reports of the evaluations are available on the web pages of the organizations involved.

[8] For brevity the section on the history of quotas has been dropped. It can be obtained by emailing the author at t.srinivasan@yale.edu.

[9] This chapter covers in some detail five G20 'summits' that have been held since the first in Washington D.C. in November, 2008 to the one in Seoul in April, 2010. Two subsequent summits held in Cannes, France in November, 2011 and in Los Cabos, Mexico in June 2012 are briefly discussed.

References

American Economic Association. 2011. 'Symposia: Financial Regulation After the Crisis'. *Journal of Economic Perspectives* 25(1): 3–248. Available at http://www.aeaweb.org/articles.php?doi=10.1257/jep.25.1 [Accessed in November, 2013].

American Economic Association. 2010. 'Symposia: Macroeconomics after the Financial Crisis'. *Journal of Economic Perspectives* 24(4): 2–233. Available at http://www.aeaweb.org/articles.php?doi=10.1257/jep.24.4 [Accessed in November, 2013].

Rahul Anand, Shanaka Peiris and Magnus Saxegaard. 2010. 'An Estimated Model with Microfinancial Linkages for India'. Working Paper: WP/10/21,Washington D.C. International Monetary Fund. Available online at: http://www.imf.org/external/pubs/ft/wp/2010/wp1021.pdf [Accessed in November, 2013].

Banque de France. 2011. 'Global Imbalances and Financial Stability'. *Financial Stability Review* 15: 1–184. Available online at: http://www.banque-france.fr/fileadmin/user_upload/banque_de_france/publications/Revue_de_la_stabilite_financiere/rsf_1102.pdf [Accessed in November, 2013].

Baumol, William. 1952. 'Transactions Demand for Cash: An Inventory Theory Approach'. *Quarterly Journal of Economics* 66: 545–56.

Bernanke, Ben. 2005. 'The Global Saving Glut and the US current Account Deficit'. Speech delivered at the Sandbridge lecture, Virginia Association of Economists, Richmond, 10 March 2005.

Bernanke, Ben. 2011. 'International Capital Flows and the Returns to Safe Assets in the United states 2003–07'. *Financial Stability Review* 15: 13–26.

Caballero, Ricardo J. 2010. 'Macroeconomics after the Crisis: Time to Deal with the Pretense-of-Knowledge Syndrome.' *Journal of Economic Perspectives* 24(4): 85–102.

CFRUSS. 2010. *The international financial institutions: A call forchange.* A Report to the Committee on Foreign Relations, United States Senate, 111th Congress, Session, 2nd session, Washington D.C.

Vasco Gabriel, Paul Levine, Joseph Pearlman and Bo Yang. 2010. 'An Estimated DSGE Model of the Indian Economy.' NIPE WP 29/2010. Available at: http://www3.eeg.uminho.pt/economia/nipe/docs/2010/NIPE_WP_29_2010.pdf [Accessed in November, 2013].

IEG. 2010. *Results and Performance of the World Bank group.* IEG Annual Report, Volume 1, Washington D.C.: World Bank.

IEO. 2011a. *IMF performance in the Run-Up to Financial and Economic Crisis*, IMF Surveillance in 2004–07.' Washington D.C.: International Monetary Fund.

IEO. 2011b. *Research at the IMF: Relevance and Utilization.* Washington D.C.: International Monetary Fund.

IMF. 2011a. *Global Financial Stability Report, Durable Financial Stability, Getting there From here, World Economic and Financial Surveys.* Washington D.C.: International Monetary Fund.

IMF. 2011b. 'Managing Capital Flows: What Tools to Use?'. IMF Discussion Note. Washington D.C.: International Monetary Fund.

IMF. 2011c. 'Recent Experiences in Managing Capital Inflows – Cross-Cutting Themes and Possible Policy Framework.' Washington D.C.: International Monetary Fund.

IMF. 2011d. 'IMF Develops Framework to Manage Capital Inflows'. IMF Survey Magazine: In the News, April. Washington D.C.: International Monetary Fund.

King, Mervyn. 2011. 'Global Imbalances, the Perspective of the Bank of England'. *Financial Stability Review* 15, 73– 80.

Mikesell, Raymond F. 1994. *The Bretton Woods Debates: A Memoir.* Essays in International Finance, 192, International Finance Section, Department of Economics, Princeton University.

Mishkin, Frederic. 2009. 'Is Monetary Policy Effective During Financial Crisis'. *American Economic Review* 99(2): 573–77.

Mishkin, Frederic. 2011. 'Over the Cliff: From Sub Prime to the Global Financial Crisis'. *Journal of Economic Perspectives*, Winter 2011: 49–70.

Ohanian, Lee E. 2010. 'The Economic Crisis from a Neoclassical Perspective'. *Journal of Economic Perspectives* 24(4): 45–66.

Ostry, Jonathan D., Atish R. Ghosh, Karl Habermeier, Luc Laeven, Marcos Chamon, Mahvash S. Qureshi and Annamaria Kokenyne. 2011. 'Managing Cpaital Inflows: What Tools to Use?.' IMF Staff Discussion Note SDN/11/06. Available online at: http://www.imf.org/external/pubs/ft/sdn/2011/sdn1106.pdf [Accessed on: 3 November, 2013].

Rajan, Raghuram. 2010. *Fault lines: How Hidden Fractures Still Threatens World Economy.* New Jersey: Princeton University press.

Reinhart Carmen M. and Kenneth Rogoff. 2011. *This Time is Different: Eight centuries of Financial Folly.* Princeton: Princeton University Press.

Reinhart, Vincent. 2011. 'A Year of Living Dangerously: The Management Of the Financial Crisis in 2008'. *Journal of Economic Perspectives* 25(1): 71–90.

Shiller, Robert. 2008. *The Sub-prime Solution: How today's Financial Crisis Happened and What to Do about It.* New Jersey: Princeton University Press.

Srinivasan, T. N. 2011. *Growth, Sustainability and India's Economic Reforms.* New Delhi: Oxford University Press.

Subbarao, Duvvuri. 2011. 'Global Imbalances: The Perspective of Reserve bank of India'. *Financial Stability Review* 15 February: 131–38.

Tobin, James. 1956. 'Interest Elasticity of the Transactions Demand for Cash'. *Review of Economics and Statistics* 38(3): 241–47.

Woodford, Michael. 2010. 'Financial Intermediation and Macroeconomic Analysis'. *Journal of Economic Perspectives* 24(4): 21–44.

WTO. 2011. 'WTO: 2011 News Items, 24 May, 201'. Geneva, World Trade organization.

Zedillo, Ernesto. 2009. *Repowering the World Bank for the 21st Century.* Report to High-level Commission on Modernization Of World Bank Group Governance. Washington D.C.: World Bank.

6 Capital Controls: Instruments and Effectiveness

Parthasarathi Shome
Jyotirmoy Bhattacharya
Shuheb Khan

Introduction

The 2008–09 global financial crisis brought up the question of whether tax and non-tax instruments should be used to contain the volatility in international financial markets. These might include a Tobin Tax, i.e., a tax on financial transactions, regulation of financial markets or direct controls on the flow of capital. So far no consensus has emerged. This chapter addresses the issue of capital controls in particular, the theory and mechanics of financial transaction taxes having been addressed by Shome (2012) in some detail recently. Even the IMF, which had earlier been a staunch critic of capital controls, now admits that they may sometimes be necessary for orderly economic growth and macroeconomic stability (International Monetary Fund, 2011).[1] Care must be taken, however, that the pendulum does not swing too far the other way. In particular, unrealistic expectations from capital controls may lead policy makers to pursue unsound macroeconomic policies that could again point the way to crises; and controls might be powerless to prevent them.

In order to consider the alternatives in perspective, in this chapter, an empirical approach is employed to test to what extent tax and non-tax modes of capital control have been successful in containing capital inflows. We have used cross-country econometric evidence and case studies of Brazil, Chile and India to assess the extent to which such instruments have been used by countries and whether the objectives have been achieved. Finally, concluding remarks over the benefits and limitations of alternative control instruments are offered.

Effectiveness of Tax and Non-Tax Capital Controls: Cross-Country Evidence

Before analysing the three individual country case studies, we first undertake a cross-country study on the effectiveness of capital controls against inflows – reflecting the vast majority of the recent capital control episodes across the world.

The advantage of a cross-country study lies in the fact that it allows us to control for unobservable factors that might influence the magnitude of capital flows to all countries in the same period. In the present context the most important such factors would be the economic conditions and policies in home countries from which capital flows originate as well as global economic conditions in general. In a single-country study it is hard to disentangle these factors from the effects of the capital control policies being pursued by the recipient country. This is particularly so once we recognize that countries choose their capital control policies not randomly but in response to economic conditions and, therefore, we are likely to see environment changes and policy changes happening at the same time, making it hard for the analyst to separate out the effects of the two.

Our cross-country methodology, using panel-data econometric models, has a chance of cutting through this difficulty. To the extent environmental factors affect all countries similarly while different countries' policies respond at different times, the comparison of outcomes across countries in a given period of time allows us to estimate the impact of policy. In terms of mechanics of the fixed-effects panel models we estimate below, country-specific and period-specific effects are captured by country- and period-dummies, leaving us with more reliable estimates of the effect of capital controls.

Cross-country studies, however, come with a difficulty of their own. Capital controls in different countries have taken different policy and administrative forms. Econometric analysis demands that we be able to find a numerical measure of the degree of capital controls that is valid and meaningful across countries. This poses a challenge.

For the present study we employ as our measure of capital controls the standard Chinn–Ito index of financial openness (Chinn and Ito, 2008) that is built using information contained in the IMF's report on *de jure* capital controls in its 'Annual Report on Exchange Arrangements and Exchange Restrictions' (AREAR). The AREAR reports regulations governing the external accounts for a cross section of countries. Chinn and Ito use the information reported in AREAR to construct dummy variables for the absence of:

1. multiple exchange rates;
2. restrictions on current account transactions;
3. restrictions on capital account transactions; and
4. requirement of the surrender of export proceeds.

The variable for the restriction on capital account transactions is averaged over a five-year window to capture the intensity of controls. The Chinn–Ito index (KAOPEN) is then constructed by applying principal component analysis to the resulting variables and taking the first principal component as the index.[2]

Our study covers 13 countries–Argentina, Brazil, Chile, China, Colombia, India, Indonesia, South Korea, Malaysia, Mexico, Russian Federation, South Africa and Thailand – for the period 1981 to 2008 (data for all periods are not available for all countries). The countries were chosen to ensure regional diversity as well as a mix of countries with and without significant capital controls. The data on the following variables shown in Table 6.1 (apart from the Chinn–Ito index itself) were obtained from the IMF's *International Financial Statistics* database. The variable *uip_gap* representing the uncovered interest gap was constructed to capture the rate of return differential between the US and the country in question.

Table 6.1: Variables Used in Cross-country Analysis

Dependent variables	
inflow	Total capital inflow (Million USD)
dir.inv	Direct investment inflows (Million USD)
portfolio	Portfolio investment inflows (Million USD)
Independent variables	
Kaopen	Chinn–Ito index of capital market openness
ln_gdp	Log of real GDP
uip_gap	Uncovered interest parity gap: Money market rate – Rate of exchange rate depreciation against the dollar – US Federal Funds rate

Estimation Results

The purpose of the estimation exercise was to judge the effectiveness of capital controls (proxied by the Chinn–Ito index) in influencing total inflows as well as direct investment and portfolio inflows separately, with the expectation that each of these flows would respond positively to a reduction in capital controls. We take the first difference of the natural logarithm of GDP (which approximately equals the growth rate of GDP) as a proxy of economic performance. To capture the effects of rate of return differentials between origin and recipient countries, we construct the variable *uip_gap* which is the differential between the recipient country's money market rate and the US Federal Funds rate with an adjustment for exchange rate changes.

For each of the dependent variables, the following country-fixed effects panel model was estimated with time dummies:

$$Y = \beta_1 \text{ Kaopen} + \beta_2 \Delta \log (\text{GDP}) + \beta_3 \text{ uip\_gap} \qquad (6.1)$$

where Y = Inflow, Dir.inv, Portfolio for successive estimates.

The results were as follows (Table 6.2):

Table 6.2: Cross-country Study: Estimation Results

	Kaopen	**Δlog(GDP)**	**uip_gap**
inflow	5270.065***	42944.93	2435.362
	(0.000)	(0.156)	(0.961)
dir.inv	2550.486***	11343.78	15326.6
	(0.000)	(0.352)	(0.442)
portfolio	707.2688	12879.08	3007.529
	(0.160)	(0.299)	(0.882)

p-values in parentheses *p<0.05, **p<0.01, ***p<0.001

While the degree of financial openness measured by Kaopen has a statistically significant and positive coefficient in the equations for total inflows and direct investment inflows, the coefficient in the case of portfolio investment is not statistically significant. Thus, while a greater degree of capital controls reduces total inflows and direct investment inflows, the evidence is consistent with its not having any effect on portfolio inflows.

The contrast in this result between the effect of financial openness on direct investment and portfolio investment is surprising. It might possibly be because foreign direct investment, being necessarily locked in to some degree in the recipient country, would be more sensitive to the regulatory environment including factors like current account convertibility as well as requirements on surrender of export proceeds that are part of the Chinn–Ito index whereas portfolio investment, as long as it was allowed, would respond to the temporary rate of return and portfolio diversification forces rather than the regulatory environment. This is not to say that capital controls would have no effect on portfolio investment. It is possible that controls would affect the composition of portfolio flows rather than their total amount. Indeed, this is what is found in the literature on the effectiveness of capital controls. Edwards (1999) and Magud *et al.* (2011) for example, show that capital controls leave total portfolio flows unchanged while shifting the composition of the inflows towards longer maturity assets. This is also confirmed in our two case studies of Brazil and Chile discussed in the following sections.

Case Studies

Brazil: The Real Plan and Thereafter

The Brazilian economy struggled with low growth and high inflation in the 1980s and early 1990s. Like many other countries, Brazil took several measures in the early 1990s to reform its economy. In July 1994, to beat high inflation, Brazil introduced a new currency Real and brought in a series of contractionary fiscal and monetary policies. Apart from stabilization policies, deeper reforms were also introduced, which involved structural changes such as continuing to open the economy to foreign trade and investment, overhauling financial market regulation, privatizing government-controlled firms and allowing markets to function more freely.[3] As a part of the reform process, significant steps were taken to liberalize the capital account. Since then restrictions on various components of the capital account were relaxed, moving cautiously towards full capital account liberalization.

Figure 6.1: Brazil: Capital and Current Account as percentage of GDP

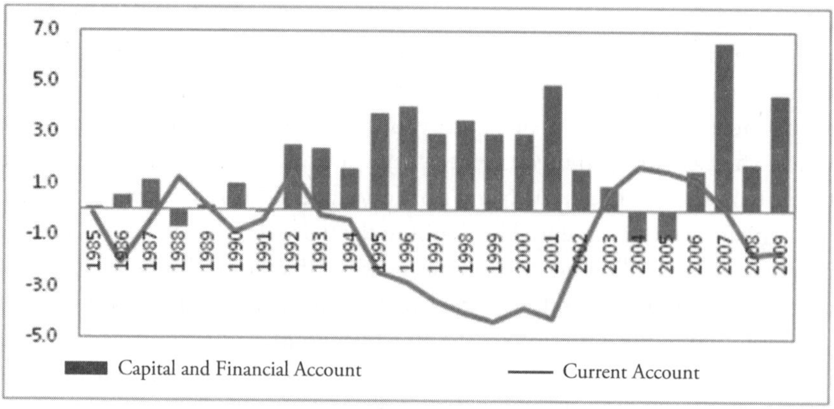

Capital and Financial Account   —— Current Account

Source: Global Development Finance and Banco Central do Brazil

Figure 6.1 shows that in the early 1990s, Brazil faced a surge in capital inflows combined with a low current account deficit, which put pressure on its exchange rate. In response Brazil introduced some capital control measures between 1992 and 1995. Between 1995 and 2001 the surplus in capital account was nearly matched by the current account deficit. After the East Asian financial crisis, investors were cautious in investing in emerging economies. Funding current account deficit through capital account surplus became difficult for the Brazilian economy. Political uncertainty, high fiscal deficit and devaluation of the Real were also responsible for capital outflow.

Recent Experience with Capital Inflows

The Brazilian economy received $89 billion of net capital inflows in 2007; portfolio investment dominated with $48 billion, followed by FDI of $27 billion. However, the global financial crisis resulted in withdrawal of funds by foreign institutional investors. As a result, net capital inflows declined to $29 billion in 2008. Strong recovery in 2009 resulted in resurgence of capital inflows. Capital inflows between January 2009 and December 2010 were very high at $169 billion; portfolio investment of $114 billion again dominated the inflows. Net foreign investment in the equity market was $74 billion, while in the debt market it was $39 billion.

The reason for heavy investment in the equity market was better returns compared to developed countries, while, in the debt market, carry trade was the reason for such a high level of investment. With the interest rate differential with the US being close to 10 per cent and, with high exchange rate appreciation, Brazil became one of the favourite destinations for investors in carry trade.

To contain the appreciation of the Real and avoid a domestic asset bubble, Brazil introduced capital control measures. The IOF tax (*Imposto de Operações Financeiras*), a Tobin-type tax on entry, of 1.5 per cent on fixed income investments by foreigners, was introduced in March 2008.[4] However, lower capital inflows due to the global financial crisis led the Brazillian authorities to withdraw this tax in October 2008. Resurgence of capital inflows resulted in the reintroduction of a 2 per cent IOF tax on capital inflows in October 2009. The tax covered equity and fixed income securities while FDI was exempted. On 4 October 2010, the Brazilian Government increased the tax on foreign investment in fixed income securities from 2 per cent to 4 per cent. On 18 October 2010 the rate was once again raised to 6 per cent. Tax on equity investment remained at 2 per cent. The tax on foreign investors' margin deposits for futures markets was also increased to 6 per cent from 0.38 per cent.[5] Brazil's central bank also made a bold move to protect the financial system from speculative trade and to curb gains in the Real, by imposing reserve requirements on banks' short positions in U.S. dollars equivalent to 60 per cent of the value of the short position above US$3 billion, or the bank's reference capital, whichever was smaller[6] (Appendix 6.1).

Effectiveness of Capital Controls

Examining the post-crisis monthly data in Figure 6.2, imposition of the first set of capital controls in 2009 was effective in terms of reducing the total inflow of capital in the economy, particularly portfolio inflows. As a result, the exchange rate depreciated marginally from 1.74 Real per dollar in October 2009 to 1.81 Real per dollar in June 2010.

However, the effect of the initial 2 per cent IOF tax was not lasting and, at the end of 2010, capital inflows, especially portfolio investment, picked up. In the month of October, portfolio investment was $18.2 billion. Alarmed by the situation, the government increased the tax rate on foreign investment in fixed income assets, twice in one month (October). Capital inflows in the next two months (November and December) dropped sharply. Net portfolio investment declined to $3 billion in November and by December gross inflows had declined so much that the net portfolio investment had reversed direction to turn into an outflow of $0.8 billion in December. The sharp decline in portfolio investment after the tax increase shows that the Brazilian government was successful in controlling the inflows and in stabilizing the exchange rate. In

Figure 6.2: Brazil: Capital Inflows

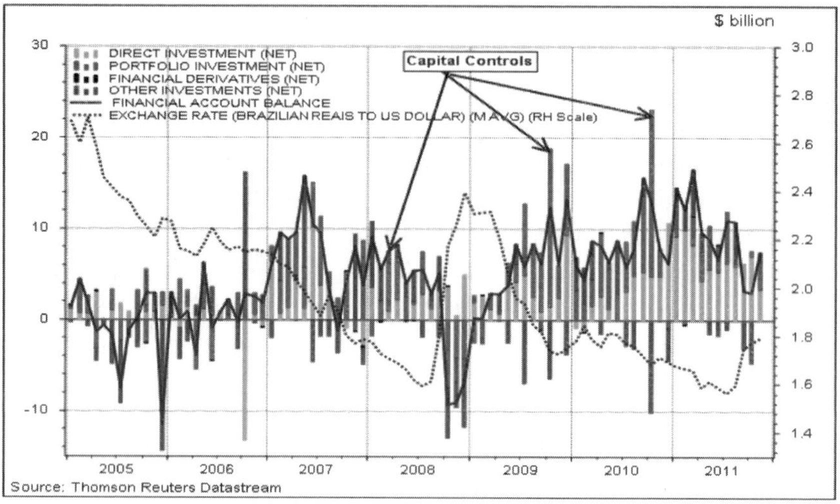

Source: Thomson Reuters Datastream

fact, the low inflow in capital account and persistent current account deficit led to a rollback of the tax rate from 6 per cent to 2 per cent in January 2011.[7] The composition of inflows also shifted in favour of long-term investment: in the $56 billion of net capital inflow that the Brazilian economy received between November 2010 and March 2011, FDI dominated at $42 billion.

Sometimes capital controls are also presented as a means for countries to regain monetary policy autonomy. A country with a fixed exchange rate is unable to use monetary policy to stabilize its economy in the absence of capital controls since arbitrage between domestic and foreign assets forces the domestic interest rates to always equal the foreign interest rate. It follows that the ability of monetary authorities to set interest rates independently of the rest of the world would be a measure of capital control effectiveness. Regarding the performance of Brazilian capital controls on this score, Gallagher (2011a) reports: 'One common test to analyze the extent to which controls are effective is to examine whether the interest rate differential adjusted for the forward discount is more or less correlated (or deviating) before and after a control is deployed. If a policy measure was meeting its stated goal the interest rates would be less correlated. In Brazil the adjusted interest rate differential does not widen until after Brazil strengthens the IOF tax to 6 per cent'. Thus, it appears that if capital controls based on a tax on inflows were to be used to regain monetary policy autonomy and not just to affect the size or composition of inflows, they would have to be imposed at a very high rate of taxation. Such high rates of taxation could be considerably more distortionary, thus raising questions about the net benefits of the policy.

Econometric Analysis

We carry out an analysis using monthly data for net foreign portfolio investment flows for Brazil from March 2008 to February 2011 to judge the effectiveness of the IOF tax. Given the evidence discussed of short-lived effects of the IOF tax on portfolio flows we do not model the absolute level of flows as a function of the IOF tax rate. Rather we model the *change* in foreign portfolio investment (FPI) as a function of the change in the IOF rate. As a control variable we introduce a measure of the differential between US and Brazilian interest rates (adjusted for changes in the exchange rate). Our variables, as shown in Table 6.3, are

Table 6.3: Brazil: Variables for Econometric Study of Capital Flows to Brazil

Dependent variable	
fpi	Foreign portfolio investment (USD millions)
Independent variables	
uip_gap	Uncovered interest parity gap: Brazilian money market rate – Rate of depreciation of currency – US Federal Funds rate
iof	Rate of IOF tax

We estimate the following equation:

$$\Delta fpi_t = \text{constant} + \beta_1 \Delta fpi_{t-1} + \beta_2 \Delta uip\_gap_{t-1} + \beta_3 \Delta iof_{t-1} \qquad (6.2)$$

We have used lagged values of the tax rate to control for contemporaneous feedbacks from the quantum of inflows to the tax rate, since it is likely that the tax rate would be increased in months with high inflows. Still the assumption of the exogeniety of the tax rate must be interpreted with caution.

We have also included the lagged value of the change in FPI in our specification to control for the possibility of negative autocorrelation in this variable. If increases in FPI above trend are likely to be followed with decreases in FPI relative to trend and if increases in FPI trigger tax increases, it is possible that the subsequent decrease in FPI would be wrongly ascribed to the tax change. The lagged change in the FPI term seeks to guard against this bias.

The estimates obtained are:

Table 6.4: Brazil: Effect of IOF on Portfolio Inflows

	Δuip_gap$_{t-1}$ LD.u	Δiof$_{t-1}$	constant-cons	Δfpi$_{t-1}$L.ar
estimates	231.1	-1293.1**	72.83	-0.510**
p-values	(0.331)	(0.007)	(0.884)	(0.004)

*p< 0.05, **p< 0.01, ***p< 0.001, N=33

The statistically significant coefficient of Δiof$_{t-1}$ in Table 6.4 shows that changes in the IOF tax rate did have a statistically and economically significant negative impact on the growth of foreign portfolio investment flows and were in that sense effective. We can interpret the coefficient to say that a 1 per cent change in the IOF tax rate leads to a mean decrease in portfolio flows of approximately $1.3 billion in the next month.

Thus, the analysis above shows that the IOF tax was indeed effective in bringing about short-term changes in portfolio inflows into Brazil and confirms the qualitative discussion above. However, this result might not generalize to a Tobin tax, which would be applicable to all foreign exchange transactions and therefore could not be levied at as high a rate as the IOF was. The effectiveness of a Tobin tax or a financial transaction tax at low rates to control the flow of capital, therefore, remains a matter of debate.

Chile

Capital Control Instruments in Chile

Although economic reform in Chile started in the mid-1970s, it was the economic crisis of 1982, that resulted in a sharp decline in GDP, which forced Chilean authorities to embark on comprehensive structural and macroeconomic reform. Reform measures led to strong recovery. The current account deficit was cut from 10.97 per cent of GDP in 1984 to 0.94 per cent in 1988, and the economy grew at an average of 5.46 per cent during the five-year period.Increased investment and higher GDP growth reduced the unemployment rate from 20.9 per cent in 1982 to 7.75 per cent in 1990.[8] Strong recovery resulted in the overheating of the Chilean economy with the annual inflation rate increasing to 27.2 per cent in 1990. Monetary tightening to counter this overheating, combined with a fall in world interest rates and an improvement in market sentiment toward Chile, resulted in a surge of private capital inflows beginning from 1989.[9]

The 1990 overheating of the economy and the surge in capital inflows created a policy dilemma. An increase in the rate of interest would have resulted in lower inflation but would encourage even higher capital inflows, which would put upward pressure on the exchange rate. Appreciation of the currency was not desirable as it would be detrimental for the external competitiveness of the economy. Although the exchange rate regime changed from a fixed exchange rate to a band arrangement within which the exchange rate could float, the focus of policy remained on stabilizing the real exchange rate against the US dollar.

The authorities initially responded to this dilemma through sterilized foreign exchange intervention and the liberalization of capital outflows. When this proved inadequate to stem the upward pressure on the currency, Chile introduced capital controls in the form of Unremunerated Reserve Requirements (URRs). Apart from reducing capital inflows, the goals of URR were to change the composition of inflows from debt to equity and from short-maturity debt to long-maturity debt, to minimize the appreciation pressures on the exchange rate and to regain some degree of independence for monetary policy.[10]

The URR regime was operative between early 1991 and late 1998. Initially, borrowers were required to keep 20 per cent of any foreign borrowing in a one-year interest-free deposit with the central bank. In response to the changing external environment and to prevent attempts at evasion, there were changes in the proportion of inflows to be kept as URR, the class of inflows covered and the currency in which the deposits were to be kept throughout the life of the regime. In late 1992, the proportion was increased to 30 per cent. In 1995, financial transactions involving less than $200,000 per person per annum became exempt from the reserve requirement. Decline in capital inflows following the East Asian crisis led to the relaxation of the regime. In mid-1998, the requirement fell from 30 per cent to 10 per cent and, later that year, it was abolished.

Though different from a Tobin tax in form, in terms of economic implications the URR was equivalent to a tax. By being required to place a fraction of their borrowings in an interest-free deposit, borrowers had to forego the returns these borrowings would have brought them if invested in return-earning assets or real-sector projects. This foregone borrowing was the tax equivalent of the URR. Moreover, since the duration of the deposits was fixed at one year regardless of the maturity of the inflow, this burden of taxation was heavier for short-duration borrowing – comparable to the case of a Tobin tax. The calculations shown in Table 6.5 below show how the implied tax rate depended on the level of international interest rates, the percentage of reserve requirement, the duration of the investment and duration of the deposits.

Table 6.5: Chile: Effective Tax Equivalent of URR

per cent

Reserve requirement rate (% of inflows)		20			30		
Interest rate on borrowed funds (%)		5	7	8	5	7	8
Required deposit duration		1 Year	1 Year	1 Year	1 Year	1 Year	1 Year
Duration of capital inflow	1 month	15.0	21.0	24.0	25.7	36.0	41.1
	3 months	5.0	7.0	8.0	8.6	12.0	13.7
	6 months	2.5	3.5	4.0	4.3	6.0	6.9
	9 months	1.7	2.3	2.7	2.9	4.0	4.6
	1 year	1.3	1.8	2.0	2.1	3.0	3.4
	3 years	0.4	0.6	0.7	0.7	1.0	1
	5 years	0.3	0.4	0.4	0.4	0.6	0.7
	10 years	0.1	0.2	0.2	0.2	0.3	0.3

Source: Laurens & Cardoso (1998)

Effectiveness of URR

Figure 6.3: Chile: Capital Inflow (Net)

$ millions

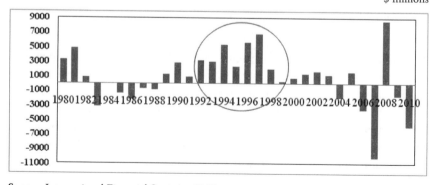

Source: International Financial Statistics, IMF

Figure 6.3 shows that net capital inflows to Chile during the period when the URR requirement was in effect was higher than in the immediately preceding and following periods. This raises doubts regarding the effectiveness of the measure, though the evidence is not conclusive since the URR was imposed precisely because of the increase in capital inflows and it is possible that inflows might have been even higher in its absence. Also, it is possible that the composition of capital inflows changed. For example, Edwards (1999) found that immediately after the implementation of the URR, short-term inflows declined very steeply. However, this decline in shorter-term flows was fully compensated by an increase in longer-term inflows and, as a result, aggregate capital inflows were unaffected.

The URR policy failed to check the upward pressure on domestic currency or give Chile greater monetary policy independence. As Cowan and Gregorio (2005) note, the real exchange rate appreciated continuously from 1990 until late 1997. The same authors also suggest a reason as to why the URR could not have been very effective in increasing monetary policy autonomy. As Table 6.5 shows, with an international rate of interest at 7 per cent, a 30-per cent URR is equal to a 3 per cent tax for a one-year inflow. Therefore, if the only instrument for arbitrage were one-year debt, domestic interest rates could differ from international rates by as much as 3 per cent without triggering arbitrage-driven flows. However, in reality investors are not restricted to using assets of only one-year maturity. Once borrowers switch to longer maturity debt, the burden of the URR, and hence the difference that can persist between domestic and foreign interest rates, decreases. Empirical studies support their reasoning. For example, De Gregorio, Edwards and Valdés (2000) find that while the URR had an effect on the interest-rate differential immediately after its imposition, this effect did not persist over the longer run.

Thus, the Chilean experience reveals that broadly the major effect of a tax or wedge on capital inflows such as the URR is on the composition of inflows. The effect on total inflows and monetary policy independence appears to be short-lived, if any.

India

India's Reform Trajectory

In 1991, the Indian economy experienced a classic external and internal disequilibrium, i.e., high fiscal deficit, inflation, rising debt service ratio, deteriorating current account and inadequate adjustment in the exchange rate. A series of reform measures were initiated to stabilize the economy. As a part of reform, the government started liberalizing various components of the capital account. Initially 'the thrust of policy reform in India was in favour of a compositional shift in capital flows away from debt to non-debt creating flows, viz., FDI and foreign portfolio investment; strict regulation of external commercial borrowings, especially short term debt; discouraging volatile element of flows from non-resident Indians' (Mohan, 2008). However, a continuously declining debt service ratio (from 35.3 per cent in 1990–91 to 6.0 per cent in 2004–05) and adequate foreign exchange reserves gave policy makers confidence to exploit the positive aspects of debt flows. Box 6.1 shows the sequencing of the economic reform process.

Box 6.1: India: Sequence of External Account Reform

July 1991: The government liberalized foreign investment policy. As against case-by-case approvals within a ceiling on foreign equity participation of 40 per cent, the new policy provided automatic approval of direct foreign investment of up to 51 per cent equity holding in 34 high-priority industries.

March 1992: The Liberalized Exchange Rate Management (LERM) system, which was a dual exchange rate system, replaced the single official rate and introduced partial convertibility of the rupee.

September 1992: Foreign investors were allowed to acquire shares in Indian companies to the extent of 24 per cent.

1994: India introduced current account convertibility.

April 1998: FIIs were permitted to invest in dated government securities subject to a ceiling.

August 1998: Several relaxations were made in external commercial borrowings (ECBs).

2001: FII and FDI policy was further liberalized.

2002: Outward FDI was liberalized.

Capital Controls in India

Capital account liberalization in India has been moving forward gradually, albeit with checks and balances. The capital control mechanism in India has evolved around sectoral concerns, adequacy of financing the current account and issues relating to financial stability.

India has preferred administrative measures[11] over market-based methods to capital flows. As evident from Box 6.2, apart from interest rate ceilings on ECBs, short-term trade credit and non-resident Indian deposits (NRI deposits), India uses administrative or quantity-based methods to control cross-border capital flows.

Box 6.2: India: Capital Control Instruments

Inflows	Foreign direct investment	Sectoral limits
	Portfolio investment	Equity: sectoral limits Debt: • Corporate bonds: cumulative investment limit • Government bonds: cumulative investment limit
	External commercial borrowings	Annual ceiling All-in-cost ceilings
	Short-term trade credit	All-in-cost ceilings
	NRI deposits	Interest rate ceiling
	Banking sector	Limits on overseas borrowings
		Interest rate ceiling on NRI deposits
Outflows	Portfolio investment	Separate investment limits for individuals, firms and mutual funds
	Outward foreign direct investment	Investment limit

Source: Various Government of India and RBI documents

Effectiveness of Capital Controls in India

Effectiveness of capital control instruments adopted by a country becomes clear at the time of a surge in capital inflow or capital flight. Capital inflows in India have generally been sufficient to finance the current account and accumulate foreign reserves for self-insurance. However, as India's emerging economy galloped to the second highest rate of growth globally, it received unprecedented capital inflows in 2007–08 (Figure 6.4), which forced the government to take capital control measures to contain an appreciating rupee. Government used mostly price-based measures to reduce debt-creating inflows such as commercial borrowings and NRI deposits. Interest rate caps on ECBs were reduced by 50 and 100 basis points for 3–5 year and above 5-year maturities, respectively, in May 2007. Similarly, the interest rates offered on NRI deposits were reduced. In August 2007, the government also announced that ECB more than US$20 million per borrower company per financial year will be permitted only for foreign currency expenditure, thus using a quantitative measure of an administrative nature.

Figure 6.4: India: Capital Inflows

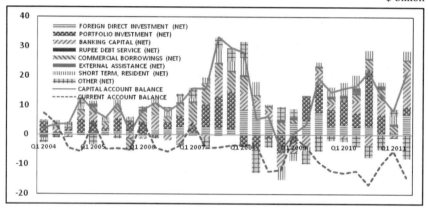

Source: Thomson Reuter Datastream

The controls were effective in containing commercial borrowings and NRI deposits. However, other components of capital inflows increased significantly. India received a massive $106 billion of capital inflows in 2007–08, resulting in criticism of the capital control policy. Patnaik and Shah (2010) showed that despite a complex regulatory structure to deal with cross-border flows and a low score (−1.14) on the Chinn–Ito index of capital account openness (Figure 6.5), India was unable to control inflows.

Figure 6.5: Chinn–Ito Index

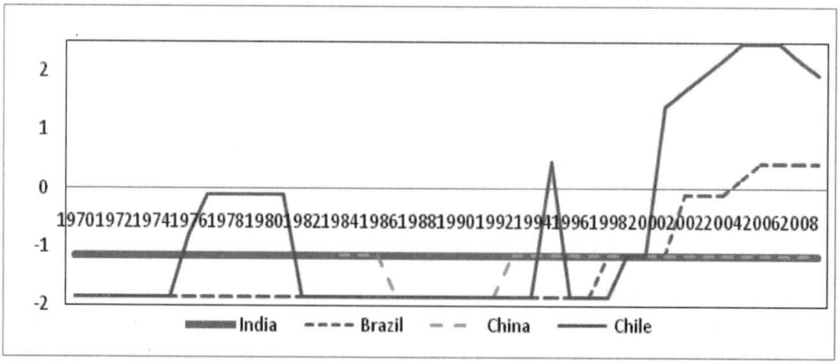

Source: http://web.pdx.edu/~ito/Chinn-Ito_website.htm
Accessed in April 2011

However, it may be misleading to draw any conclusion from the Indian case regarding the effectiveness of capital controls in general. Despite the myriad regulations, capital controls in India actually covered only a very limited set of flows and therefore there is no reason to expect them to have had an effect on the overall volume of flows. The extent of capital account openness in India is not well captured by the Chinn–Ito index. While India has significantly liberalized its capital account since 1991, the value of the Chinn-Ito index still remains at its 1970 level[12] (Figure 6.5). As we discuss below, while formulating its capital controls policy the Indian government may have had in mind objectives other than containing total inflows and exchange rate movements. Because of these multiple objectives, India used capital controls only on two components of inflows, viz. ECBs and NRI deposits and it was this selective use of controls which was responsible for the large inflows of 2007–08.

1. Portfolio investment: By the end of 2006, the developed countries were heading towards lower growth rates, while India registered GDP growth of more than 8 per cent. The search for yield resulted in massive capital inflows by foreign institutional investors. $27.4 billion of portfolio investment (net) (25.7 per cent of total net capital inflows) came in. Thus, despite having some sectoral caps, India had no instrument to check portfolio investment. It is not impossible that an apprehension that investors may not return for a long time, prevented the government from using tax or other strong restrictions, despite heavy upward pressure on the rupee.

2. Foreign direct investment (FDI): Long-term funds also surged because of high GDP growth and a positive investment climate. India received $34.7 billion of FDI in 2007–08. However, due to large outward FDI, the net FDI inflow was $15.89 billion (14.9 per cent of total net capital inflows).FDI is considered the best way to finance the current account deficit since, unlike other inflows, it also brings benefits such as technological upgradation and access to global managerial skills and practices. Given the considerable benefits attached to FDI inflows, the government never contemplated controlling it.

3. Banking capital: The emergence of the subprime lending crisis in the US forced Indian banks to draw down assets held abroad,[13] as a result of which, inflow from the assets side was $6.9 billion in 2007–08. On the liabilities side, the government was successful in reducing NRI deposits from $4.3 billion in 2006–07 to $0.18 billion in 2007–08, by reducing the interest rate ceiling; however, other foreign currency deposits by

non-resident banks and official and semi-official institutions went up. The total increase in liabilities was $5.2 billion. Consequently, the net increase in banking capital was $11.7 billion (11.03 per cent of total net capital inflows).

4. Other capital: Other capital inflows increased from $4.2 billion in 2006–07 to $10.96 billion in 2007–08 (10.3 per cent of total net capital inflows). Disaggregated data show that the increase reflected primarily, advances received pending the issue of shares under FDI, which increased by $7.2 billion in the same period (Table 6.6). Although inflows were coming in as FDI, government, concerned about the misuse of the facility, strengthened the regulation relating to share transfers on 29 November 2007.[14]

Table 6.6: India: Details of 'Other Capital' (Net)

$ million

	2006–07	2007–08
Lead and lags in exports[15]	217	–899
Net funds held abroad	619	–2,682
Advances received pending issue of shares under FDI		7,200
SDR allocation		
Other capital not included elsewhere (Inclusive of derivatives and hedging, migrant transfers and other capital transfers)	3,373	7,350
Total	4,209	10969

Source: RBI

5. Short-term loans: Short-term trade credit to India increased from $6.6 billion in 2006–07 to $15.9 billion in 2007–08 (14.9 per cent of total net capital inflow). 'The significant rise reflected the increased financing requirements of crude oil imports led by higher crude prices'.[16] The government could have controlled the inflow by lowering the permissible borrowing limit. However, the all-in-cost ceilings throughout the fiscal year remained at 50 bps and 125 bps over six-month LIBOR for loans upto 1 year and 1–3 years, respectively.[17]

6. External commercial borrowings (ECB): 'An analysis of movements in ECB mobilization and the growth in industrial production, *prima facie*, establishes a conclusion that external borrowings are greatly influenced by the pace of domestic activities. The coefficient of correlation between

IIP growth and ECB mobilization is observed to be relatively high (0.71)' (Singh, 2007). Large external borrowings by the corporate sector exerted pressure on the exchange rate in 2007–08. In response to this, the government reduced interest rate caps in May 2007. However, this did not have any significant impact on the ECB inflows. Rather than reducing interest rate ceilings further, in August 2007 the government announced that ECBs more than $20 million per borrower company per financial year will be permitted only for foreign currency expenditure. The rationale behind this policy seems to have been to contain the appreciation of the rupee without hurting the ability of firms to raise foreign loans for capital goods imports and overseas investment. This policy had a significant impact on the composition of ECBs. Borrowings for rupee expenditure for local sourcing of capital goods and modernization/expansion of existing units declined from $8.2 billion in 2006–07 (32.7 per cent of total ECB) to $3.7 billion in 2007–08 (12.2 per cent of total ECB). However, import of capital goods and overseas investment increased from $7.2 billion (28.2 per cent of total ECB) to $16.6 billion (53.7 per cent of total ECB) in the same period.[18]

Assessment of Capital Controls in India (2007–08)

One objective of capital controls on portfolio investment and FDI, which constituted more than 40 per cent of total capital inflows (net) in 2007–08, appears to have been to protect domestic industry. Government used sectoral caps to protect industries that are of a strategic interest or sectors with livelihood concerns for large sections of the population. Foreign investment liberalization coincided with periods of low capital inflows; however, liberalization measures lacked reversibility and be converted to capital controls to deal with periods of excess capital inflows. Hence, they could not be expected to achieve the primary objectives of capital control outlined by Magud et al. (2011):

- reduce the volume of capital flows;
- alter the composition of capital flows (towards longer maturity flows);
- reduce real exchange rate pressures; and
- allow for a more independent monetary policy.

Capital control instruments on foreign loans have been designed mainly to keep the cost of borrowings within prudent limits so that corporations do not take excessive risk.[19] However, these instruments have also been used to achieve macroeconomic objectives as already mentioned. In 2007–

08, excessive capital inflows created pressures on the exchange rate, and government responded by reducing the interest rate ceilings on ECB and NRI deposits and imposing restrictions on end-use of ECBs. Policy decisions had an impact on concerned categories of inflows. However, other components of capital inflow went up dramatically and exerted pressure on the exchange rate. It was primarily because of unavailability of instruments to control foreign investment, non-utilization of all-in-cost ceilings on short-term trade credits and drawdown of assets held abroad by Indian banks due to the emergence of the subprime lending crisis in the US. More focus on altering the utilization of ECBs rather than reducing the quantity of it was also a factor.

Sterilized Intervention

Capital controls are not the only instruments with which a country could respond to volatile or otherwise undesirable capital inflows. Another alternative is for the central bank to intervene in the foreign exchange markets to contain the adverse impact of inflows.

By itself, intervention in foreign exchange markets to stabilize exchange rates has the negative consequence of taking away the autonomy of the central bank in determining domestic monetary policy. Since any purchase (or sale) of foreign currency by the central bank increases (or reduces) the stock of domestic money in the economy, it must be the case that once the central bank targets the exchange rate, the stock of high-powered money is determined by the volume of capital inflows or outflows. One way that the central bank may try to avoid this dilemma is by also carrying out domestic open market operations (buying or selling government bonds) in an attempt to offset the effect of capital flows on the stock of high-powered money. Intervention in the foreign exchange markets combined with offsetting open-market operations of this sort is known as sterilized intervention.

The efficiency of sterilized intervention has been a source of debate in the academic literature. In a world of perfect substitutability between the assets of different countries and no capital controls, the *uncovered interest* parity theorem says that arbitrage in financial and foreign exchange markets would ensure that the difference between domestic and foreign interest rates would exactly equal the expected rate of depreciation of the domestic currency. Therefore, given foreign interest rates and market expectations, the only way in which the central bank can influence the exchange rate is by allowing the interest rate to vary. But because sterilized intervention is designed precisely to keep the money supply and the interest rate fixed, intervention of this sort may be expected to be ineffective.

In the literature on this topic (see Sarno and Taylor, 2001, for a survey), two mechanisms have been suggested through which sterilized interventions might influence the exchange rate. First, the central bank's intervention might signal its long-term intentions regarding the exchange rate and thereby influence exchange rate expectations. Second, domestic and foreign assets may not be perfect substitutes, thereby breaking the uncovered interest parity relation and introducing a risk premium as an additional source of divergence between domestic and foreign interest rates – a risk premium that might be influenced by the central bank's actions of increasing or decreasing the stock of domestic bonds in the hands of the public. Apart from these two factors, the existence of capital controls themselves can break the uncovered interest parity condition–thus suggesting the possibility of a complementary relation between capital controls and sterilized intervention as tools for managing the balance of payments and exchange rates.

Exchange Rate Regime in India

Between 1975–92 the exchange rate was determined by the RBI within a nominal band of ±5 per cent of a weighted basket of currencies of India's major trading partners (Jadhav, 2005). In March 1992, LERM, a dual exchange rate system replaced the single official rate. In a significant policy change in 1994, India introduced current account convertibility.

Figure 6.6: India: Foreign Exchange Intervention by RBI and Exchange Rate

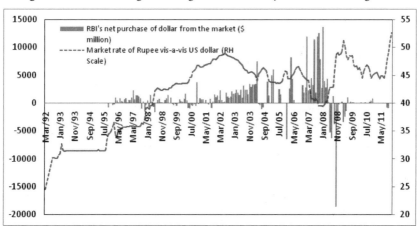

Source: CMIE database

Since 1994, the RBI has been following a policy of managed floating exchange rate. It has been intervening in the foreign exchange market during periods of excess volatility in the exchange rate (Figure 6.6). As capital inflows in excess of current account deficit have exerted upward pressure on the rupee, the RBI has been purchasing dollars to protect the competitiveness of the export sector. In the process, it has accumulated around $300 billion in foreign exchange reserves.

Rapid accumulation of reserves has significant implications for the balance sheet of central banks. Intervention injects liquidity in the economy, which results in downward pressure on short-term interest rates. 'Bank credit would tend to expand and inflationary pressures would eventually mount. If central banks have a target for the short-term rate (usually the policy rate), they would attempt to offset increases in bank reserves through changes in other balance sheet items (usually selling domestic assets or issuing their own securities) over which they have control (sterilized intervention)' (Mohanty and Turner, 2006).

Table 6.7: India: Sterilization Operations by the Reserve Bank of India

Rs. billion

		2003–04	2004–05	2005–06	2006–07	2007–08	2008–09
Market purchases(+)/Sales(-) of foreign currency by RBI		1407	911	329	1190	3121	−1786
Management of liquidity (I + ii + iii)		-1398	-1076	-429	-1219	-2804	1574
(i) Policy actions (a to c)		-356	-732	459	-607	-1389	2870
	(a) Change in CRR (first round)	35	-90	0	-275	-470	1023
	(b) MSS operations	0	-642	351	-339	-1054	803
	(c) OMOs	-391	0	107	7	135	1045
(ii) Other factors (a to c)		-720	-497	-1009	-976	-1626	-778
	(a) Currency with public	-434	-409	-573	-698	-856	-979
	(b) Existing CRR	-108	-93	-209	-267	-504	-402

		2003–04	2004–05	2005–06	2006–07	2007–08	2008–09
	(c) Surplus cash balance of the central government with RBI	-178	5	-227	-12	-266	604
(iii) LAF operations		-322	153	121	364	212	-518

Source: Mohan and Kapur (2009).
Note: CRR: Cash Reserve Ratio; MSS: Market Stabilization Scheme; LAF: Liquidity Adjustment Facility; OMOs: Open Market Operations
(–) indicates absorption of liquidity from the banking system and (+) indicates injection of liquidity.

India has been following the sterilized intervention route, i.e., purchasing foreign currency and selling domestic assets (Table 6.7). In the early 2000s, the sterilization process was hampered because of depletion of government securities with the RBI. In April 2004, a new instrument named Market Stabilization Scheme (MSS) was introduced for sterilization purposes. Under MSS, the RBI was empowered to issue treasury bills and medium duration dated securities for the purpose of liquidity absorption (Subbarao, 2011).

In the case of India, sterilized intervention has a quasi-fiscal cost as payments on domestic bonds are higher than the return on foreign assets. Interest payments on MSS securities, which are shown in the budget documents, have averaged 0.13 per cent of GDP over the period 2004–09 (Mohan and Kapur, 2009). The long-term fiscal impact of sterilization policies needs to be taken into account by policy makers (Subbarao, 2009). Also, the increasing weight of foreign assets in the RBI's balance sheet exposes it to greater interest rate and exchange rate risks (RBI, 2006). Given these potential costs of intervention, it becomes even more necessary to judge the effectiveness of sterilization as a policy. We attempt to do so in the econometric exercise which follows.

Econometric Analysis

We carry out a simple econometric exercise to judge the effectiveness of RBI's intervention in foreign exchange markets to reduce exchange rate volatility. We use monthly data for the rupee/dollar exchange rate and the quantum of RBI's intervention in the foreign exchange market for the period January 2000–11.

The dependent variable in this analysis is the volatility of the exchange rate as measured by the standard deviation of the daily rupee/dollar rate for each month of the study period (Table 6.8). Our explanatory variables are the amount of dollars bought or sold by RBI in that month. We use the buy and sell amounts separately rather than the net value since we seek to distinguish between the effectiveness of interventions against inflows and outflows. Intervention against inflows would take the form of purchase of dollars by RBI whereas intervention against outflows would take the form of sale of dollars by RBI (Figure 6.7).

Table 6.8: India: Variables Used in Econometric Study of Exchange Rate Volatility

Dependent variable	
msdev	Month-wise standard deviation of daily rupee/dollar exchange rate
Explanatory variables	
buy	RBI's purchase of dollars from the market (US $ million)
sell	RBI's sales of dollars to the market (US $ million)

Figure 6.7: India: RBI Intervention and Rupee/USD Volatility

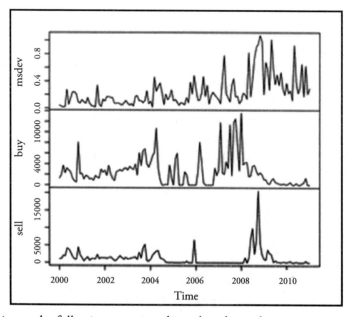

We estimate the following equation through ordinary least squares:

$$msdev_t = constant + \beta_1\, buy_t + \beta_2\, buy_{t-1} + \beta_3\, sell_t + \beta_4\, sell_{t-1} + \beta_5\, t \qquad (6.3)$$

Table 6.9: India: RBI Intervention and Exchange Rate Volatility:
Estimation Results

msdev	Coef	Robust Std. Err.	t	P>|t|	[95% Conf. Interval]	
buy$_t$	-.0000113	4.67e-06	-2.41	0.017	-.0000205	-2.03e-06
buy$_{t-1}$	1.67e-06	4.37e-06	0.38	0.703	-6.97e-06	.0000103
sell$_t$	.0000218	6.65e-06	3.27	0.001	8.61e-06	.0000349
sell$_{t-1}$	.0000309	5.08e-06	6.08	0.000	.0000209	.000041
t	.003479	.0004013	8.67	0.000	.0026849	.0042731
constant_cons	-1.700976	.2093083	-8.13	0.000	-2.115191	-1.286761

We find that the contemporaneous value of buy and the contemporaneous as well as lagged value of sell are statistically significant at the 5 per cent level of significance (Table 6.9). From this, we conclude that RBI's intervention is associated with changes in exchange rate volatility.

While the coefficient of *buy* is negative, that of *sell* and its lagged value is positive. This is significant since it shows that while RBI's intervention against inflows is associated with reduced exchange rate volatility, its intervention against outflows is associated with increased exchange rate volatility.

One possible explanation for this result might be that capital inflows and capital outflows are driven by different forces. While capital inflows are driven by country-specific pull factors, capital outflows might be more affected by what is happening in the capital's country of origin. If this is so, then RBI's intervention against inflows was effective by signalling RBI's commitment to maintaining a stable exchange rate. On the other hand, RBI's intervention against outflows was ineffective as outflows, at least in the period under consideration, were not driven by India-specific factors and hence could not be influenced by signals from India's policy stance that embodied its market interventions.

Conclusion

Both the cross-country econometric analysis as well as the case studies of Chile and Brazil show that capital controls are ineffective in influencing the overall volume of capital inflows in the long run unless the instruments are used so heavily (as when Brazil's IOF was at 6 per cent) as to simply cut off the inflows.

Our econometric study of Brazil does show, however, that they bring about short-term changes but it would be dangerous to think of capital controls as being capable of isolating an economy from global economic forces. Indeed, use of capital controls in a situation of fundamental disequilibrium might land policy makers in a sense of complacency, hence laying the grounds for even more serious crises than those already experienced.

On the other hand, our evidence does show that capital controls are effective in influencing the composition of inflows, by dampening short-term flows. To the extent that short-term flows are more destabilizing than long-term flows, this must be seen as some vindication of the proponents of such controls. While observers of Chile and Brazil have commented on the different means employed by the private sector to circumvent the controls, the evidence tends to reveal that perfect enforceability is not necessary for a policy to be effective.

The case of sterilized intervention in India is complementary to the discussion on capital controls. On the one hand it shows that the list of instruments available to a country facing destabilizing flows is longer than the Tobin tax or its variants. Pursuit of the limited objective of stabilizing the exchange rate seems much more sensible in the light of our discussion on the inability of capital controls in Chile and Brazil to achieve the more ambitious goals of countering long-term appreciation pressures and win independence of monetary policy. Moreover, by acting primarily on the expectations of asset holders, a policy of intervention need not impose the deadweight loss on society that a tax does.[20] On the other hand, one of the reasons of the effectiveness of the sterilized intervention policy might be the continuing controls on capital account in India which prevent perfect substitutability between Indian and foreign assets. To the extent that this is the case, capital controls and interventions may be seen as complements instead of substitutes.

Appendix

Appendix 6.1: Capital Control Policy in Brazil (2008–11)

Mar–08	Capital control	The IOF tax (*Imposto de Operações Financeiras*), a Tobin-type tax on entry, of 1.5% on fixed income investments by foreigners, was introduced.
Oct–08	Capital control	IOF tax on fixed income investments by foreigners reduced from 1.5% back to zero.
Oct–09	Capital control	The Ministry of Finance reinstated a 2% financial transaction tax (IOF) on equity and fixed income portfolio inflows.
Oct–10	Capital control	(i) IOF increased twice (from 2 to 4%) for fixed income portfolio investments and equity funds. (ii) IOF increased to 6% for fixed income investments.
Oct–10	Exchange rate management	(i) IOF on margin requirements on derivatives transactions increased from 0.38% to 6%. (ii) Some loopholes for IOF on margin requirements closed.
Jan–11	Prudential regulation	BCB requires banks make non-interest bearing deposits equivalent to 60% of short dollar positions in the spot FX market that exceed US\$3 billion or their capital base, whichever is smaller (to be implemented over 90 days).
Mar–11	Capital control	Increased to 6% the IOF on new foreign loans (banking loans and securities issued abroad) with maturities of up to a year. Companies and banks previously paid only a 5.38% IOF on loans up to 90 days.
Apr–11	Capital control	(i) 6% IOF extended for the renewal of foreign loans with maturities of up to a year. (ii) 6% IOF extended for both new and renewed foreign loans with maturities of up to 2 years.

Jul–11	Prudential regulation	BCB changed the non-remunerated deposits on banks' short positions. From now on a 60% reserve requirement was mandatory for amounts over US$ 1 billion or their capital base (whichever is smaller).
Jul–11	Exchange rate management	(i) The government extended the IOF on currency derivatives. The IOF charged at a rate of 1% on the notional adjusted value, on the acquisition, sale, or maturity of financial derivative contracts implemented which, individually, result in an increase in short currency (dollar) exposure or a reduction in long currency (dollar) exposure. Net long real positions with a notional value of $10 million or less are exempt from the tax. (ii) The government also laid down new legislation whereby the National Monetary Council became the agency responsible for regulating the derivatives market; this tax could be increased up to 25%; all FX derivatives to be registered in clearing houses; the FX exposure of all agents to be consolidated.

Source: Prates (2011) and Magud *et al.* (2011)

Endnotes

[1] However, the IMF's conditional endorsement of capital controls has been accompanied by the proposal of a framework restricting the use of such controls only as an instrument of last resort and even then as a temporary measure. As Gallagher (2011b) reports, this attempt by the IMF to impose a 'code of conduct' after the fact has not been well received by developing countries which have borne the brunt of the risks introduced by volatility in capital flows and which in some cases have already introduced capital controls on their own initiative. This conflict of views further highlights the importance of more independent academic research in this area.

[2] Principal Component Analysis is a statistical technique for optimally approximating the information contained in a large number of variables by a smaller number of variables (Jolliffe, 2010). In this case the Chinn–Ito index is chosen to be that linear combination of the four dummy variables which captures the variation in these variables between the countries/periods to the greatest possible extent.

[3] CRS Report for Congress (http://congressionalresearch.com/98987/document.hp?study =BRAZILS+ECONOMIC+REFORM+AND+THE+GLOBAL+FINANCIAL+CRISIS) Accessed in April 2011.

[4] Magud *et al.* (2011).

5   Prates (2011).
6   http://www.forextradinglb.com/news.php?go=fullnews&newsid=375. Accessed in April 2011.
7   http://www.reuters.com/article/2011/01/03/brazil-economy-tax-idUSN0313052220110103
8   World Economic Outlook Database (2010).
9   Laurens (2000).
10 Cowan (2007).
11 Administrative controls are considered more effective in terms of controlling capital flows. However, they are not considered market friendly, as investors cannot build their cost into their portfolio calculation, which they can, for example, in the case of a financial transaction tax. In addition, the ability of administrators to keep up with new forms of derivatives is limited (Fitzgerald, 1999).
12 Similarly, for countries like Thailand, Korea and Philippines, indices are also seen to suffer from inertia for extended periods. Perhaps this can be attributed to the fact that such studies and the IMF's AREAR view capital account openness as a binary event: either open or closed, when in fact it should be seen as a process (Mohan and Kapoor, 2009).
13 RBI (2008).
14 It was decided that the equity instruments should be issued within 180 days of the receipt of the inward remittance. If the equity instruments are not issued within 180 days from the date of receipt, the amount of consideration so received should be refunded immediately to the non-resident investor (RBI, 2007).
15 'Leads and lags' in exports represent differences between the merchandise exports data recorded through the banking channel and the data recorded through Customs due to timing and the valuation differences (Balance of Payment Manual of India (RBI, 2010). 'Leads & lags in exports' also include trade credit extended by Indian exporters to non-residents [Developments in India's Balance of Payments during First Quarter (April–June) of 2011–12 (RBI, 2011)].
16 RBI (2008).
17 Non-utilization of the available capital control instrument indicates that government was trying to provide some relief to oil companies.
18 Singh (2007).
19 Verma and Prakash (2011).
20 Though continuous sterilized intervention to prevent currency appreciation incurs quasi-fiscal costs which may need to be met through distortionary taxation, Indian authorities seem to have avoided this temptation and restricted themselves to a stabilization mandate.

References

Chinn, Menzie D. and Hiro Ito. 2008. 'A New Measure of Financial Openness'. *Journal of Comparative Policy Analysis* 10(3): 309–22.

Cowan, Kevin and José De Gregorio. 2005. 'International Borrowing, Capital Controls and the Exchange Rate: Lessons from Chile'. *Central Bank of Chile Working Papers* No 322.

De Gregorio, Jose, Sebastian Edwards and Rodrigo O. Valdés. 2000. 'Controls on Capital Inflows: Do They Work?'. *Journal of Development Economics* 63(1): 59–83.

Edwards, Sebastian. 1999. 'How Effective Are Capital Controls?'. *Journal of Economic Perspectives* 13(4): 65–84.

Fitz Gerald, V. 1999. 'Policy Issues in Market Based and Non Market Based Measures to Control the Volatility of Portfolio Investment'. *Queen Elizabeth House Working Paper Series* No. 26.

Gallagher, Kevin. 2011a. 'Regaining Control? Capital Controls and the Global Financial Crisis'. *PERI Working Paper* No. 250.

Gallagher, Kevin. 2011b. 'The IMF, Capital Controls and Developing Countries'. *Economic and Political Weekly* 7–13 May:12–16.

International Monetary Fund. 2011. 'Recent Experiences in Managing Capital Inflows Cross-Cutting Themes and Possible Policy Framework'. Prepared by the Strategy, Policy, and Review Department, IMF.

Jadhav, Narendra. 2005. 'Exchange Rate Regime and Capital Flows: The Indian Experience'. Presented at Chief Economists' Workshop, 4–6 April, Bank of England.

Jolliffe, I. T. 2010. *Principal Component Analysis*. 2nd ed. New York: Springer Verlag New York Inc.

Laurens, Bernard and Jaime Cardoso. 1998. 'Managing Capital Flows: Lessons from the Experience of Chile'. IMF Working Paper No.WP/98/168, December.

Laurens, Bernard. 2000. 'Chile's Experience with Controls on Capital Inflows in the 1990s'. In *Capital Controls: Country Experiences with Their Use and Liberalization*, by Ariyoshi, Akira, Karl Habermeier, Bernard Laurens, InciÖtker-Robe, Jorge Ivan Canales-Kriljenko and Andrei Kirilenko. IMF Occasional Paper No. 190. Washington: International Monetary Fund.

Magud, Nicolas E., Carmen M. Reinhart and Kenneth S. Rogoff. 2011. 'Capital Controls: Myth and Reality - A Portfolio Balance Approach'. NBER Working Papers 16805.

Mohan, Rakesh. 2008. 'Capital Flows to India'. *RBI Monthly Bulletin*, 2048, December.

Mohan, Rakesh and Muneesh Kapur. 2009. 'Managing the Impossible Trinity: Volatile Capital Flows and Indian Monetary Policy'. Stanford Center for International Development Working Paper, No. 401.

Mohanty, M. S. and Philip Turner. 2006. 'Foreign Exchange Reserve Accumulation in Emerging Markets: What are Domestic Implications?'. *BIS Quarterly Review*, September.

Patnaik, I. and A. Shah. 2010. 'Did The Indian Capital Controls Work as a Tool of Macroeconomic Policy?'. NIPFP Working paper, 2011–87.

Prates, D. M. 2011. 'Dealing with Capital Flows in the Post-Crisis Context: The Brazilian Experience'. Paper presented at IE/UNICAMP and HTW Berlin workshop on 'Financial Sector Development for Sustained Growth', Berlin, Germany.

Reserve Bank of India. 2006. 'Report on Currency and Finance 2004–05'. Mumbai: Reserve Bank of India.

RBI. 2007. 'Foreign Direct Investments (FDI) – Issue of Shares under FDI and Refund of Advance Remittances'. RBI/2007–08/213 A. P. (DIR Series) Circular No.20.

RBI. 2010. 'Balance of Payment Manual of India'. Mumbai: Reserve Bank of India.

RBI. 2008. 'India's Balance of Payments Developments during Fourth Quarter of 2007–08'. Mumbai: Reserve Bank of India.

RBI. 2011. Developments in India's Balance of Payments during First Quarter (April–June) of 2011–12'. Mumbai: Reserve Bank of India.

Sarno, L. and Mark P. Taylor. 2001. 'Official Intervention in The Foreign Exchange Market: is it Effective, and, if so, How Does It Work?'. *Journal of Economic Literature*. [Accessed in April 2011].

Shome, Parthasarathi. 2012. 'Financial Transactions Taxes'. In *Essays in Honour of Raja Chelliah*. New Delhi: Sage Publications, 11–36.

Singh, Bhupal. 2007. 'Corporate Choice for Overseas Borrowings: The Indian Evidence'. *Reserve Bank of India Occasional Papers* 28(3), Winter.

Subbarao, Duvvuri. 2009. Remarks at G30 International Banking Seminar in Istanbul on October 5, 2009 organized on the occasion of the IMF-World Bank Annual Meetings. Available at: http://www.rbi.org.in/scripts/BS_SpeechesView.aspx?Id=441 [Accessed in April 2011].

Subbarao, Duvvuri. 2011. 'Implications of the Expansion of Central Bank Balance Sheets'. Comments of Governor, Reserve Bank of India at the Special Governors' Meeting in Kyoto, Japan, on 31 January.

Verma, R. and Anand Prakash. 2011. 'Sensitivity of Capital Flows to Interest Rate Differentials: An Empirical Assessment for India'. RBI Working Paper Series, W P S (DEPR): 7 / 2011.

WEO. 2010. 'World Economic Outlook Database'. International Monetary Fund, October.

The International Monetary System: Mitigating Risks from Dominance of the Dollar and India's Stance

Renu Kohli[1]

Introduction

Surveying the financial battlefield after the crisis, the world is in a corrective mood. The advanced economies are limping to normalcy but are not yet there. Having fared better, the emerging and developing countries are in lead economic position. The aftershocks linger, prompting a sombre realization across both groups; there can be further, perhaps more serious, eruptions if the present international monetary system is not reformed to ensure its safety and stability. There is concurrence for the need of a coordinated global effort towards its reform among stakeholders, even though the views on the precise mechanics are divergent. Unfortunately, so are the national interests. The question is how to reconcile this divergence and weave it into a common thread of global agreement.

This chapter is concerned with the anchor of the current international monetary system – the dollar. With the unfurling of the global financial crisis in 2008, the tensions between the dollar's role as the world's reserve currency and a national currency have reached a flashpoint threatening global stability. The scale of trade and investment flows across the globe has risen significantly from the time the dollar became the medium of international payments and exchange. The resulting need for additional international liquidity has been increasingly met by the use of the dollar as a reserve currency. The rules and institutions governing these flows however, have neither functioned in the manner originally intended nor kept pace with changes in the global monetary landscape. As a result, national interests have often overlooked broader obligations and commitments of countries to abide by a code of conduct for the international exchange of goods, services and capital. Orderly conditions for global growth and stability, the goals that international monetary rules were intended to achieve, have not prevailed. To the contrary, unrestrained macro policies have exacerbated imbalances much of which are centred upon the dollar, heightening the risk of systemic instability. This has prompted countries to consider ways to alleviate the risks from the dollar's supremacy.

Loosely, these rules of exchange constitute the current International Monetary System (IMS)[2] with the International Monetary Fund (IMF) as a back-up institution for liquidity, controls and parity adjustments and the dollar as the reserve currency.[3] Replacing the pre-1971-Bretton Woods[4] system of fixed parities vis-à-vis the dollar, this IMS – a 'non-system' – did not bind any country to establish a par value for its exchange rate. Instead, countries could choose their own exchange rate arrangements. IMF, the institution overseeing these arrangements, was assigned no mandate to interfere in this matter as the rules of exchange that replaced the Bretton Woods arrangement permitted all exchange rate regimes except pegging to gold (Williamson, 2009). Therefore, the manner in which exchange rate parities were set among the transacting countries came to determine how well or not the new IMS functioned.

As international capital mobility rose, especially from the 1990s, the trilemma – wherein a fixed exchange rate system with free capital mobility can work only when there is monetary policy independence – confronted developing economies with ever-increasing intensity (Obstfeld and Taylor, 2003). Capital controls in these countries started to lose their grip. And the US – the reserve-issuing country of this monetary structure – followed an increasingly lax monetary policy to counter recession in its economy from 2000 onwards. The confluence of conflicting domestic economic policy goals and international responsibilities of the reserve-issuing country on one side with global capital flows and the self-preserving policies of the developing world on another thus led to a significant divergence in exchange rate policies of the two groups. As a result, a polarization of free floating currencies emerged at one end with a group of currencies managed/stabilized vis-à-vis the dollar at another.

This division of 'free floaters' and 'intermediate' regimes has emerged in a specific context and is not without reason. One, the rise in international capital mobility was accompanied by an increased frequency and intensity of financial crises in several parts of the world, e.g., Latin America in the 1980s; East Asia, Russia and Mexico in the 1990s and Argentina and Brazil in the 2000s. These developments triggered a wave of precautionary reserves' accumulation among emerging and developing countries who sought to 'self-insure' themselves from future liquidity shocks (Eichengreen, 2004).[5]

Two, perceptions of unfairness or inequity of the existing international financial architecture gathered force, especially during the East Asian crisis of 1997–98, when liquidity support from international financial institutions like the IMF was either delayed or conditional. This pushed the afflicted Asian nations towards creation of liquidity buffers and build regional reserve pools. Three, commodity-exporting countries have smoothened terms-of-trade shocks by accumulating surpluses to contain real appreciation-driven expansions in domestic demand and avoid adverse effects upon productivity.[6] Finally, export-oriented countries have accumulated reserves by saving surpluses to avoid exchange rate appreciation that could otherwise hurt export competitiveness.[7] As a result, the pace of reserves' accumulation accelerated from the nineties (Figure 7.1).

Figure 7.1: Global Imbalances (in per cent of world GDP)

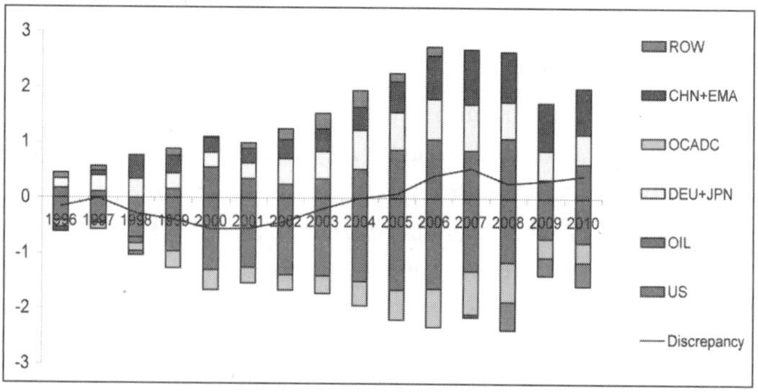

Source: IMF, WEO database
CHN+EMA: China, Hong Kong SAR, Indonesia, Korea, Malaysia, Philippines, Singapore, Taiwan Province of China and Thailand;
DEU+JPN: Germany and Japan, OIL: Oil exporters, ROW: rest of the world; US: United States.
OCADC: Bulgaria, Croatia, Czech Republic, Extonis, Greece, Hungary, Ireland, Latvia, Lithuania, Poland, Portugal, Romania, Slovak Republic, Slovenia, Spain, Turkey and United Kingdom.

Globally, the concentration of savings in one set of countries is offset by growing deficits in the reserve-issuing country, the US (Figure 7.1). The build-up of this global imbalance exposes the fault lines in the current IMS structure. First, and as mentioned earlier, the system lacks a mechanism to address such distortions except through mutual agreement and cooperation between the major surplus and deficit countries. Second, the instability stemming from this asymmetry is compounded by the fact that much of these savings are held in dollars. Post-crisis, the value and safety of these assets is now in danger of erosion as the dollar reflects the weak economic position of a crisis-ravaged US; further, the US is not bound to maintain the value of its currency in the current IMS, unlike the Bretton Woods system where it was obliged to maintain the gold convertibility of the dollar. Finally, the absence of any commitment of the reserve-issuing country to the rest of the world makes all other countries dependent upon US monetary policy, which is transmitted through financial linkages and trade flows in an increasingly interconnected global economy. For example, creation of excess liquidity in global markets through expansionary US domestic polices to stimulate domestic demand can be inflationary and destabilizing for other countries; on the other hand, too few issues of the reserve currency to meet domestic price objectives can be contractionary.

These deficiencies bring to fore the inherent conflict between the national economic objectives of the reserve-issuing country and its international responsibilities. In particular, post-crisis compulsions to kick-start growth have triggered a repeat of past trends by the US: unprecedented loose monetary settings stimulating speculative, destabilizing capital flows in search of quick and high returns in the fast-growing emerging nations, eliciting foreign exchange intervention by the latter. Moreover, this excess liquidity is placing an enormous burden of adjustment on recipient countries that are loath to bear the brunt, especially at this juncture.

On the part of reserve-holders, the linkage to the ups and downs of US economic policies exposes them to a cycle of risks and benefits that is not always in harmony with domestic economic structures or policies (UN, 2009). To elaborate, a weaker dollar is precisely what the US might need at this point to boost its economy as its traditional driver, domestic demand, remains depressed and below trend. But that is not what the rest of the world wants. However, the current IMS neither binds the reserve-issuer to international responsibilities nor does it prevent countries from keeping exchange rate values at their desired levels, each being a matter of sovereign rights. Whereas, the point of an international monetary system, say Eichengreen and Temin (2010) is '...to be a system in which countries on both sides of the exchange rate contribute to its smooth operation'.

The problems with dollar supremacy extend beyond global reserve-holdings. It towers over other currencies in international private usage. It is unparalleled in the range and depth of its markets, instruments and liquidity. Its omnipresence in official and private transactions compounds financial instability risks with the slightest hint or threat to the sustainability of its value. As the deteriorating economic strength of the US, its high level of unemployment, record fiscal deficit and financial sector troubles question the sustainability of the dollar's value, one dimension of the reform of the international monetary system is devoted to find alternatives to its dollar dependency. See Figures 7.2 and 7.3.

Figure 7.2: Dollar as the Reserve Currency

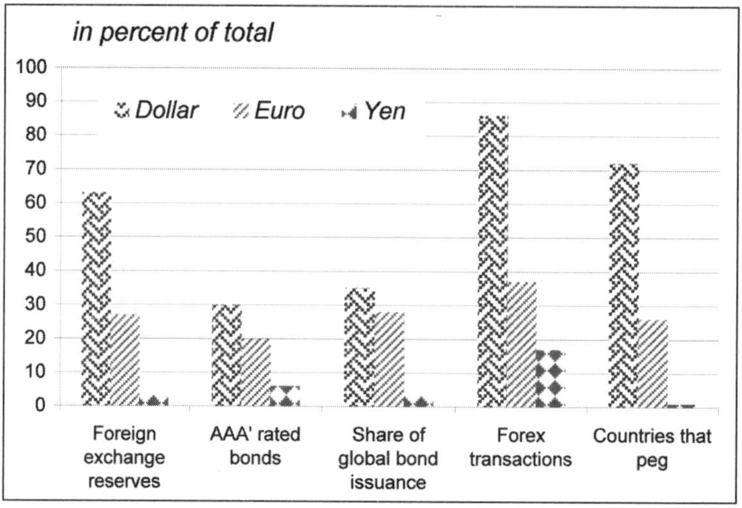

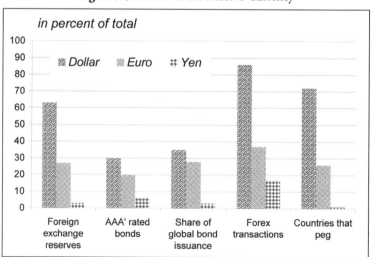

Source: McKinsey (2009) & author's calculations

Figure 7.3: Dollar as the Reserve Currency

Source: McKinsey (2009) & author's calculations

Several proposals have been mooted since then to minimize the risks arising from the dominance of the dollar in the international monetary system. For obvious reasons, one of the first calls for international monetary reform has come from China, the largest surplus country in the world. Assessing the post-crisis situation, the Governor of its central bank called for a shift away from the US dollar to a more broad-based, stable and equitable reserve-currency for the global economy (Zhou Xiaochuan, 2009). International organizations like the UN (2009) and IMF (2009) have also come forth with proposals and comprehensive discussions on the matter. The ideas for reform range from building the SDR as a reserve currency (Zhou Xiaochuan, 2009) to instituting a truly global reserve currency (UN, 2009) and realistic assessments like the unstoppable emergence of a multicurrency system that reflects the shifting axis of global economic power (Eichengreen, 2011).

The third section of the chapter deals with these reform proposals. Each of these proposals has strengths and limitations. A realistic assessment however, has to transcend efficiency considerations. For what is of more relevance is the readiness, or otherwise, of players – especially the key stakeholders – to accept one or another alternative. For the history of international monetary arrangements, of which a reserve currency is a key constituent, is littered with episodes of non-cooperation among members as national interests override the needs and desire for convergence to a stable outcome. Thus, any alternative to the US dollar will eventually be acceptable more for its political viability than pure efficiency.

This is where an international forum like the G20 is especially relevant. The broader subject of reforming the international monetary system, with the replacement of the dollar as an important constituent, has been discussed and continues to dominate discussions at various platforms like the UN, IMF and the G20. Both the IMF and UN have been explicit in recognizing the risks attached to the dominance of the dollar in the international monetary system and put forth a set of proposals to launch a debate. However, any attempt at reform has to be made politically viable through the provision of leadership and international cooperation. The G20 offers one such platform.

It is noteworthy that major countries, also the key stakeholders in this regard, are critical deciders for the direction that IMS reform takes. China, because of its sizeable reserve-holdings of $3.2 trillion (September 2011), runs a high risk of capital losses on its assets if the dollar were to slide suddenly and/or substantially; incompatibly, the US needs a weaker dollar in order to boost growth, with adjustments from the rest of the world. A multilateral solution to this non-cooperative game therefore has to be found. Second, it is important to separate out the short-term needs vis-à-vis long-term requirements in order to set the reform ball in motion. Third, the pace of the shift or diversification away from the dollar has to be gradual and orderly to avoid disruption in global financial stability. It is possible to resolve these issues at the G20, which has emerged as the main vehicle for coordinating global responses in the post-crisis world and for the engagement among nations for international monetary reforms.[8]

National thinking on these issues is important for each country's interests may be better served in backing one or another idea. Countries like India may be considerably less exposed than China and therefore less vulnerable to dollar depreciation, but long-term geopolitical considerations and the prestige that active participation and facilitation of international economic cooperation brings could shape a specific stance. France, for instance, has been vocal against the domination of the dollar, as has been Russia for reasons of international prestige. Likewise, the BRICS (Brazil, Russia, India, China and South Africa) nations called for a stable, predictable and more diversified international monetary system, to which India was a signatory (BRIC summit 2010). Although India recognizes the merit in diversifying away from the dollar, so far, no specific position has emerged on the subject. The chapter also considers the various possibilities: it assesses India's macroeconomic risks and geopolitical considerations that serve as inputs to evolve its stance. As the Co-Chair of the G20 Working Group which is charged with studying these problems, India can play a useful role.

This chapter argues that a beginning must be made to address the fundamental flaws of the current IMS. The push for reform must originate from a perspective of a globally integrated world in the long term. In the light of the worst-ever financial crisis in a century, it considers that the timing is ripe for such reforms. However, it acknowledges the difficulties of reconciling national interests and achieving international cooperation, especially at this juncture when many countries are focussed on recovering output losses suffered during the crisis and returning growth to pre-crisis levels. It also factors in the absence of any clear alternative to the US dollar at this point. Against this backdrop, it suggests that the starting point of a shift away from the dollar could be in official transactions, viz. the conversion of dollar reserve-holdings into SDRs. From a short-term perspective, this has the merit of reducing some of the risks from dollar dominance. Over a longer period, the rise of other currencies in private usage will further reduce the risks from dollar dominance and provide a broader base for international payments and settlements.

Pre-eminence of the Dollar: History, Implications and Risks

This section traces the trajectory of the dollar to the status of the world's reserve currency. It charts its rise to dominance in trade and financial transactions, which outweighs that of any other currency; it also considers the conflicts and problems caused by this dominance. The risks associated with this supremacy are discussed at length as also how these might bear upon international monetary reform.

The Dollar's Rise to World Reserve-currency Status

How the dollar came to dominate the international monetary system is a combination of historical opportunities and economic fortune. At the start of the twentieth century, the British sterling was the dominant world currency. But the decline of Britain as an imperial power, the two World Wars between 1914 and 1945 and the growing economic strength of the US in this period led to a rise of the dollar as a currency of international usage (Eichengreen, 2005; Eichengreen and Flandreau, 2008). Effectively, the pound and the dollar coexisted in a dual-reserve currency system from the mid-1920s until about the World War II, by which time the dollar had clearly emerged as the dominant world currency. It therefore became the natural choice of an anchor for the Bretton Woods system of fixed exchange rates set up in 1945.[9]

The dollar continued as the leading currency in the international exchange rate system when the Bretton Woods system was effectively abandoned in 1971[10] by the US (Eichengreen 2008); thereafter, the world shifted to a system of largely floating exchange rates, later termed as Bretton Woods II. Legacy and economic strength again played a key role in the persistence of the dollar in the global exchange rate system in this round of global monetary arrangement as well. The US' leading geopolitical role at the time was reflected in its domination of the global financial system, substantially derived from the rapid growth and deepening of its own financial system. Countries that did not float their currencies in the post-Bretton Woods world also chose to peg or manage their currencies vis-à-vis the dollar, thereby making it a global benchmark for exchange rate parities. This dominance continues to this day with some 66 countries pegging or stabilizing their exchange rates vis-à-vis the dollar; by comparison, only 27 countries anchor their currencies against the Euro.

The 'network externalities' – the more a currency is used, the more it becomes attractive and acceptable to others – further multiplied dollar usage. By the 1990s, when the scale and pace of foreign exchange reserves' accumulation accelerated considerably, the dollar was the natural choice as currency for such investments too. The fact that there was no other currency that matched the dollar's attributes also contributed towards establishing its position as the global reserve currency. For example, the Euro – although representing a considerable portion of world output and trade – was introduced only in the new millennium, took some time to establish confidence in its value and to this day, does not match up to the dollar in terms of liquidity across a wide range of instruments and maturity.

History, however, can repeat itself. The dollar's rise was built upon the decline of the sterling. That the strength of the dollar's tide might now well be ebbing is manifest in many visible signs, the most important of which is a weak US economy with little promise and potential in the future. In an unmistakeable irony of history, this decline also coincides with a tilt in economic power towards fast-growing Asia, especially China, that is evenly balanced vis-à-vis the US in terms of size and trade but outweighs it on many other attributes like demographics, catch-up dynamics, future potential and so on. The uncertainty surrounding the dollar's future can be observed from the responses of surplus countries, which are steadily diversifying their reserve-holdings to other currencies, gold and other hedges to spread their risks. Still, the reduction of risks stemming from dominance of the dollar is limited for lack of alternatives; for example, the Euro lacks the financial depth and liquidity in its markets, the region's economy is under significant fiscal stress and it is unclear as to whether it is ready, or has the necessary capacity to bear the costs of being a reserve issuer.

There is therefore, no real challenge to the dollar's supremacy at this point. But the wheels of history turn slowly but inexorably. And, it is not hard to imagine an eventual dilution of the dollar in the foreseeable future with a multicurrency system instead of the bipolar example from history.

Trade and Finance Domination

Being the major currency in the global monetary system for more than half a century, it is no surprise that the US dollar dominates global trade and financial transactions. This applies for practically all measures of global use of the dollar (Figure 7.4). According to the IMF, 66 countries peg to or manage their exchange rates vis-à-vis the dollar. Nearly 62 per cent of the official foreign exchange reserves were held in dollars in 2010 compared to 27 per cent in the Euro. This however, could be an underestimate, as many countries, e.g., China, do not report the currency composition of their reserves. Reflecting apprehensions about debasement in its value, however, dollar holdings of official reserves show a gradual decline, especially from 2005, as many surplus countries have started to diversify their risks.

Figure 7.4: Dollar Share in Global Reserves

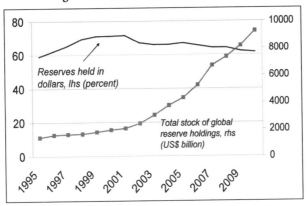

Source: Author's calculations with data from COFER, IMF

Currency distribution of global foreign exchange market turnover (Percentage shares of average daily turnover, April 2010)

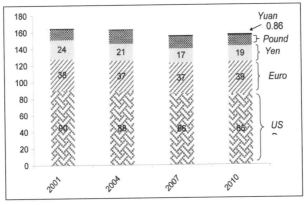

Source: BIS

   The BIS Triennial Central Bank Survey of Foreign Exchange and Derivatives Market Activity, 2010 shows that nearly 86 per cent of forex transactions take place in the dollar; by comparison, forex transaction in the Euro have remained at around 38 per cent since its launch in 2000; a majority of these are intra-EU transactions. Much of the liquidity in global bond markets comes from dollar-denominated bond issuances that are little more than a third of total all such issuances. According to Eichengreen (2011), nearly three-quarters of all $100 bills circulate outside the US (while China's official dollar holdings are at $1000 per Chinese resident!).

Figure 7.5: Proportion of Trade Settled in USD (x-axis) Against Proportion of Trade with the US

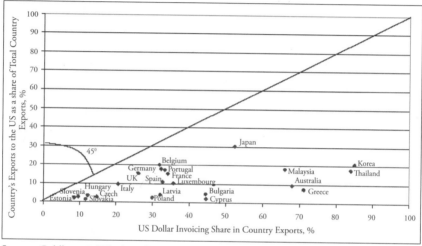

Source: Goldberg & Tille (2008)

Figure 7.6: Net Foreign Holdings of the US Treasury

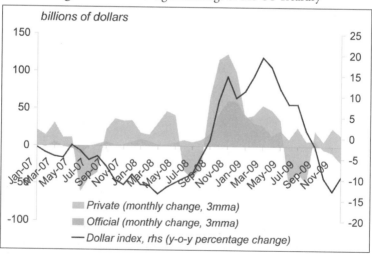

Source: Datastream and author's calculations

The dollar dominates global trade as well. It is the primary invoice currency of choice in the invoicing of both exports and imports by countries outside Europe, with substantial variation in the extent of its usage across countries (Goldberg and Tille, 2008). The dollar's usage in trade invoicing is far greater than what would be expected purely on the basis of direct trade flows and is particularly strong for Korea, Thailand, Australia, the UK and Greece (Figure 7.5).[11] Other than trade settlements and usage as reserve currency, the dollar also dominates through its use in the pricing of primary commodities. Despite the risk and uncertainty surrounding the value of the dollar as well as unease about US monetary policy, the dollar continues to serve as a safe haven for global investors in periods of increased uncertainty and risk.

Finally, the dollar's role as a safe haven is repeatedly borne out in crisis events (Figure 7.6). The precise reasons for this role remain unknown, notes Obstfeld (2010), who suggests that the liquidity of dollar funding markets and their effect upon the size of gross dollar positions could be one of them. So, high liquidity generates large gross dollar positions; when credit market conditions tighten in a crisis the demand for dollar to pay off short-term debts is disproportionately high, leading to a rise in the dollar price relative to other currencies (Ibid.).

Problems with Dollar Dominance

Why is the strong presence of the dollar such a problem? One of the main arguments relate to a problem identified by Robert Triffin (1961): the use of a national currency as an international reserve currency. Commonly referred to as 'Triffin's Dilemma', the argument is that as the scale of global trade in goods and assets rises, the growing transactions' demand for the reserve asset would generate deficits in the reserve-issuing country. Originally presented in the context of the old Bretton Woods system – when the dollar was convertible into gold – the contradiction referred to a future situation wherein the growing demand for the reserve currency reached a point where the outstanding dollar liabilities of the US exceeded its holdings of gold, thereby triggering a confidence crisis over the credibility of US authorities to honour their commitment of converting dollars into gold. Under the current international monetary arrangement, which is not backed by gold, the 'Triffin's Dilemma' is rather reflected in the belief of economic agents about the credibility of the US Federal Reserve's monetary policy. In principle, the US does not really have to run persistent current account deficits; it can, instead, issue a range of liquid assets to the world's reserve-holders offsetting these through matching investments in overseas' assets to achieve external balance. Likewise, a decline in the dollar's value will not bring about a collapse of the entire system. There are, however, risks associated with these situations that are spelt out in detail in the next section.

A second problem is the 'exorbitant privilege'[12] this accords to the US. There are substantial benefits to the issuer of the global reserve currency. One major advantage is income derived from seigniorage or the effectively interest-free loan received from the non-resident holders of its currency. For instance, whenever the dollar depreciates vis-à-vis that of its financial partner-countries, a capital gain accrues to the US; Clarida (2009) estimates that such capital gains amounted to $1 trillion from gradual dollar depreciation for several years to the crisis. The second benefit is a reduced cost of capital accruing from the high demand for reserves by foreign governments and which is reflected in lowered yield on US government securities. McKinsey (2009) calculates that this effect contributed to lowering the US cost of capital between 50–60 basis points over 2008–09. Applying this to borrowings by the US government, households and corporates, their computations show an annual savings of $130 billion on this count; these, however, are reduced by some $30 billion due to interest income foregone by households and corporations by the lower interest rates. Finally, the US derives enormous policy latitude due to the greater liquidity of its markets, its ability to borrow freely in its own currency abroad at reduced costs and the seigniorage it earns from issuing a global currency.[13]

The 'exorbitant privilege' has costs though. One, the increased demand for dollar-denominated assets by non-residents results in exchange rate overvaluation,[14] which directly impacts the US economy through competitiveness losses translating into lower exports and the creation of additional demand for imported goods and services that become relatively more competitive. McKinsey (2009) estimates the former to be around $30 billion for every 5 per cent overvaluation, while the latter are in the of $10–20 billion range; US consumers benefit from lowered import prices to the tune of $25–45 billion a year. A second cost is of increasing current account deficits in the US resulting in an adverse impact upon domestic demand as the excess demand for dollar assets by surplus countries – without any forthcoming adjustment in foreign demand – forces the US to maintain a persistent fiscal deficit; periodic adjustments to this growing deficit would then demand contractionary macro policies, thereby lowering output (UN, 2009). Last are the sharp fluctuations in asset prices that can result in valuation losses in the net international investment positions during such events pointing to an asymmetry in the roles of exorbitant privilege and safe haven (Obstfeld, 2010).[15]

A third problem with the dollar underpinning the global monetary structure is the instability associated with tying the rest of the world to a single economy. This assumes special relevance at this point as the expansionary policies of the US to boost its economy are imposing the burden of adjustment upon the rest of the world. There are also other destabilizing sources like the persistent payment imbalances that contribute to undermine confidence in the value of the dollar.

Last is the unfairness of such a system. This concern was flagged by the Chinese Premier Zhou in 2009 with a call for reform of the international monetary system through a shift from the dollar towards the SDR as the anchor currency (Xiaochuan, 2009). The UN Report on the Reforms of the International Monetary and Financial System (2009) also notes the inequities of such a system that results in a transfer of resources from the developing to developed countries – mainly the United States – at ultra-low interest rates, placing the estimates at $3.7 trillion for 2007; these transfers exceeded the foreign assistance received from developed countries. Put differently, this view holds a dollar-centred IMS as a US-controlled structure within which the rest of the world must operate. It allows it to simply pursue its sovereign policies while the emerging markets have little say or influence over these choices, which have a tangible, often destabilizing, impact upon their economies.

Risks of Continued Dollar Dominance

The problems arising from the supremacy of the dollar throw a number of identifiable risks. A major risk is that of being a hostage to the reserve-issuing country's ability to debase the value of its own currency. This is a source of great uncertainty as the US remains in a weak economic position due to the impact of the financial crisis of 2008. The dollar, whose fundamental value is determined by these factors, is on a downward path with waning confidence on the part of investors that its value will sustain in the near future. These fears were partly realized with the recent downgrading of outlook for the US Treasury's long-term debt from 'stable' to 'negative' in early April, 2011. The belief that the US will continue to run 'irresponsible' policies, i.e., gear its policies to domestic economic objectives without commitment to its international role, is also by now well entrenched. There are also fears of that the extremely loose monetary policy might eventually lead to inflation, thereby reducing the enormous debt overhang of the US, but causing losses to investors. And there is a risk that the 'exorbitant privilege' accruing to the US shifts the burden upon the non-reserve or deficit countries to adjust vis-à-vis the surplus, reserve-issuing countries.

Another risk is the export of 'deflationary' bias to the rest of the world if the US were to offset its growing claims on the rest of the world, i.e., foreign purchases of US assets, by accumulating foreign assets through either public or private sector mechanisms. The ensuing deficit-reduction or increased net savings in the US would contribute significantly towards depressing global aggregate demand. Alternately, if the rest of the world were to become reluctant in accumulating further dollar assets, then the adjustment of global imbalances would necessarily have to come from a fall in global income, as UN (2009) points out, adding the risk is high in the light of the expansionary policies of the US so far.

Further, an unmet demand–supply gap by the reserve-issuer could possibly stimulate alternative reserve assets of poor quality and limited use that, in turn, could contribute to a 'debasement' and further destabilize the international monetary system (IMF, 2009). On the other hand, if the demand for reserves is accommodated ad infinitum, the risk is of an unsustainable build-up of public debt. Either way, the imperatives of national economic policies militate against those of broader, international significance.

In balance, it would be fair to say that the international monetary system has reached a point where its single, national currency anchor poses significant instability risks, among other things. At the same time, the pervasiveness of dollar-denominated transactions across trade, finance and global reserves suggests that any shift has to be gradual and evolutionary; certainly it is hard to see private transactions moving entirely away from the dollar, except briefly when uncertainty is very high. The dollar also remains, despite all the fears about US' economic prospects, a refuge of safety; this role cannot diminish overnight. This points to a segmented approach to mitigate the risks from the universal dollar, possibly distinguished by official and private categories. The next section considers the proposals made in this regard.

Alternative Proposals to Reduce the Dollar's Role

The proposals to replace the dollar-centred global monetary system with one that is broader, fairer and more stable are not new. These have been around for some time, surfacing periodically in times of financial turbulence but relegated to the backburner for lack of political commitment and cooperation after the storm has passed. Some are more a reflection of the reality of the changing world patterns. These are discussed in this section. Before that however, it would be apt to list the desirable properties that a global reserve currency must possess to better illuminate the appraisal of the proposals that follow.

Theoretically, and like national currency arrangements, a reserve currency also needs to have a stable value linked to a benchmark and must be issued according to a set of rules that are flexible enough to allow adjustments to changes in demand. It should also have the property of confidence in its value, so that official reserves can be invested in it and the private sector can denominate their trades in it.

Unlike national currencies, however, a reserve currency should not be tied to the economic conditions or national interests of any single or group of countries. A primary consideration for a viable alternative to the dollar would be to resolve the Triffin's dilemma. Further, a reserve currency like the dollar is also a unit of account in which oil and other commodities are priced, contracts drawn and transactions invoiced (McKinsey, 2009). Private sector acceptability is also a must for international usage. Since it is also eventually a medium of exchange, it should also have international acceptability, sufficient depth for a multitude of transactions to take place, liquidity for borrowing–lending operations of global scale and magnitudes and the necessary range across maturities to resolve the inter-temporal constraints of users (McKinsey, 2009).

Reviving the SDR

One of the oldest and currently popular proposals is that of converting the SDR into a reserve asset. The SDR is a claim upon a basket of currencies operated through the IMF membership. A synthetic reserve asset, it was created in 1969 in a context somewhat similar to the present: the conflict between the gearing of economic policies of the reserve-issuing country towards domestic objectives vis-à-vis requirements of global liquidity and exchange. At the time, the contractionary monetary policy of the US had sparked fears of a liquidity deficit (or shortage of dollars) that led to the emergence of the SDR to plug the funding gap.

The SDR proposal dates back to the formation of the Bretton Woods institutions and is already embodied in Article VIII of the Articles of Agreement of the IMF, which tasks the latter with the goal of making the SDR a principal reserve asset in the international monetary system. In the most recent thinking on IMS reform, a number of academics (e.g., Bergsten, 2009; Williamson, 2009), countries like China (Xiaochuan, 2009) and international agencies like the UN (2009) have called for its activation and revival to secure global financial stability and facilitate world economic growth. The UN (2009) suggests that an institutional way of establishing a new global reserve system would be a simple broadening of the existing SDR arrangements, making their issuance automatic and regular. This would also fulfil the original purpose of creating the IMF.

The SDR is unlike a reserve asset in that the reserve-holdings of countries are not denominated or held in the form of SDRs; for example, only 0.4 per cent of the world's total non-gold reserves were held in SDRs in 2009. It is also unlike a global currency in that it is not in use as a medium of international private transactions. But it can be held and converted among the IMF membership. For instance, a country holding SDRs can convert the same into another member-country's currency through the IMF. A general allocation of SDRs is decided by the IMF's Board of Governors, whose decision is based upon an assessment of the long-term global reserve requirements. Originally, its value was fixed in terms of gold. But with the collapse of the Bretton Woods, its value is constructed from a basket of currencies that at present (November, 2010) are weighted with the dollar (41.9 per cent), the Euro (37.4 per cent), the Pound Sterling (11.3 per cent) and the Yen (9.4 per cent). These weights are reviewed at five-year intervals by the IMF Executive Board.

The supply of SDRs has therefore remained small, at 21.4 billion until 2009. In April 2009, the G20 summit in London called for an increase in general SDR allocation of $250 billion as well as a ratification of the Fourth Amendment to the Articles of Agreement of the IMF in 1997 that was to double the SDR allocation. The general allocation was approved by the IMF's Board of Governors in August 2009 while the Fourth Amendment was ratified by the US Congress and enforced from September 2009. The supply of SDRs from the IMF has therefore increased the holdings in SDRs to 204 billion or nearly 4 per cent of global reserves. These magnitudes, however, have to rise considerably for the SDR to figure meaningfully in the world monetary system.

The proposal of the SDR, if promoted as the principal reserve asset of the global monetary system, possesses a number of attractive properties (IMF 2009). These are:

- First, it has the appeal of not just diversifying away from the US dollar at present but also to bring about a reform by effectively delinking the global monetary system from the vagaries of a linkage with any national currency. It therefore, spreads out the 'exorbitant privilege' attached to a reserve-issuing country across a range of countries whose currencies form the SDR basket.

- Two, the SDR-based system would be more stable as it would have a broader base, a feature it shares with a multiple-currency system. It would also be more convenient to manage compared to a portfolio diversified across different currencies. As a store of value however, the SDR's value would reflect the relative stabilities of its components: the IMF (2009) discussion notes that since the different currency weights are defined in absolute terms, e.g., 44 US dollar cents per SDR, the relative weights would adjust with currency movements, a feature that would serve as a policy disciplining device for the reserve-issuing countries.

On the flip side, promoting the SDR proposal for a universal acceptance requires considerable efforts on the part of the international community. They are:

- First of all, it has to be made more liquid in order to increase its usage as a currency. For this the supply has to increase and the reserve-holdings of different countries must be converted into SDRs. This is not an easy task for several reasons. For one, this demands agreement of the US at the IMF Board given the current distribution of voting rights. It is unlikely that any proposal that would dilute the dollar's strength through a diversification would find favour with it.

- Second, an SDR-based system would also come to depend upon the provision of liquidity by the IMF, i.e., how much or how little reserves are provided? A restrictive reserves policy, for example, could be deflationary for the world, as was witnessed in the last days of the Gold Standard, while a liberal reserves policy would be inflationary. Judgments regarding the global macroeconomy could diverge significantly between the IMF and other countries. So the diversity of views could render the IMF's task extremely difficult. Moreover, this also brings into focus the structure of the IMF Board that is currently unrepresentative of the world balance, but would get to decide on the quantity of SDR issuance.

- A practical drawback is that it would be difficult to match the depth and liquidity of dollar-denominated assets for a very long time. Central banks intervene in foreign exchange markets with the dollar because there is a market for it with takers and instruments. In contrast, the SDRs could be deployed as an intervention currency only after being converted into a traded currency through an official channel between the central bank of a country and the IMF. As such, an enormous liquidity has to be imparted to the currently illiquid SDR to induce central banks to intervene and hold foreign exchange reserves in this form.

- A major limitation of the SDR proposal is its transformation beyond official international transactions. Eichengreen (2011) argues that SDRs are currently neither used to settle cross-border transaction nor as a unit to denominate international bonds. These markets currently do not exist and it will be very hard to create such markets (for example, incentives to induce private agents to transact in SDRs vis-à-vis other convertible currencies). Further the IMF would have to be empowered as a global central bank, a proposal unlikely to find political consensus.

- Another problem associated with providing an SDR base to the IMS is that it needs to replace a current glut of dollar reserves, not add to it. The transition therefore has to be such that the diversification from dollar holdings does not depreciate its value and thereby, the value of the reserve-holding as well. One suggestion to overcome this difficulty is to create a 'substitution account',[16] originally conceived in the 1970s when similar concerns about the safety of the dollar as a reserve asset arose; the idea however, never fructified due to differences over the cost sharing of transfer risks.[17] If operated transparently with clear rules, a substitution account could make for an orderly unwinding by the large reserve holders and reduce the current dollar 'overhang' in the global monetary system (Williamson, 2009). Creation of a substitution account at the IMF, however, would require agreement among countries to socialize the exchange rate risk that is currently concentrated on large balanced positions of countries like China.

Nevertheless, the SDR proposal is not impossible to achieve. China's reform proposal suggests how to impart liquidity to the SDR (Xiaochuan, 2009). This involves setting up a settlement system between SDRs and other currencies; promotion of SDRs in trade and investment; creation of SDR-denominated securities and improvements in valuation and allocation of the SDR including expansion of the basket of currencies of its composition to make it more representative.

The UN (2009) proposes that the creation of new SDRs could either be based upon the incremental demand for reserves or could be countercyclical. The countercyclical version would provide a more active role for the IMF during crises. Another way to manage the SDR would be Jacques Polak's suggestion made more than three decades ago: provide all the financing during a crisis with SDR loans, which could be automatically extinguished once they are repaid. This would create a global equivalent to the issuance of reserves by central banks of industrial countries. The G20 has also endorsed a countercyclical approach during the current crisis as exemplified by the decision to issue $250 billion worth of SDRs. The problem with this, however, is that less than $100 billion of these emissions are likely to benefit the developing countries that need liquidity financing and support as the SDR issuance is tied to IMF quotas.

How realistic and achievable are these reforms? While some, like setting up a settlement system and improvements in valuation and allocation of SDRs, require political agreement. The promotion of the SDR as a currency for invoicing international trade and conducting financial transactions across borders appears far-fetched at present, as there would have to be very strong incentives to induce private participants to make a switch from dollar transactions.

However, to actualize the SDR proposal, one need not look that far ahead for now. For the SDR to emerge as a reserve asset in the near-term, a priority would be to create a liquid market in SDR-denominated assets to encourage it as an intervention currency. The main problem with this would be that of 'network externality': the first-mover to create SDR-denominated assets would find substitution vis-à-vis dollar assets unattractive due to the low liquidity and low returns on the former. Overcoming this problem would require coordinated action from countries that have an incentive to shift to an SDR-based monetary system (Eichengreen, 2009). The UN (2009) proposes that one way to propagate SDR usage would be to further development objectives by allowing the IMF to invest funds made available through SDR issuance in the bonds of multilateral institutions.

Multicurrency System

A multicurrency system, in which other internationally convertible currencies emerge in usage while that of the dollar declines, is less of a reform proposal and more a reflection of the emerging reality of realigning economic power in the world. Just as the ascendancy of the dollar is associated with the unchallenged economic and financial strength of the US as Europe and Japan rebuilt their economies after the two World Wars, it is possible for the dollar's role to dilute while that of other currencies rises as the centre of economic gravity shifts away from the US.

There is the historical precedent of dollar–pound coexistence as currencies of international usage in a bipolar currency system. The dollar eventually eased the pound off the global arena as the US gained economic and geopolitical power after World War II. It is therefore, not difficult to contemplate a repetition of history many decades down the line as the US' power as the world's economic engine wanes while other stronger economies fill the vacuum. It could be, of course, equally argued that there's only been a bi-currency world historically (IMF, 2009); logically too, network externalities ensure that users gravitate towards one currency. However, that was in the context of two continents, Europe and America, whereas this time round, the Asian region is also a hub of economic activity, so it would not be too far-fetched to imagine a regionally strong base for different currencies as currently exists in the case of the Euro.

Pending reform of the IMS, which requires enormous cooperation among countries, the multicurrency system remains the most feasible and quickest option available for diversifying risk from the dollar. Indeed, this has been happening at the level of official reserve-holdings. Another factor prompting a shift away from the dollar towards other viable currencies like the euro, yen and in time, the renminbi, would be the absence of any serious overhaul of the existing IMS. The crisis has exposed the instability and dependency upon one country as the world's reserve-issuer. It is unlikely therefore, that major powers like China would risk such dependency if a *status quo* were to prevail.

Judged by the metric of stability, a multiple-currency system ranks higher than the single-currency system today, as it eliminates or largely reduces the vulnerability of being linked to one country's economic policies. It provides the reserve-holding or surplus countries room for diversification although there could be an element of additional instability from the exchange rate volatility among the reserve-assets currencies themselves, especially if central banks were to respond to exchange rate fluctuations by rebalancing their reserve portfolios (UN, 2009).[18] The advantage offered by the disciplinary effect upon macro policies, in that case, would be offset by the fact that the ensuing reserve switches would not guarantee stability; this could even lead to calls for fixed parities between currencies (although it seems unlikely in the context of high levels of capital mobility that define the global financial economy today).

From the perspective of inequity, a multicurrency system offers a broader distribution of privileges associated with being a reserve-issuer, but does not eliminate these altogether. However, it does not really solve the problems associated with having a national currency – particularly from major industrial countries – in use as a reserve asset. Although no country would be the sole issuer in such an arrangement, the problems associated with the duality of a national and global reserve currency would exist to a significant extent.

How feasible is the emergence of this structure? The assessment can be in terms of many yardsticks. One is the readiness of countries in the reckoning to don the mantle of a reserve issuer. In this regard, Bergsten (1975) has argued that countries may dislike this prospect because of the instability that peremptory withdrawals of its debt and reserve-switches by monetary authorities could prompt as well as the leverage it would accord to debt-holders or creditor nations. While each country would get the exorbitant privilege, they would also have to bear the costs associated with national currencies serving as a reserve currency. These costs are primarily the exchange rate overvaluation that results from an increased demand for the currency.

Currently, the three prospective conkenders in the multiple currency system – the Euro, Yen and the Chinese Renminbi – appear unlikely to be economically or politically ready to bear those costs (McKinsey, 2009). On a practical measure, all are unmatched by the dollar in usage. The Euro, although now making up 27 per cent of the $5.1 trillion global reserves, lacks integrated capital markets and the size and liquidity of $600 billion a day US bond market (McKinsey, 2009).

On a measure of economic readiness, the macroeconomic stability required to inspire confidence in the currency as a global reserve is also weak, except for China. For instance, there is uncertainty about the Euro area over fiscal sustainability and lack of institutional structures within the union to address such issues; the rigidity of its labour markets and reluctance over structural reforms are other sources of fragility. Next, Japan is also in poor economic shape with low consumption and investment levels that have not recovered since its 'lost decade'; recent natural disasters have further weakened it economically and its public debt position (over 200 per cent of GDP) is worse than the US and Euro region. The third claimant, China, is being hailed as the next big emergent threat to the primacy of the dollar. This possibility cannot be ruled out, but currently the yuan is a long way from matching the three major currencies in terms of their financial market strength. However, there is ample evidence in the last two years that China regards internationalization of its currency as an element of IMS reform. It has made a series of moves setting off a process that it expects will likely take 15–20 years;[19] in this, it appears to be following the US nearly a century ago to popularize the use of the dollar internationally wherein the dollar eventually replaced the British pound by the end of World War II (Eichengreen, 2011). *Inter alia*, these are:

- Active pushing of the Yuan in invoicing trade with reported targets of 50 per cent of its trade to be invoiced in the domestic currency in five years;[20]

- Allowing offshore trading in yuan by banks and individuals, expanding it to include US customers in January 2011;

- Creating financial infrastructure through establishment of an offshore centre in Singapore, in addition to an already flourishing market in Hong Kong;

- 'Actively considering' new rules to make it easier to bring yuan funds raised offshore back onto the Chinese mainland;[21]

- Yuan-denominated trade rose to about 7 per cent of China's foreign trade in the first quarter of 2011, compared to just 0.5 per cent in the first quarter of 2010.

To summarize, the emergence of a multicurrency world is perhaps an inevitable process over the next 10–20 years, as has been argued by Eichengreen (2011) who adds that countries like Brazil, India and even China, although large sized, still worry about cost competitiveness in international markets, retain or levy capital controls to insulate their markets from capital flows and possess relatively low levels of financial market development.[22] For these reasons, he excludes any significant threat to the primacy of dollar in the near or even medium-term, although usage of the Euro, Yen and Renminbi will significantly rise. Over a longer period however, the Renminbi could be a major international player.

A New Global Reserve Currency

A sweeping proposal by the UN (2009) is to launch a new currency that is truly global in nature to address the gaps and anomalies discussed here. The idea is akin to John Maynard Keynes' idea of having a global currency (Bancor) issued by a global bank (the International Clearing Union or ICU). Keynes proposed that the global currency's value could be based upon 30 representative commodities; it would be exchangeable against national currencies at fixed rates and could float alongside them and be used for international transactions (Cf. Mateos et al., 2009).

On similar lines, the UN proposal suggests that the institutional framework to administer the global reserve currency could be either the IMF or a new institution specifically created for the purpose. In case of the IMF, it would depend upon needed reforms. Countries could exchange respective currencies for the new global currency (International Currency Certificate or ICC) in a system similar to swaps among central banks, except that it would be universal and therefore, fully backed by a basket of currencies of all members. An alternate structure could be to simply have global currency issues without any backing except for central banks' promise of exchange. Countries could agree to hold an agreed percentage of their reserves in this global currency, which would fetch an interest rate set to induce countries to invest in it. Allocations of the global reserve currency could be based upon a formula incorporating the relatively higher demand for reserves by developing countries, which would address the existing anomaly of 'quota-based allocation' of SDRs at the IMF that results in exactly the opposite outcome. The allocations would have in-built incentives to discourage large surpluses while the size of annual emissions would be targeted to offset reductions in global aggregate demand arising from reserve accumulations.

The merits of this proposal are obvious. It corrects for Triffin's dilemma and the generation of large, global imbalances. It is an improvement upon the SDR proposal as it addresses the governance and equity concerns linked with it. The acceptability of the proposal, however, may not be favourable to the major industrialized countries, which stand to lose their economic power and dilute the leverage they currently exercise through their domination of the boards of the existing international institutions. Over a longer period, the hold of national currencies over trade and financial transactions could also be weakened.

Incremental Reforms

Yet another approach to reform is an incremental one. As a radical redesign or shift away from the dollar involves too much international cooperation and as different countries – notably the major parties, the US and China – have divergent incentives, some have argued that risk-mitigation by countries could be based upon diversifying reserve-holding away from the dollar towards other currencies and by creating reserve pools through bilateral and/or multilateral cooperation for self-insurance purposes (Xiaochuan, 2009; UN, 2009). This would satisfy the demand for reserves due to self-insurance reasons and reduce the accumulation of idle assets by emerging nations who would also gain from reduction in valuation risks.

Status Quo

There is also the possibility of matters remaining where they are. This could be for several reasons. Any reform produces winners and losers. In this instance, it would be the US that would lose from a dilution of the dollar's role and status if any one of the reform proposals, including broader use of the SDR, were to be chosen. Lowering the prestige of its own currency is obviously of disinterest to the US. A third reason to support a *status quo* on the matter is that the costs of inaction on the part of major deficit and surplus countries, i.e., US and China, are mounting. The two countries therefore, despite occasional tension, continue to be engaged in the US–China Economic and Strategic Dialogue to discuss, among other things, their unsustainable external positions.

Further evidence in support of this outcome is offered by efforts to rebalance growth, especially on the part of China, who appears frustrated by the lack of any progress in improvements in international financial architecture. Summarily, these include:

- Repeated hints at diversification of its $3 trillion of currency reserves from dollars. If this gathers pace, it would reduce a significant source of dollar-buying globally.[23]

- It has also allowed the Renminbi to appreciate steadily, which reduces its need to buy dollars. This also encourages Asian currencies competing with the Renminbi to appreciate, thereby contributing to lower overall global demand for the dollar. Renminbi appreciation is expected to sustain for longer periods as it evident from an oft-repeated assertion of Chinese officials that the country's reserves exceed 'reasonable requirements'.[24]

- As against this, the dollar's decline so far has been orderly too. The dollar has fallen approximately 9.1 per cent in 2011 over last year; by comparison, it registered annual declines of close to 10 per cent in 2003–04 in the previous period of very low interest rates (Figure 7.7).

Figure 7.7: Dollar and Renminbi Movements

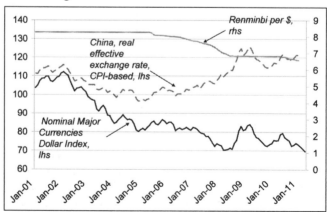

Source: Datastream and author's calculations

- China, as reflected from its Twelfth Plan, is already starting to shift away from the export-led growth model, although this transition will happen over the medium to long term. It has already taken several measures to encourage consumption and provide broader domestic base to its growth.[25]

In contrast, the US is yet to signal a credible plan or strong commitment to reduce its unsustainable external and internal positions. One source of its sanguinity over IMS reform in this direction is the lack of incentive for any surplus country, especially China, to stage a run on the dollar as France did in the 1960s (Bordo, 2010). Nevertheless, a currency's value is determined by both structural and cyclical factors. In this regard, the US public debt that has reached 100 per cent of GDP, its monetary policy currently carries little or no credibility on the dollar despite affirmations by the Federal Reserve Chairman, Ben Bernanke, in his first-ever press conference (April 2011) – backed by the US Treasury Secretary – that a strong dollar was in the interest of the US. This cannot be ruled out as the US economy is dominantly consumption based; a weaker dollar is politically expensive for it hits American consumers by raising the price of imported oil, although it helps its exporters by a more competitive pricing of their goods. It also increases domestic inflation risks and diminishes the global standing of the country.

Scenario Assessment

The acceptance of any of the above proposals is contingent upon, among other things, reconciliation of diverse national interests. This convergence requires strong commitment, shared need, common political ties and a leader country's supervision of the process, the identifiable common and principal elements of past reform initiatives (Oliva, 2011). Although the G20 is a relatively small group compared to the 187 members of the IMF, its heterogeneity of interests is reflected in that its members face diverse economic situations, political features and national goals that are sometimes in direct conflict. This weakens commitment to international cooperation even at a smaller group like the G20. Further, strong leadership to forge a consensus to shift the dollar from the centre of global economic gravity is missing. Against this background, this section attempts to appraise the odds of success of the few proposals discussed above.

Table 7.1 presents a summary position of the different proposals against their relative merits and disadvantages as well as the political acceptability to major countries. As the table reveals, there are winners and losers from each

Table 7.1: Alternatives to the Dollar Dominance: Summary Position

Proposal	Advantage	Drawback	Acceptability (Major stakeholders)	Issues for cooperation
SDR	• Not tied to any national currency; Stable; ensures purchasing power • Can be adapted to address inequity concerns • Addresses exorbitant privilege • Existing base to build upon • Rule-based, orderly issuance	• Demands reform of IMF quotas • Socialization of costs	• China - √ • US – Resists • Emerging nations/BRICS- Qualified	• IMF governance reform to address demand for reserves by developing countries • SDR composition reforms • Mechanism for conversion of existing reserves • Rules of issuance
Multicurrency System	• Diversifies risk away from the dollar in the near term. • Fairer as seignorage is distributed	• Does not correct for Triffin Dilemma • Reserve-switching could be destabilizing. • Reserve-issuers may be reluctant to accept costs, policy discipline or responsibility.	• China - √ • US – √ • Other countries - √	• Evolutionary, so does not require any negotiation. • Reserve-issuers might be reluctant to bear the costs, viz. loss of competitiveness due to higher demand for their currency
New global currency	• Not tied to any national currency • Stabile, rule-based issuance • Would evolve through • International consensus • Comprehensively addresses • Existing deficiencies of the IMS	• Requires administering institutions that could be new, or existing (e.g, IMF); therefore, agreement could be hard to obtain.	• All countries (187)	• All issues, i.e. administering institutions, rules, etc. would have to be devised and accepted by all.
Status Quo	• No abrupt shifts to a news ystem • Orderly, gradual unwinding of global imbalances	• Perpetuates inequitable structures • IMS remains unstable • Risky • Demand for reserves, other issues unaddressed	• China – No • US – √ • Emerging nations- No	• Both the US and China must agree to orderly unwinding and change in exchange rate and macro policies.

of the reform proposals, which has an obvious bearing upon their relative political acceptability. There are inevitable trade-offs that countries, especially the major stakeholders China and the US, have to make. The key intractable problem in this regard is how to get these countries to go beyond their limited national interests, which appears very unlikely in the post-crisis world. Both the US and China are equally concerned about social and political costs arising out of low growth and unemployment and therefore, unwilling to risk reforms to rebalance growth; e.g., China is unlikely to relinquish capital controls and free its exchange rate and it appears implausible that the US will tighten its monetary policy and address its current account and fiscal deficits.

China has openly called for and is pressing ahead with the SDR proposal, apprehending the danger of significant capital losses in the event of a run on the dollar. Further, it is moving rapidly to garner support for the SDR proposal. One, it organized a conference in Beijing on reform of the IMS[26] from where emerged a consensus favouring the SDR as the principal reserve currency. This came ahead of a G20 seminar in Nanjing, attended by President Sarkozy of France, the then chairman of G20. Three, it narrowed down common interests to the BRICS countries by organizing a summit that called for the IMF to expand its use of SDRs. It is also rapidly expanding usage of its currency in trade payments and settlements (see the discussion in the next section) and creating financial market infrastructure for trading in its currency to eventually reach a point of full convertibility, a move that has the dual advantage of accelerating the move towards a multicurrency arrangement as well as meeting the criteria for inclusion in the SDR composition basket in time for the next IMF review in 2015.

The gains to China from the SDR proposal are reduction in risks from capital losses on its assets in the event of dollar depreciation; these would be lessened as the rest of the world would agree to a substitution account in the process (Williamson, 2009). Over a longer period, China's interests are served by a combination of multicurrency arrangement: it has a greater say and role in the international financial architecture as well as private, international transactions.

In contrast, the US' interest in the SDR proposal is exactly the opposite. An extension of the SDR implies curbing the international role and importance of the dollar. Although it would gain by being able to finance its debt relatively cheaply and assuredly through this route, it would risk instability due to sudden outflows on account of past build-up of liabilities (Williamson, 2009; Bergsten, 2009). A multicurrency system, however, would be in the interests of the US as it would allow the dollar to depreciate.

From a broader international perspective though, creation of the SDR as the official reserve-holding currency parallel to the evolution of a multicurrency world would stabilize the IMS, provide a viable financial safety valve and reduce dollar dominance at the same time (Williamson, 2009). Even if the private sector were to have little incentive to switch to SDRs, its usage for official reserve-holdings would significantly reduce dependency upon the dollar and alleviate the Triffin's Dilemma. In this light, the SDR proposal appears to be the only one that reconciles the stability and equity attributes of a reserve currency with those of political acceptability. It is perhaps the most practical and feasible of all alternatives.

The relative merits and acceptability of the reform proposals can be assessed against the yardsticks of fairness, feasibility, efficiency, stability, political choice and ease of implementation (IMF, 2009). The accompanying heat map (Figure 7.8) provides a crude assessment. As can be observed, the yellow codes correspond to a medium score to each criterion, reflecting a moderate reform against the two extremes of the 'weak' (blue code) current IMS structure and the 'ideal' new global reserve currency (red). Both multicurrency and SDR proposals are in the middle; while the former is evolutionary and unstoppable, requiring no action on the part of any country, the latter is an immediate reform that needs considerable cooperation amongst the international community.

Figure 7.8: Heat Map of Alternate Proposals to Replace the Dollar

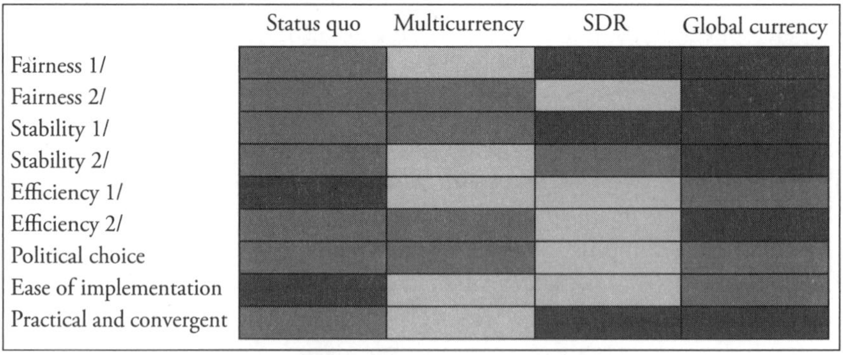

	Status quo	Multicurrency	SDR	Global currency
Fairness 1/				
Fairness 2/				
Stability 1/				
Stability 2/				
Efficiency 1/				
Efficiency 2/				
Political choice				
Ease of implementation				
Practical and convergent				

Source: *Features, as defined below, obtained from IMF, with author's mapping*
Fairness 1/ Capital flows from poor to rich; Fairness 2/ Exorbitant privilege
Stability 1/ Intertemporal stability; Stability 2/ Exchange rate volatility
Efficiency 1/ Scale economies (network effects)
Efficiency 2/ Efficient and effective insurance arrangements for reserves

Explanatory Note:
Colour codes correspond to extent proposal meets the reserve currency criteria
Red - High; Yellow – Reasonable; Green – Low; Blue – Negative

The positive part of the SDR proposal, however is many countries, including the core BRICS, have endorsed the proposal; the US, however has not committed itself so far. Against the nearly 17 per cent voting share of the US at the IMF Board and the tendency of the European countries to vote en bloc with the US, the success of the SDR rests critically upon reforms in the IMF governance. As such, it requires enormous coordination and cooperation among member countries. The key stumbling blocks in this regard are:

- Weight revision to include the renminbi in the composition basket for a more representative currency basket. This is already resisted by the US on the ground that the renminbi is not a fully convertible currency. This opposition however overlooks that at the time of SDR formation, the German mark and the franc themselves were not fully convertible.[27]

- Another obstruction would be the associated proposal to create a substitution account were the SDR proposal to be agreed upon. There are several possibilities how this could be resolved (Willamson, 2009): normally, any country's accounts are denominated in SDRs, but if this rule was extended in this instance, then the US would bear the cost of a dollar depreciation. Alternately, if the substitution account was to hold dollars and all members of the IMF were to make up any losses or profits arising out of changes in the dollar–SDR rate by utilization of IMF's gold stock. A third route would be a balanced book at the IMF so the acquisition of dollars would be exchanged for euros, yen and sterling (56 per cent). All three scenarios lead to lesser losses for China.

The benefits of transiting to an SDR system can also be viewed through the prism of immediate and longer-term benefits. In the near–term, the advantage of diversifying the reserve-portfolios of central banks will lead to significant reduction in risk arising from possible fall in the dollar's value (depreciation). This indeed is the primary reason underlying the Chinese call for a shift towards the SDR-based system as it has the maximum exposure to the dollar with about 67 per cent of its reserves being denominated in it. Over the long–term, it would lead to a broader underpinning of the international monetary system.

India's Policy Stance

This section focuses upon risks to India from dominance of the dollar and a possible debasement in its value. It considers India's macroeconomic interests and supplements these with other geopolitical considerations to then evolve the country's stance at the G20 over reform of the IMS to make it safer, more stable and equitable.

Although economic risks to India from the dominance of the dollar can be assessed from a variety of perspectives, it would be most useful to analyse it over short- and long-term horizons. This is due to two reasons. One, there is an immediate risk from a possible, further deterioration in US economic conditions leading to an erosion of investor confidence and consequent undermining of the dollar's value because of reduced demand for the currency. Two, the preceding section suggests a very low probability of a fundamental overhaul of the IMS that could dislodge the dollar's global occupancy; even the SDR proposal is yet to be endorsed by the key shareholder, the US. Therefore, a realistic near-term approach for countries like India would be to shield themselves from volatility and depreciation risks from the dollar movements while setting the ball in motion for structural reform of the global monetary system.

Macroeconomic Risks

India's overall macroeconomic framework is characterized by three key vulnerabilities: current account deficit, fiscal deficit and inflation. From the standpoint of the dollar's role in the world economy, a major factor impacting these variables is the price of oil, to which India is extremely vulnerable over both time horizons: A rise in oil prices leads to a deterioration in the current account through higher import payments. It also worsens the fiscal position due to subsidization of fuel and fertilizer prices to protect domestic consumers and directly as well as indirectly contributes towards inflation pressures in the economy. Currently, India imports close to three-fourths of its energy requirements. Over a longer time period, energy demand is poised to accelerate with rapidly rising incomes and consumption; energy-intensity, already relatively high, will also increase as the production base widens.

Near–term

Near-term macroeconomic risks to India can be disaggregated by official and private exposures to the dollar; the latter can be further distinguished by trade and financial transactions denominated in the dollar. Considerations for India in the short–run reduce to whether it stands to gain or lose from any sudden changes in the value of the dollar and the impact of any run on the dollar upon global financial markets. See Figure 7.9.

Figure 7.9: India: Foreign Exchange Reserves: Composition

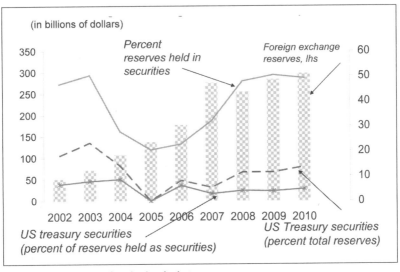

Source: Datastream and author's calculations

Corresponding to the worldwide trend among emerging and developing countries, official reserve-holdings by India have risen significantly from 2000 onwards. Like most countries, the currency composition of international reserves is not known.

- However, an analysis from the foreign official holdings of dollar-denominated securities[28] shows that nearly 14 per cent of foreign exchange reserves – or nearly one-third of the stock of reserves held as foreign securities (49 per cent) – were invested in dollar-denominated securities in 2010; this assumes that all holdings of US Treasuries by India are official. Holdings of US Treasury securities in the overall securities portfolio have declined since the peak of 2004, although raised relative to 2007 levels. By this measure, India does not attract any significant risk of value-erosion of its foreign currency assets.

- Moreover, what is lost on the swing could be partially recovered from gains on the roundabout: assuming that rest of the securities' portfolio is deployed in other convertible currencies like the euro and yen, these would appreciate in adjustment to the dollar as well due to increased demand from investors. Unlike official exposure, however, the private sector is more vulnerable to adverse movements in the dollar.

- The dollar is extremely important in export pricing decisions. Up to

80 per cent of India's external, private transactions are invoiced in dollars, it being the major currency of invoicing even in trade with countries other than the US (Table 7.2). The exposure of software services' exports, close to two-thirds of which are directly to the US, is equally high as all pricing other than exports to the EU (30.5 per cent share) is in dollars.

Table 7.2: Trade with Major Countries/Regions
percentage to total

	Exports	Imports	Currency of invoice
Asia+ASEAN 1/	54.1	61	Dollar
European Union	21.6	19.3	Euro
United States	7.6	6.6	Dollar
China	6.5	10.7	Dollar
1/ includes China			

Source: Economic Survey with representative estimates from Godlberg & Tille (2008) and author's calculations

- Assuming the exchange rate is allowed to adjust fully, a fall in the dollar's value directly impacts India's exports, and the current account balance, through a rupee appreciation. This could result in significant loss of external competitiveness as decisions by existing and prospective foreign buyers are made on the pricing in the invoicing currency and not the bilateral exchange rate between the importing country's currency and the rupee. Many of India's exports are price-sensitive, e.g., textiles, and operate upon thin margins and high volume turnover.[29] Alternately, if the rupee's rise were to be restrained through intervention-cum-reserve accumulation, official exposure to dollar could be raised; in addition, there would be sterilization costs. See Figure 7.10.

- These losses could be offset by the impact of rupee appreciation on lowered prices of imported inputs and help dampen price pressures from abroad.[30] This applies especially for oil, other commodities and metals etc., the prices of which contribute significantly to overall inflation.

- Bilateral rupee–dollar movements are not the only source of currency

Figure 7.10: Dollar and Commodity Prices

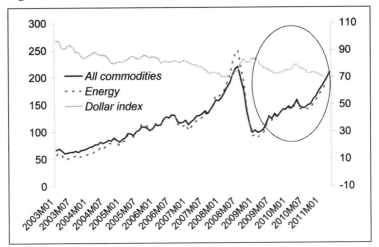

Source: Datastream

risks for India. One, a sudden shift from dollars into currencies like euro and yen would see a sharp rise in these two currencies and therefore, a downward adjustment in the rupee value that would benefit exports. Two, the renminbi will fall with the dollar as China is unlikely to respond with a flexible exchange rate adjustment. This could result in significant competitiveness losses.[31]

- In addition to the direct adjustment of the rupee in response to a weaker dollar, its impact upon commodity prices is a key source of vulnerability for India. The dollar is the pricing currency for oil, metals and other key commodities in global markets and oil-exporters abroad respond to such events by seeking higher dollar-denominated crude prices to offset the dollar's waning value. The loss from higher oil and commodity prices would thus offset the appreciation gains.

- Finally, India is impacted through the financial channel by increased stock price volatility and uncertainty regarding direction of capital flows. It is difficult to predict the direction of global capital flows in the event of a sinking dollar in view of its 'safe haven' role.

- In a scenario of risk-diversification towards currencies like the euro and yen, even though economic conditions in these regions are not better than in the US, capital flows could reverse from Indian markets. Shrinkage in capital inflows, although it would offset the upward adjustment in domestic currency, would have an adverse impact upon the current account and it's financing, nearly three-fourths of which is financed by volatile capital inflows.

- An alternate scenario in which capital surges into emerging markets would be helpful in mitigating current account pressures but would impact asset prices, inflation and aggregate demand; it would also compound currency appreciation with consequences for the real economy.

- An appreciating currency – higher domestic borrowing costs combination will be beneficial to firms that can borrow abroad but will also result in an increase in India's short- and long-term liabilities, with implications for India's external investment position.

Long term

Over a longer period, India's macroeconomic interests are likely to change somewhat although the key risk – that of being a net oil and commodity importer – will persist. Indeed, demand for these items will increase exponentially in the light of India's long-term growth targets (9–9.5 per cent according to the Draft Twelfth Plan), growth drivers like demographic change, rising savings and investment rates and the catch-up dynamics of convergence. Past trends show that higher growth rates in India are always accompanied by a widening current account deficit as demand for world output increases.[32] These factors point to a clear structural upward trend in India's demand for all sorts of commodities, ranging from oil, metals including precious metals to food commodities.

In this regard, the role of alternate currencies in the pricing of oil and other commodities is of some macroeconomic interest to India. Although it is hard to predict whether, when and how the shift in global pricing of key commodities – currently indexed in dollars – takes place, it would be fair to factor in moves by China, which currently accounts for nearly half of world demand for commodities and who has recently moved to play a more meaningful role in global pricing of these items. This includes, *inter alia*, the setting up of commodities trading exchange in Hong Kong with the aim of making it a global centre for trading of these items in the future. This would suggest an increasing weightage of the Chinese renminbi in pricing in the future.

Geopolitical Considerations

India has geopolitical interests in contributing towards the evolution of a viable risk-mitigation mechanism against the dominance of the dollar that is acceptable to all countries at the G20 forum. These can be identified as:

- A common interest with the developing world on equity and fairness grounds.

- It is the Co-chair of the G20 Working Group charged with responsibility of studying these problems. The Finance Minister is also the current Vice Chair of the G24, and will become Chair next year. Both these placements provide an opportunity to India to display global economic leadership and distinguish itself.

- Self-interest to secure its future presence and role at international institutions and to have a share in any risk-mitigating arrangement in the IMS. This assumes importance in the recent reciprocal backing between Europe and China for the posts of IMF Managing Director and First Deputy Managing Director, which points towards increasing Chinese influence at the IMF.

- Safeguard against future risks that could arise from an exclusive multicurrency reserve arrangement with the renminbi becoming the most dominant currency. This raises concerns about China's future role in pricing of oil and commodities for trust and confidence in Chinese macro policies and currency is so far, not well entrenched.

India's Stance

Based on the preceding discussion and considerations, India's strategy should be a composite balance of macroeconomic and geopolitical considerations. The suggested stance to mitigating risks from domination of the dollar can be divided into short-term responses and a more flexible and considered view over a longer period. The suggestions factor in a low-probability of any reform proposal materializing in the near future, some success on the SDR initiative in view of China's expanding influence at the IMF and a parallel emergence of a multi-currency reserve arrangement.

Near- and medium-term Policy Stance

- India should retain its intervention-cum-reserves' accumulation strategy as one of the policy tools to manage heavy volumes of capital inflows predicted[33] because of the divergent monetary policies of advanced and developing countries and which is expected to persist.

- As a deficit country, India should limit the burden of adjustment upon itself in the realignment of global imbalances. Exchange rate adjustments on account of a weakening dollar should therefore, be restrained to guard against competitiveness losses, the creation of additional import demand and import substitution effects that could adversely impact the domestic production base.[34]

- The benefits from an appreciating currency – dampening inflation and lowered costs of borrowing abroad – must be actively assessed against the negative income and employment effects from reduced exports, rising import substitution, etc.

- India should associate itself with a regional reserve pool arrangement like the Chiang Mai Initiative to limit reserves' accumulation and diversify towards other forms of liquidity insurance mechanisms. This will minimize the costs of holding excessive reserves, help resolve conflicts in macroeconomic management caused due to large capital flows and simultaneously realize geopolitical goals of regional coordination.

- The country should also consider bilateral currency swap agreements to manage its foreign exchange reserves on the lines of the People's Bank of China (PBOC).[35]

- The current policy of gradual diversification of reserve-holdings away from the dollar should be retained to protect the value of reserve assets from abrupt swings and weakening value of the US dollar.

- The private sector should be encouraged to diversify away from the dollar to the extent possible to limit exchange rate risks and widen the trade invoicing base of the tradable sector. Participants should also be educated and encouraged to take a longer view and incorporate the possibility of a multicurrency worlds in pricing decisions.

Policy Stance in the Long Run

So far, India's stance on one or another reform proposal appears to be observational and ambivalent. For instance, the RBI Governor's statement at the IMFC, on behalf of the Finance Minister, said:

> …it is desirable to develop a multi-currency system with several currencies operating as broad substitutes and reflecting changing economic weights and global realities. In this context, we note that there have been recent efforts by the IMF to promote the use of SDR as a potential reserve asset

for the evolving international monetary system. For the SDR to take on this significant role, several prerequisites have to be in place. The SDR has to be accepted as a liability of the IMF, has to be automatically acceptable as a medium of payment in cross-border transactions, be freely tradeable and its price has to be determined by forces of demand and supply. As the SDR does not satisfy these conditions, it cannot be a reserve currency in the international payment system. In principle, one needs a global central bank to issue SDRs which take the characteristic of unit of global payment and settlement system. Thus, we see the move to multicurrency world as a gradual evolution. Another dimension of this issue is to change the composition of the SDR basket. Going by the recent initiatives, if at all there is a move to alter the composition of the SDR basket, we could consider including currencies of those dynamically emerging market economies that satisfy the existing inclusion criteria: in particular, a fully convertible capital account and a market determined exchange rate (*Statement by RBI Governor on behalf of the Finance Minister at the IMFC meeting on 16 April 2011*).

In the intervention statement the RBI Governor said the move towards a multicurrency world needs be assessed on the criteria of full convertibility, market-determined exchange rate, significant share in world trade, liquid, open and large financial markets in the reserve-issuing country as well as confidence-inspiring policy credibility for potential investors (India's intervention statement at the IMFC meeting on 16 April 2011).

India is also participating in moves to circumvent the dollar, e.g., at the BRICS summit organized by China in April, 2011, where development banks of these countries agreed to facilitate and expand the system of settling trade in local currencies, which is an important part of Beijing's agenda. And at the BRICS leaders' meeting at Sanya, China (April 2011) India welcomed the '...current discussion about the role of the SDR...including the composition of ...basket of currencies' in the declaration statement.

Against this context, India's suggested stance in the long run can be distributed between support for the SDR – for official reserve transactions– and the multicurrency system. This would spread India's risks, contain Chinese domination at the IMF and in international private transactions and secure some space for India in a new IMS. Specifically,

- India should pursue and support the move to convert reserves into SDR holdings to broaden the currency base of the IMS and to reduce linkages to the dollar or any other currency in the future. This would be ideal for a number of reasons.

- ○ It is useful to view the risk-mitigation proposals from the prism of whether or not India can be a future aspirant to reserve-currency status in the long run for the interests of reserve-issuers and non-reserve issuers are quite contradictory (Williamson 2009). Since it is unlikely that India can fall into the former group,[36] India would gain more from '…boosting the role of the SDR and achieving a portion of the seigniorage gains…' as a non-reserve issuer country (Ibid.).

- ○ Pending establishment of confidence and trust in Chinese economic policies and currency – an essential pre-requisite for acceptance of a currency as the international medium of exchange – and from a geopolitical standpoint too, it would be in India's long-term interest to not have the Chinese currency eventually dislodge the dollar. Securing the official part of international transactions in SDRs, even if private transactions continued in multiple currencies with proportionate regional presence, would serve to limit exposure to the Chinese currency and also restrain it from eventual domination as in the historical precedent of the dollar.

- ○ It would offer a good opportunity to India for gathering support and providing a leadership role at the G20. Currently, there is no country that has done that, except China, which has a vested interest. Specifically, India can suggest a viable, practical reform proposal in this regard, canvas broader support for it at the G20 and gain from contributing towards international policy formulation and governance reforms.

- ○ The proposal implies significant reforms in governance at the IMF, which would be in India's interests as it would benefit from an expanded quota and vote share at the IMF Board.

- Specifically, the Chinese proposal for entrusting part of the member countries' reserves to the centralized management of the IMF and deploying these towards domestic development and growth should be supported as a first step towards promoting SDR usage as a reserve currency. This is politically feasible and acceptable to a wide range of countries with diverse national interests.

- Since China will eventually dominate world output, trade and financial markets possibly, it would be in India's interests to press for and assume leadership for de-politicization of the IMF. If the renminbi were to become the reserve currency over the medium to long-term clearly, a strong possibility – then a policy of SDR allocations at the IMF would not just yield seignorage benefits to China, but also to India.

Conclusion

The global financial crisis has deepened the cracks in the international monetary system, threatening its safety and stability as never before. It has also resurrected long-held concerns among the international community about the safety, stability and the fairness of a system that hinges upon just one currency, viz. the dollar. This chapter is concerned with issues surrounding the supremacy of the dollar. It discusses in detail the different reform proposals that have been offered in the wake of the crisis. Starting with the Report of the UN Commission on the Reform of the International Monetary System (2009), IMF discussion paper also calls for reform backing one or another proposal by different countries, the chapter attempts a comprehensive assessment of these proposals with specific reference to the G20. The guiding perspective in the assessment is dominantly the political acceptability of a particular proposal as also the practical ease with which it can be adopted, partially or fully. Based upon these and other criteria of efficiency, flexibility, etc. it maps the relative advantages each of these proposals.

The chapter concludes that the SDR proposal is the most feasible of all the suggestions for reform. Post-crisis developments also endorse this conclusion. For instance, a beginning in this direction has already been made since 2009. The G20 already agreed to issue $250 billion worth of SDRs that was accomplished in September 2009. Two, a beginning has been made to change the IMF practices by instituting the Flexible Credit Line of financing support (with only ex-ante conditionality) in March 2009, doubling of all credit lines and the elimination of structural benchmarks in conditional lending to address the reluctance of countries in seeking IMF support. More recently, the G20 agreed to a criteria-based path to broaden the composition of the SDR. However, it notes that countries, especially the major surplus and deficit nations, have to arrive at significant agreements and converge for any progress on the SDR proposal.

The chapter next shifts to domestic considerations for India as a country, in this context. It considers India's interests – macroeconomic and geopolitical– in the short run as well as over a longer time horizon. It finds that India does not face any major threat to erosion to the value of its reserve-holdings in the event of a risk to the dollar value. It argues that an appropriate stance towards IMS reform in which India's interests would be best served should be a composite balance of macroeconomic and geopolitical considerations. In the short run, India should continue to pursue an intervention-cum-reserves' accumulation strategy to deal with heavy volumes of capital inflows triggered by monetary easing in the developed world; limit the burden of adjustment upon itself in the realignment of global imbalances as a deficit country; carefully assess the trade-offs between an appreciating currency against the negative income and employment; associate itself with a regional reserve pool arrangement like the Chiang Mai Initiative to limit reserves' accumulation and diversify towards other forms of liquidity insurance mechanisms. It should also consider bilateral currency swap agreements to manage its foreign exchange reserves and encourage the private sector to diversify away from the dollar to the extent possible to limit exchange rate risks and widen the trade invoicing base of the tradable sector.

Over a longer period, India should pursue and support the move to convert reserves into SDR holdings to broaden the currency base of the IMS and to reduce linkages to the dollar or any other currency in the future. This, the chapter argues, would be useful as India is an unlikely future aspirant to reserve-currency status; moreover, such a move would limit the country's exposure to the Chinese currency in the long run, which is in its geopolitical interest. Other than this, this provides India the opportunity to display a leadership role at the G20 as practically no other country besides China has an interest in shifting towards the SDR. It could therefore present a viable, practical reform proposal in this regard and canvas broader support for it at the G20, thereby gaining from a contribution and facilitation role in international policy formulation and governance reforms.

Endnotes

[1] The author is Senior Consultant to the G20 project at ICRIER and former staff member of the IMF and RBI. The chapter is the sole responsibility of its author and does not represent the views of neither past nor present employers.

[2] Throughout this chapter, the acronym IMS is used to denote the International Monetary System.

[3] A more specific characterization of the IMS would refer to the internationally agreed rules and conventions of cross-border trade and investment flows; it includes the institutions backing these arrangements if there are problems of liquidity support, controls or parity changes (IMF, 2009).

4   See Corden (1993) for a detailed explanation on the collapse of the Bretton Woods System. Summarily, he identifies that the post-war macroeconomic policy framework assigned no clear responsibility for preventing inflation so that the divergence across countries created unsustainable differences in competitiveness, eventually requiring exchange-rate changes; countries were unwilling to adjust their currency values in the face of fundamental disequilibria (especially the United States); and the growth of international capital flows helped to undermine the Bretton Woods system.

5   Research studies confirm the pervasiveness of insurance motives among this group of countries. Obstfeld, Shambaugh and Taylor (2010) explain nearly two-thirds of the growth of international reserves through a model based on financial stability and financial openness, and outperforming traditional models as well as those based on external short-term debt. They find that the size of domestic financial liabilities that could potentially be converted into foreign currency (M2), financial openness, the ability to access foreign currency through debt markets, and exchange rate policy are all significant predictors of reserve stocks. And they show that countries with large reserves (as proportion to M2) did not suffer significant currency depreciations during periods of global instability, contributing proof of reserves as a useful buffer (Obstfeld *et al.*, 2009).

6   Known as 'Dutch disease', the term – with its origin in Holland after the discovery of North Sea gas – describes the adverse effect of a natural resource discovery that boosts the export earnings of the economy, but the ensuing surplus appreciates the currency value leading to a loss of competitiveness in the manufacturing sector as exports decline and imports become more competitive.

7   Bordo (2010) notes that like France in the 1920s and 1930s and the Unties States in the 1960s, important countries like China are not playing by the rules of the IMS. These countries accumulated surpluses for national objectives: France feared return to high inflation of the 1920s, so did the US, while China undervalued to pursue a successful export-led growth strategy.

8   D'Arista and Erturk point to another route, viz. the impact of increasing costs of inaction upon various policymakers.

9   The Bretton Woods System, in operation from 1946–1971, was based upon a fixed dollar-gold parity.

10 It broke down under the dual pressure of countries – primarily the US and Europe – needing to re-adjust parities for balancing their external and internal positions [See Eichengreen, 2008].

11 Nearly a third of exports by Eurozone countries and close to 40 per cent of their imports are invoiced in dollars while the euro dominates the rest of the transactions. Both Korea and Thailand use it for more than 80 per cent of trade transactions. Similarly, Japan, Australia and Malaysia use the dollar in more than 50 per cent of trade transactions (Goldberg and Tille, 2008).

12 The term is ascribed to the French President Valery Giscard d'Estaing who accused the US in the 1960s of enjoying an 'exorbitant privilege' because of the dollar's role as the global reserve currency.

13 The UN Report points out that the global monetary system has been afflicted by cycles of declining confidence in the US dollar as its monetary policies have been implemented with little, if any, consideration of impact upon global aggregate demand or demand for global

liquidity. These cycles have intensified from the 1980s making the US current account particularly volatile with consequent impact upon the exchange rate, the dollar.

[14] Overvaluation of the dollar is a common finding across several studies. For example, Cline and Williamson estimate the dollar remained overvalued by about 5 to 8 per cent (May 2010); Isaard (2007) also found similar values.

[15] He points out the study of Gourinchas, Rey and Govillot (2009) which assigns the lower returns paid by the US on its external liabilities relative to its earnings on comparable external assets to an insurance payment to foreigners that they purchased by lending to the US at relatively lower interest rates in normal circumstances.

[16] The idea of a 'substitution account' is that of an off-market mechanism wherein the reserve holders exchange their excess dollar holdings into SDR-denominated assets, transferring the risk to the IMF. The dollars received by the IMF in exchange – primarily short-term US Treasury bills – would be converted into longer-term claims on the US Treasury. The spread – the difference between the short-term rate paid to SDR-holders and the long-term yield – would help cover the exchange rate risk. However, it is not assured that the exchange rate risk is eliminated as the yield curve itself could shift. See Williamson (2009) for details.

[17] Alternative methods to offset the exchange rate risk were also considered, viz. investments in sovereign bonds of SDR component currencies or using a part of the IMF's gold stock to absorb the costs.

[18] In this context, Williamson (2009) recalls an unpublished research project in the early 1980s to establish whether there had indeed been (net) destabilizing reserve switches in the 1970s. He concluded that had, indeed, been the case. The evidence, presented at a meeting at a European central bank, was received coldly; the central bank in question had actually moved a large stock of reserves into the yen just before it peaked, making significant losses. He comments that central bankers are not good speculators, but nevertheless speculate if given the opportunity!

[19] See, for instance, statement of Dai Xianglong, Chairman, China's National Council for Social Security Funds, at an annual economic forum in Beijing, January 2011 (http://news. xinhuanet.com/english2010/china/2011-01/15/c_13692144.htm).

[20] See, A.V. Rajwade: 'Why the yuan is gaining currency', *Business Standard*, 14 February 2011. He reports that many orders by Indian firms from Chinese suppliers are being contracted in yuan; importers are even offered discounts over the dollar price to get them to agree to yuan pricing. On their part, the Chinese exporters have an incentive to quote prices in the yuan rather than the dollar in view of its steady strengthening over time.

[21] See 'China Speeds Yuan Push'. *Wall Street Journal*, 20 April 2011.

[22] Ranjan, Rajiv and Anand Prakash. 2010. 'Internationalization of Currency: The case of the Indian Rupee and Chinese Renminbi.' RBI Staff Studies. DEAP 3/2010.

[23] However, as of March 2011, China still owned 25 per cent of the marketable US Treasuries held by foreigners.

[24] Governor of China's central bank, quoted in *Business Standard*, 10 May 2011.

[25] These include lowering consumption taxes, abolition of agricultural taxes in rural China, expanding credit markets, improving the social safety net and boosting workers' disposable incomes.

[26] 'Reforming the Global Monetary System', Beijing, 18–19 March 2011, co-organized by the Columbia Global Center East Asia in partnership with Policy Dialogue at Columbia University and the Central University of Finance and Economics. This conference brought together over 20 renowned scholars, including Nobel laureate Joseph Stiglitz; Dr Yi Gang, Deputy Governor of the People's Bank of China; Dr Jacob Frenkel, former Governor of the Bank of Israel and former Finance Minister of Colombia Jose Antonio Ocampo.

[27] Rajwade, A.V. 2011. 'End of dollar dominance?' *Business Standard*, 25 April.

[28] US Treasury International Capital Reporting System.

[29] Up-to-date estimates of pass through of exchange rate changes on US$ export prices for India are not available. An older study (Mallick and Marques 2006) calculates (for post-1990s) that a 10 per cent appreciation raised export prices by 7 per cent in US dollar terms, with much sectoral variation. The pass through was nearly full in machinery, but almost zero in the chemical sector. The appreciation impact is the largest on industries with thin profit margins, weak or no price-setting power in foreign markets and low import content, e.g., textiles.

[30] The pass-through from exchange rate into the aggregate price index cannot be large in India as a significant portion of the index is directly or indirectly administered. Econometric estimates of the RBI indicate that a 10 per cent rupee appreciation lowers overall WPI inflation from 0.6–1.3 per cent at a 6-month horizon. Studies for earlier period (e.g., Mallick and Marques 2006; Barhoumi 2006) find there is wide sectoral variation, with the impact ranging from 0.4 per cent for fuels to 19 per cent for edible oils, although a 10 per cent rupee appreciation could reduce overall import prices in rupee terms, on average, around 7.5–8.5 per cent.

[31] Recent estimates of the RBI (2011) show that percentage point depreciation in the rupee–yuan exchange rate increases the value of India's exports to China – mostly primary commodities, which are sensitive to terms of trade – by 1.1 per cent. On the other hand, a similar movement reduces imports from China – chiefly machinery and electronic goods – by around 0.43 per cent.

[32] Although this could be partially offset by an increasing share of exports in GDP from the current 20 per cent, which is significantly lower than all other Asian countries.

[33] The Institute for International Finance projects net private capital flows to emerging economies to rise to US $960 billion in 2011 (a 50 per cent increase over 2010 levels) and $1009 billion in 2012 (IIF 2011). The IMF notes that gross inflows have already reached 6 per cent of emerging world GDP in a quarter of the time it took to reach a similar peak before the crisis (World Economic Outlook, April 2011).

[34] Not much is known about these effects at present for lack of studies as well insufficient time period. In a 2011 research note, Sonal Varma of Nomura points out for 2009–10, a period characterized by steady appreciation of the rupee that import substitution has accelerated in recent years; while cases like coal and oil can be explained by resource constraints, she points out that imports are replacing domestic production even in segments capacity can be augmented, viz. metals, project goods, chemicals, wood products and textiles. India, in fact, has become a net steel importer in recent years with an expected 43 per cent increase in imports by the industry in 2011–12.

[35] Since the outbreak of the global financial crisis, the PBOC has entered into a series of bilateral currency swap agreements (BSAs) whereby the PBOC and other central banks have agreed to exchange the renminbi (not the US dollar) with the respective counterparty currencies. These

are with South Korea (2008) followed by agreements with Hong Kong, Malaysia, Indonesia and Belarus; in Latin America, a 70 billion yuan (or $10.2 billion) currency swap agreement with Argentina (2009) that allows yuan-denominated orders for Chinese imports. Other than reducing dependency upon the dollar these inter-central bank arrangements are expected to expand China's trade with its respective partners by providing renminbi-denominated funds to counterparty countries and regions (Ranjan and Prakash, 2010).

[36] An RBI Study Internationalization of Currency: The case of the Indian Rupee and Chinese Renminbi (Rajiv Ranjan and Anand Prakash, RBI 2010) assesses the rupee's potential for internationalization and concludes that the necessary preconditions for this are far from met at present.

References

Auerbach, Alan J. and Obstfeld, Maurice. 2010. 'Too much focus on the Yuan?' *VoxEu.org.*

Barhoumi, K. 2006. 'Differences in Long Run Exchange Rate Pass-Through into Import Prices in Developing Countries: An Empirical Investigation', *Economic Modeling* 23: 926–51.

Bergsten, C. Fred. 1975. *The Dilemmas of the Dollar.* New York: New York University Press for the Council of Foreign Relations.

Bergsten, C. Fred. 2009. 'The Deficits and the Dollar'. *Foreign Affairs*, November–December. NYU Press for CFR.

Bordo, Michael. 2010. *The Future of the International Monetary System.* Remarks prepared for the Conference on the International Monetary System: Old and New Debates, Paris, December.

Clarida, R. 2009. 'With Privilege Comes…?' Available at: http://www.pimco.com/LeftNav/Global+Markets/Global+Perspectives/2009/With+Privilege+Comes+Clarida+Oct+2009.htm# [Accessed in May–June 2010].

Cline, W. R. and J. Williamson. 2010. 'Estimates of Fundamental Equilibrium Exchange Rates', Policy Brief PB10-15. Peterson Institute of International Economics, Washington D.C.

Corden, W. M. 1993. 'Why Did the Bretton Woods System Break Down'. In *A Retrospective on the Bretton Woods System*, edited by Bordo, M. and B. Eichengreen. Chicago: The University of Chicago Press.

D'Arista, Jane and Erturk, K. 2010. 'The Case for International Monetary Reform'. *Real-World Economics Review* 54: 58–80.

Eichengreen, Barry. 2004. 'The Dollar and the New Bretton Woods System'. Henry Thornton Lecture delivered at the Cass School of Business, London, 15 December.

Eichengreen, Barry. 2008. *Globalizing Capital: A History of the International Monetary System.* 2nd ed. Princeton: Princeton University Press.

Eichengreen, Barry. 2005. 'Sterling's past, dollar's future: Historical perspectives on reserve currency competition'. *NBER* Working Paper No. 11336.

Eichengreen, Barry. 2009. 'The dollar dilemma,' *Foreign Affairs* 88(5): 53–68.

Eichengreen, Barry. 2011. 'The bear of Bretton Woods'. *Project Syndicate*, Project Syndicate Column.

Eichengreen, Barry and Flandreau, Marc. 2008. 'The rise and fall of the dollar or when did the dollar replace sterling as the lead international currency?'. *NBER Working Paper* No. 14154, July.

Eichengreen, Barry and Temin, Peter. 2010. 'Fetters of Gold and Paper'. *VoxEu*. July 30.

Goldberg, L. S. and Tille, C. 2008. 'Vehicle currency use in international trade'. *Journal of International Economics* 76(2): 177–92.

Gourinchas, Pierre-Olivier, Rey, H. and Govillot, N. 2010. 'Exorbitant Privilege and Exorbitant Duty'. Paper presented at the IMES International Conference, Bank of Japan, Tokyo, May.

IIF. 2011. 'Capital Flows to Emerging Market Economies'. Institute of International Finance, January 24.

Khundrakpam, J. 2007. 'Economic Reforms and Exchange Rate Pass-through to Domestic Prices in India'. *Bank of International Settlements.*

Mallick, S. and H. Marques. 2006. 'Sectoral Exchange Rate Pass-Through: Testing the Impact of Policy Reforms in India'. *Scottish Journal of Political Economy.* 53: 280–303.

Mateos Lago, I., R. Duttagupta and R. Goyal. 2009. 'The Debate on the International Monetary System'. *IMF Staff Position Note*, SPN/09/26, Washington D.C.

McKinnon, Ronald. 2010. 'China Bashing over Yuan Needs a Long Rest'. Commentary. Available at: http://www.businessweek.com/news/2010-07-05/ [Accessed in May–June 2010].

Obstfeld, Maurice. 2010. 'Expanding Gross Asset Positions and the International Monetary System'. Remarks at the Federal Reserve Bank of Kansas City symposium 'Macroeconomic Challenges: The Decade Ahead'. Jackson Hole, Wyoming, August 26–28, 2010.

Obstfeld Maurice and Alan M. Taylor. 2003. 'Globalization and Capital Markets'. In *Globalization in Historical Perspective*, edited by Michel D. Bordo, Alan M. Taylor and Jeffrey G. Williamson, Chicago: University of Chicago Press, 121–83.

Obstfeld, Maurice, Jay C. Shambaugh and Alan M. Taylor. 2009. 'Financial Instability, Reserves and Central Bank Swap Lines in the Panic of 2008'. *American Economic Review* 99(2): 480–86.

Obstfeld, Maurice, Jay C. Shambaugh and Alan M. Taylor. 2010. 'Financial Stability, the Trilemma, and International Reserves'. *American Economic Journal: Macroeconomics* 2(2): 57–94.

Oliva, Juan C.M. 2011. 'Can the G-20 Reform the International Monetary System?' *Real Time Economic Issues Watch*. Peterson Institute for International Economics, 2 March.

Prasad, E. 2009. 'Rebalancing Growth in Asia'. NBER Working Paper No. 15169.

Robert Triffin. 1961. *Gold and the Dollar Crisis: The Future of Convertibility*. Revised edition. New Haven: Yale University Press.

Truman, Edwin M. 2011. 'International Monetary System Reform: Will the G-20 Make Significant Progress?'. *Real Time Economic Issues Watch*. Peterson Institute for International Economics, 23 February.

Williamson, John. 2009. 'Why SDRs could rival the Dollar?'. Peterson Institute for International Economics, Policy Brief PB09-20.

Xiaochuan, Zhou. 2009. 'Reform the international monetary system'. Essay by Dr Zhou Xiaochuan, Governor of the People's Bank of China, 23 March 2009. Available at: http://www.bis.org/review/r090402c.pdf?frames=0 [Accessed in May–June 2010].

8 Challenges in IMS Reforms: Emerging Markets' Perspective[1]

Alok Sheel[2]

The subject of reforms in the international monetary system has in recent years seen perhaps the most intense debate since the inception of the Bretton Woods system. Policy-makers from both developed and developing countries, intergovernmental organizations and prominent academics are proposing a number of reforms to the international monetary system to maintain financial and price stability, and to ensure economic growth going forward. The French Presidency had also placed the subject high on the priority of the G20 agenda for the sixth Summit at Cannes.

Weaknesses in the extant international monetary system, including those of the 'non-system' in place following the breakdown of the Bretton Woods system, that are now being highlighted, have long been known[3]. The system had nevertheless served the global economy reasonably well, ensuring price and financial stability, and also delivering on global growth. Indeed, the post-war period was a period of unprecedented prosperity and growth sustained over a long period – half a century to be precise. Is there now a lurking fear that this is coming, or has come, to an end, and that a major overhaul of the international monetary system is, *inter alia*, necessary to get the global economy back on a sustainable track?

I will not even pretend that I have an answer to this question. I would instead try to put some questions on the table by looking at the issue from two perspectives, namely stability and equity.

The question of stability derives from the intellectual debate on the origins of the recent global financial crisis. While the US subprime housing problem is by consensus the trigger that initiated this crisis, its ultimate causes are usually traced to mounting global imbalances and underlying weaknesses in the financial and monetary systems.[4] Global imbalances generated a flood of liquidity that drove down interest rates, and thereby encouraged excessive leverage and risk taking in search of higher returns. The lax supervisory and regulatory structure in the financial system in advanced countries, and the extant monetary policy framework, translated risky behavior into investment in risky high yielding financial instruments.

Role of the IMS and its Limitations

So, where does the international monetary system come into all this? One of the main objectives of a well-functioning international monetary system is to prevent the build-up of large, unsustainable external imbalances in the first place. The weakness of the extant international monetary system lies in the fact that it does not have institutional or market-based mechanisms for preventing or correcting certain kinds of imbalances. The issue is no doubt complex, with several interrelated problems, and I will mention four that come to my mind.

First, the market forces only deficit countries to adjust through the threat of market revolt, and not surplus countries, something pointed out by Lord Keynes decades ago.[5]

Second, there is little pressure on both deficit and surplus countries within currency unions to adjust because the exchange rate between them is fixed. Thus the Eurozone can be seen as a microcosm of the global economy, with the north–south imbalances mimicking the US–China imbalances.

Third, reserve currency issuing countries also have little pressure to adjust, as they can continue financing large internal and external deficits with seeming impunity, on account of a large external demand for their financial assets. This 'exorbitant privilege' is magnified when most required during crises as there is a flight to safe reserve currency status. This is the equity issue. Indeed, it was noted quite some time ago by Robert Triffin that reserve issuing currencies may need to run larger and larger deficits to meet the needs of global liquidity. This problem has since been made more complex by the increasing importance of the liquidity multiplier through a sophisticated financial system.[6]

Fourth, the capacity of the G20 and other multilateral fora such as the IMF to address the reserve currency issue is limited as policy-based solutions need to find market acceptance.

Following the breakdown of the Bretton Woods system it was expected that floating exchange rates would prevent the build-up of large imbalances, as current accounts would tend to move towards balance through appreciation and depreciation of currencies. The impact of exchange rate movements is however hotly contested and frequently misunderstood because of the disproportionate attention showered on the nominal exchange rate. Thus, although Japan's fixed nominal exchange rate may have contributed to its large current account surplus in the period leading to the Plaza accord, the subsequent appreciation of its nominal exchange rate did not abate its large current account surplus.

How could this have happened? One way of looking at the issue is through relative shifts in productivity. Let us suppose that a country's current account is balanced at the beginning. *Ceteris paribus*, an improvement in productivity relative to other countries would tend to move its current account into surplus through improved competitiveness, and vice versa. Counterpart capital flows should over time move the current account back towards balance through adjustments in the nominal exchange rate. The *ceteris paribus* condition, alas, rarely holds in the real world. This self-correcting mechanism may not work if real wages do not keep pace with productivity gains. To take another scenario, if capital flows exceed the level required to finance the current account in the event of a downward shift in relative productivity, the nominal exchange rate could even appreciate. What matters, therefore, is not the nominal exchange rate, but the real effective exchange rate, that takes into account relative movements in productivity and inflation. Movements in the REER are, however, non-observable and notoriously difficult to compute.

Adjustments in the nominal exchange rate therefore may not correct imbalances.[7] The latter are really the counterpart of savings, investment and consumption patterns in different economies, captured in the national income equation[8] in which external balances play a key balancing role. These patterns in turn are linked to stages of development and cultural differences. Thus savings rates tend to increase in young societies undergoing rapid growth; they tend to decline as societies age; they are generally higher in developing Asia than in developing Latin America; and within OECD countries, the savings and consumption behaviour of the Swabian housewife in Germany is very different from that of the stylized American housewife.[9]

It is also possible to argue that the development of global imbalances was inherent in the pattern of globalization based as it was on international mobility of capital, goods and services combined with relative immobility of labour. This lowered returns to labour relative to capital on the one hand, even as capital moved to areas where productivity gains, and therefore returns, were highest. On the flip side, real wages failed to keep pace with productivity increases,[10] depressing consumption and increasing reliance on external sources of demand. Since income from labour rose relatively modestly, global growth increasingly relied on investment (in developing countries) and leveraged consumption (in OECD countries, especially the US which emerged as the global consumer of last resort) enabled by a combination of loose monetary policy, financial innovation and lax regulation. Excessive consumption should ordinarily lead to rising current account deficits which in turn should be self-limiting through the market mechanism. However, since markets didn't penalize current account deficits of reserve issuing currencies under the extant international monetary system, it is hardly surprising that these deficits were concentrated in the United States and within the so-called 'Club Med' Eurozone countries, both of which had access to cheap capital derived from the reserve status of their domestic currencies.

The picture drawn above indicates that global imbalances are commonplace, their cause complex and multiple, and may they not be easy to correct through some silver bullet, such as adjustments in the nominal exchange rate, as is sometimes argued. Arguably, policy makers are better advised to spend their energies on managing them than on trying to eliminate them.

Reforming the IMS: Three Alternative Approaches

What, then, should our level of ambition be in the circumstances? Should we try and reform the international monetary system which can prevent the accumulation of imbalances through market mechanisms? Alternatively, should we try to inoculate the financial system through reform of regulatory and monetary policy frameworks in such a manner that imbalances do not destabilize the global economy? Or do we rely on institutional mechanisms like the IMF and the G20 to keep imbalances within reasonable limits, which would need to be defined, consistent with financial stability? Let me turn to each of these three options, beginning with the last.

Institutional Mechanisms

The IMF was expected to be the institutional mechanism for making the adjustments to prevent the build-up of large global imbalances. Under Article IV of its Articles of Agreement, it has an internationally agreed mandate 'to exercise firm surveillance over the exchange rate policies of members' to 'assure orderly exchange rate arrangements and to promote a stable system of exchange rates'. This surveillance was mostly done through a process of bilateral consultations, with limited multilateral surveillance as a relatively late entrant.[11] Be it as it may, the IMF and other eminent economistshad clearly sounded strong warnings of a possible financial crisis emanating from a disorderly unwinding of global imbalances leading to a collapse of the dollar.[12] The predicted financial crisis did occur, and global imbalances also had something to do with it, but not in the manner prognosticated. As a result, the current crisis has only strengthened rather than weakened the dollar. This rather counter-intuitive phenomenon largely derives from the dollar's status as the global reserve currency, an issue to which I shall turn at present.

It is clear that IMF's surveillance mechanism to prevent and correct imbalances did not work well.[13] The Independent Evaluation Office of the IMF has identified analytical and organizational weaknesses within the IMF for this failure.[14] I would however like to highlight three major reasons. First, there are inherent difficulties in aligning 'visible' nominal exchange rates with 'non-observable' real effective exchange rates for abating imbalances as such measurements are eminently contestable. We have seen that the problem is complex. Second, the IMF had limited leverage with major countries in enforcing its policy advice, as this is usually done through conditionalities imposed on countries that borrow from the IMF. Major countries that accounted for the big imbalances never felt the need for IMF financial support: surplus countries do not need its funds, while the big deficit countries had no problems financing them But perhaps the most important reason was IMF's crisis of legitimacy. Its governance and ownership structure remained basically the same as it was at the time it was set up at the end of World War II. Its major shareholders never felt the need, let alone urgency, to adjust its governing structure to accommodate the rising emerging economies whose weights in the global economy was rising dramatically. There was therefore always the feeling that IMF's policy advice was not even handed, and that this reflected the viewpoint of its majority shareholders. This perception prevails to this day, despite the marginal shift in quota in favour of EMEs following a push given in this direction by the G20.

The G20, which has a more balanced governing structure in which major advanced and developing countries are represented as equal partners, has emerged as a new premier forum for global international co-operation. It now appears to be taking over the IMF's mantle as the institutional mechanism for making adjustments to keep global imbalances within the limits necessary to ensure strong and sustainable growth going forward. The IMF plays an important role in this 'Mutual Assessment Process (MAP) , initiated at the third G20 Summit at Pittsburgh[15], but only as a technical advisor. The new process is purely multilateral and is owned by the G20 countries themselves who take decisions through mutual consultations and assessment. The MAP has come to occupy centre stage within the G20, and is often described as its heart and soul, almost as though the G20's credibility depends on the MAP outcome.

The G20 MAP has featured prominently in all G20 summits since Pittsburgh, with countries increasingly committing to specific, and indeed measurable, short-term and medium-term policy actions. This is still work in process, and we have still to see how this new Framework would work, and to what extent countries are willing to harmonize country and multilateral frameworks. The two assessments of progress done so far by the G20 itself are not very encouraging.[16] The benefits of policy coordination are manifest. Apart from policy spillovers, in an increasingly integrating global economy, it is apparent that an un-coordinated rebalancing of the global economy, such as a rise in savings in one part of the global economy in the absence of a rise in consumption or investment in some other part, would lead to lower growth in the aggregate. Through the WTO it has been possible to arrive at globally agreed and enforceable agreements on trade, so could the same happen in the case of macro-economic policies? Welfare gains from trade can however be symmetric, since most countries have at least some comparative advantage. However, gains from macro-economic policies may be asymmetric, on account of the inherent advantages accruing to issuers of global reserve currencies. A working agreement on macro-economic policy coordination within the G20 may therefore be more difficult and hinge on the overhaul of the reserve currency system.

Reforming Financial and Monetary Frameworks

The second option is to reform financial regulatory and monetary policy frameworks. Consumer price deflation was one of the chief features of the 'Great Moderation' preceding the recent global financial crisis.[17] This was largely on account of the downward pressure on real wages in a fast globalizing world with large productivity gains through the entry of big developing countries like China and India into the international market for labour, as goods and services increasingly moved more freely across borders. As a result, instead of overheating the economy through inflation, excessive demand simply widened the current account deficit. Global imbalances increased the demand for reserve assets, hence widening current account deficits did not put pressure on the currency, re-inforcing consumer price stability. Excessive liquidity meanwhile spilled overseas into emerging markets in search for higher yields and into financial asset and commodity markets, inflating their prices.

This dramatic decoupling of consumer and asset prices should have rung alarm bells for financial market regulators and central banks alike, but they did not.[18] As a result, since monetary policy responded to consumer prices rather than to asset prices – because, as famously articulated by Alan Greenspan, central banks cannot call asset bubbles and so should only clean up afterwards[19] – US Federal Reserve's monetary policy remained unusually accommodative even by its own yardstick of the Taylor Rule.[20] In retrospect at least, Alan Greenspan's argument does not seem convincing. Quite apart from the decoupling in prices, returns on financial assets also far exceeded returns in the real economy. This was easily measurable through a comparison of returns in financial and non-financial companies. This was potentially destabilizing as financial assets are ultimately only claims on real economy activities. This unusually loose monetary policy encouraged risky behavior and innovation that sought to drive up yields, and ultimately the excessive leverage that the world is still struggling to unwind. Central banks also lost control of liquidity management by the emergence of a lightly regulated shadow banking system.[21] The question now is whether a shift in the monetary framework to cover both consumer price and asset inflation might abate the deleterious impact of global imbalances by reining in the build-up of excessive leverage through shadow banking.

The deleterious impact of global imbalances was amplified through the financial system through risky innovations that gave rise to what is often described as the 'shadow banking system'. This resulted in a dangerous build-up of leverage and opaque and risky financial instruments. Much of the spurt in growth during the 'Great Moderation' was based not on rising labour incomes, which remained stagnant in real terms, but on leveraged, and therefore unsustainable, consumption enabled by financial innovation. Major financial regulatory reform is being attempted by through the restructured Financial Stability Board under the aegis of the G20 to address these flaws. It is however still unclear as to whether this will go far enough to keep leverage and asset booms in check, especially since the Basel II 'mark to market' accounting standards are not being revisited. No distinction is still being made between leveraging for investment in the real economy, and leveraging for investment in financial assets and for consumption. Comprehensive reform of the shadow banking system is still to be addressed head on to mitigate the risks it generates in the financial system. It is at best work in progress.[22] Moreover, while regulatory reforms might ensure that leveraged private consumption booms are kept in check, there seem to be few constraints on public sector leveraging to plug in the gap in leveraged private demand. It may just be the case that the source of risk in the financial system is changing and not the underlying risk as such. It is not clear as to how this new risk to the financial system[23] would be addressed by regulators as there is a clear conflict of interest. There is already talk of the unsustainable Bretton Woods II international monetary system giving way to an equally unsustainable Bretton Woods III, where private leverage is replaced by government leverage.[24]

Reforming the International Monetary System

This brings me to the third option, namely the reform of the international monetary system itself, which is closely linked to the issue of equity. The G20 has so far reached some sort of consensus on a number of issues relating to reform of the international monetary system,[25] such as policy approaches on handling large volatile capital flows, enhancing the capacity of developing countries to absorb capital inflows, coping with sudden stops of capital in developing countries, and reviewing the composition of the SDR basket. No consensus has however been reached on the bigger issues relating the measurement and metrics of global liquidity, accumulation of reserves, exchange rate management, and the reserve currency question itself. I will handle the issue of reform of the international monetary system in two parts. Firstly, the issue of capital flows, and secondly the issue of the international reserve currency.

Capital Flows

From the viewpoint of the widely accepted Mundell–Fleming open economy model,[26] a country can have only two of the following as part of its macro-economic framework: an open capital account, a stable exchange rate and monetary independence. While several developing countries, including India, have at times tried – with little success I may add – to get around this impossible trinity, countries have mostly adopted different solutions to this equation. Thus, the United States has an open capital account, independent monetary policy but a floating exchange rate (India's solution resembles this model the most). China has adopted a stable exchange rate, independent monetary policy but a closed capital account. The Eurozone solution to the equation was to have a fixed exchange rate within the monetary union, an open capital account, while its countries sacrificed monetary independence.

From the perspective of national macro-economic balance or stability, any of the three solutions are equally valid; however, this is less clear from a multilateral perspective or from the viewpoint of global stability. Is one of the solutions likely to lead to a greater build-up of global imbalances? In its recent reports the IMF seems to have made clear its preference for the combination of flexible exchange rates, open capital account and monetary independence to prevent the build-up of global imbalances.[27] The Mundell–Fleming trilemma however indicates that there are other tools through which external adjustments can be made. Indeed, those countries that adopted a model with floating exchange rates were never in a position to use the exchange rate tool for adjustment at all.

From the IMF perspective, global imbalances kept rising under Bretton Woods II because some developing countries adopted other combinations of the impossible trinity, such as a fixed nominal exchange rate, closed capital account and monetary independence. The IMF however seems to have overlooked the equally destabilizing impact of a fixed nominal exchange rate, open capital account and monetary dependence followed by Eurozone countries. At any rate it did not sound the alarm bell on intra-Eurozone imbalances with the same shrillness as it did in the case of US–China imbalances. In retrospect it does not seem in the least bit coincidental that the two countries with the largest trade surpluses, namely China and Germany, have fixed nominal exchange rates – the first relative to the US dollar, and the second within the Eurozone. Therefore, an open capital account may not in itself prevent the build-up of external imbalances.

From a developing country perspective, the IMF prescription may well have worked had capital flows remained merely the counterpart of current account imbalances. However, with greater integration, openness and sophistication of financial markets, capital flows gradually decoupled from the current account. Cross-border capital flows rose sharply from around $ 1 trillion in 1990 to $ 11.5 trillion in 2007, before falling to an estimated $ 4.6 trillion in 2012 in the wake of the global financial crisis. Capital inflows into developing countries however have recovered to their 2007 highs, and comprise about a third of all cross-border flows compared to just 5 per cent in 2000.[28] This led not only to greater volatility in such inflows, but also to excessive inflows in times of plenty, and outflows when external capital was most needed. This at any rate has been India's experience, which needs foreign capital on account of a structural current account deficit. This volatility can make the nominal exchange fluctuate sharply over relatively short periods, with a very damaging fall out on the real economy. Thus, starting out from the mid-forties to the US dollar, the last few years has seen the rupee appreciate all the way down to the mid-thirties, then depreciate sharply to exceed fifty, before falling back to the mid-forties, then settling into the mid-fifties, almost breaching the sixty-nine barrier consequent on indication by the US Federal Reserve in May 2013 that it was preparing to exit from unconventional monetary policies before falling back to around sixty on fresh expectations that early rollback was not imminent after all.

This excessive volatility has repeatedly tested the Central Bank's resolve to stick to its solution to the Mundell–Fleming equation and try to beat the impossible trinity by intervening in foreign exchange markets. Good macroeconomic management was no guarantee of stable flows, as a crisis in one part of the globe spreads rapidly to other parts of the world through financial markets, leading to safe haven flows. Since cross-border capital flows are denominated in reserve currencies, and increasingly in US dollars, this meant capital flight to the reserve issuing countries, and particularly the US. This happened even in cases where the source of the crisis itself lay in reserve-issuing countries, such as following the collapse of Lehman Brothers, the credit downgrading of US long-term debt, in the midst of the Eurozone crisis and again on indications of exit from unconventional monetary policies.

Even in non-crisis situations, however, reserve-issuing countries can influence the direction of capital flows through their domestic monetary action which can impact the flow and cost of capital in developing countries. From this perspective it can indeed be argued that open capital accounts are supportive of monetary policy frameworks of reserve issuing countries, who are also the major shareholders of the IMF. It is easy to see why the IMF has a crisis of legitimacy. It is also easy to see why the IMF has now relented on the issue of capital account convertibility,[29] and why the consensus on 'coherent conclusions' arrived at by the G20 at Cannes in the matter of managing capital flows retains the option of imposing capital controls in certain circumstances.[30]

There was of course always the IMF that was expected to provide liquidity support to developing countries in just such an eventuality, when liquidity was a problem. However, the experience of several developing countries with

IMF programmes has not been pleasant – although I may add that India has little ground for complaint in this regard – procedures were tardy, the structure of the programmes reflected the interests of creditors or the majority developed country shareholders, leading to contractionary policies in times of stalling growth – or the exact opposite of what it is now recommended for developed countries in crisis currently – and the stigma attached by markets to approaching the IMF. Many countries have complained that as soon as markets got wind of their intention to even engage the IMF on standby arrangements, this was interpreted by markets as the first sign of crisis and they started penalizing them for their foresight! In these circumstances is it surprising that developing countries turned increasingly to building their own financial safety nets through accumulation of reserves? Countries with such large reserves also seem to have fared better during the recent crisis. The other response has been to develop regional financial safety nets, such as the Chiang Mai initiative, and now the EFSF in the Eurozone. The effectiveness of such regional safety nets however still has to be tested. Accumulation of large reserves by developing countries, therefore, is not simply the by-product of export-led strategies of growth. It is also a self-insurance mechanism to manage large and volatile capital inflows that can be hugely destabilizing.

International Reserve Currency

Lastly, I come to the issue of the international reserve currency itself. I have already referred to the perception that the issuer of reserve currencies has certain inherent advantages. There has therefore been talk of negating this advantage by moving to a multi-currency system, or to a new currency, such as the SDR, which is not linked to any nation state. Apart from rhetoric, however, these suggestions have led nowhere, and the G20 has even stopped discussing this aspect of reform of the International Monetary System. We therefore need to explore this issue a little deeper, even at the cost of covering some basic, well-known territory, including the very nature of money itself.

Trade and exchange are among the most ancient of human transactions. Money emerged as a form of universal exchange that enabled human societies to move beyond barter that was very cumbersome as you needed to trade in a large number of articles to eventually get what you wanted to consume.

Different forms of money, or currencies, were until recently local phenomena, because bulk trade, and society itself, was local until major technological advances following the Industrial Revolution. Despite poor communications, however, there was always a flourishing long-term trade, such as the overland silk trade, or the maritime Indian ocean trade, in luxury goods for which there was stable demand from the ruling classes of opulent empires. The currencies issued by big empires were generally acceptable across borders for trade and financial transactions, especially since these were not fiat currencies, and there was always a relationship between its extrinsic value and the intrinsic value of its scarce metal content, such as gold, silver, copper and so on. No sophisticated financial, monetary or legal system was required to back up currencies issued by major empires, such as the Roman and later the British, which could be considered to be the original global reserve currencies.

Reserve currencies always had a strategic and extra-economic dimension, which is the case even to this day. The US dollar has been the world's reserve currency since as far back as most people can remember, and certainly since the end of the British Empire. Its continuing resilience has long been an unexplained macro-economic puzzle, as its relative value does not seem to respond to current account and fiscal deficits in the manner other currencies do. Indeed, a number of intrepid theories have been floated to explain its continuing strength, such as that by the economists Hausmann and Sturzenegger[31] who invoked the 'dark matter' analogy from quantum physics. The fact of the matter is that in a globalized world the macro-economic rules of the thumb applicable to other currencies do not apply to the international reserve currency as the latter has a strategic and safe haven status that cannot be captured in financial models.

It is this unfair advantage[32] devolving on the international reserve currency that has time and again led to calls for either competing reserve currencies or for replacing the dollar by a currency at arms length from Nation States, such as the SDR, and even for a return to the gold standard.[33]

However, the same economic logic that gave rise to money itself as a form of universal exchange makes it likely that as economies integrate further and become seamless, a single reserve currency would become the measure of universal international exchange and value. The international reserve currency itself might change in future with shifting geo-political and economic fortunes, just as it transited from the pound sterling to the US dollar in the inter-war period. However, a shift to a more legitimate multi-currency system would run against the tide of history. Arguably, a fast globalizing world has space for just one international reserve currency. The problem of the reserve currency advantage, attendant moral hazards and legitimacy issues will not go away.

It is still possible that one reserve currency could be replaced by another, just as the pound sterling yielded to the dollar in the first half of the twentieth century as the US economy became the biggest economy and trading nation, and also the dominant technological and military power.

The only currency area that comes even close to the US in economic size is the Euro area. Even before the Eurozone's current travails, however, trend growth in the latter was slower than in the US. The relative size of the US economy was therefore actually increasing with respect to the Euro area, and the technological and military gap was also widening. It could however be argued that a further expansion of the Euro area could in future have dwarfed the US economy, and the Euro could have replaced the Dollar going forward. However, over the last fifteen years beginning 1998, the US dollar has not conceded space to the Euro in the foreign exchange market, with its share at a steady 45 per cent or so. This is because trade flows account for a very small, and diminishing, share of all cross currency transactions.[34] Any thoughts of the Euro taking on the US dollar have perished at a time the survival of the Euro itself is at stake.

The large Chinese and Indian economies are growing much faster and rapidly bridging the gap with the US, but are still a small fraction of the latter at market exchange rates. A time may nevertheless come in the foreseeable future when major emerging markets match the economic size of major advanced economies. Even so, since trade-related transactions comprise an insignificant share of total cross currency transactions, emerging market financial systems would need to match those of advanced economies in depth before they can aspire to reserve currency status, let aspire to become the international reserve currency. Beyond this, economic and financial convergence would need to be matched by technological and military convergence. At this point in time, therefore, it is difficult to see the renminbi or any other emerging market currency challenge the US dollar as the international reserve currency in the foreseeable future.

While the G20 at Cannes asked the IMF to take a re-look at the current SDR basket, even a major recast of the SDR basket is unlikely to amount to much since the SDR is currently simply an accounting unit and not a payments currency accepted by markets. It could make a transition to becoming a currency only if there was a market maker on a monumental scale to negate the first mover advantage of the dollar, with all associated risks and costs.[35] This appears unlikely. The most likely candidate, the IMF, is unlikely to be given the powers of an international central bank with full discretion to print SDRs at will. There is no good reason for the international reserve currency issuer to give up its enormous advantage in the matter of financing internal and external deficits at low costs, especially when it appears that no other currency has the market depth or intrinsic strength to take over the mantle of an alternative reserve currency from the dollar. The inescapable conclusion therefore appears to be that currently there is no alternative currency that can rival, let alone replace, the US dollar as the international reserve currency in the foreseeable future.

Conclusion

So where do we go from here? I should have really stopped here at what appears to be a dead end, since the remaining option of reverting to the gold standard did not seem practicable as governments and central banks would lose flexibility in the use of monetary and fiscal policies to stabilize the economy. It may be recalled that the origins of the Great Depression are often traced to the absence of these macro-economic tools.[36] The current debate on the international monetary system has also not treaded on this dangerous territory. While I am no longer so sure, I would nevertheless have kept these doubts to myself had this not been an academic seminar where ideas are expected to germinate and struggle for survival.

The reason why I raise this rather subversive thought is that extant fiscal and monetary frameworks developed alongside the fiat currency system since the seventies are under undue strain. The chief economist of the IMF is also on record to confessing that we are no longer sure as to what parts of the extant macro-economic framework still works.[37]

The seventies saw unbridled use of fiscal policy to counter what was a permanent rather than a cyclical demand shock deriving from the severe oil price shock, leading to stagflation. This was tamed through aggressive monetary action. It was soon recognized that fiscal policy is too political a tool to be used optimally in macro-economic management. The burden of stabilizing growth therefore passed on to central banks through monetary policy, which in turn became increasingly rule based.

The ageing of Western societies however continued to strain the fiscal framework, while the great moderation, as we saw, had features, such as 'good deflation' and 'shadow banking' that strained the monetary framework. Policy spillovers were also making the task of macro-economic management enormously complicated. Now a sovereign debt crisis in western economies alongside near recessionary conditions is making monetary policy unusually accommodative and innovative through quantitative and credit easing to the point that the divide between fiscal and monetary policy has all but collapsed, as private deleveraging has yielded first to government leveraging and finally to central bank leveraging without addressing the underlying problem of excessive leveraging that lay behind the current crisis.

Exit from extraordinary monetary policies in advanced, reserve currency-issuing countries has renewed concerns about their spill overs on emerging markets. This raises the question whether emerging markets are better off subjecting themselves to the vagaries of US monetary policies by floating their currencies against the dollar, or by adopting a nominal anchor, such as gold.

Macro-economic policies and the international monetary system now seem to be at a historic tipping point, just as they were during the Great Depression. Reshaping them are the great challenges for the future. How might this be done? Does the past provide some guidance? How can monetary and fiscal tools be reshaped?

If both fiscal and monetary policies have been debased within just 40 years of the end of the gold standard, the question may soon be asked, as it indeed was by the World Bank President, Robert Zoellick, some time back,[38] and if it is not already being implicitly asked by markets, as to whether the gold standard was no worse than, and arguably superior to, fiat money?

The gold standard imparted a degree of inflexibility to using macro-economic policies to stabilize growth, since money could not be created at will. Fiat money, however, suffers from the obverse problem that has seen policy-makers succumb to moral hazards inherent in excessive policy flexibility. The gold standard at least delivered on price stability over the long term. Since the stock of gold is limited and finite, its value could not be eroded significantly. The stock of fiat money, on the other hand, is potentially unlimited and policy-makers cannot be trusted to use it wisely.

A return to fiscal and monetary rectitude may well entail re-anchoring fiscal and monetary tools, and with it money itself, to gold (or some other scarce natural material) in some manner. How this re-anchoring could be done is not clear at this stage. However, the concept itself might not be entirely fanciful. The market response to the debasement of macro-economic policies since the onset of the recent financial crisis seems to be to turn to gold as an alternate safe haven alongside the US dollar.

If gold is now behaving more like a currency than a commodity, this could be a classic illustration of the age-old Gresham's Law that bad money drives good money out of the market. The question is whether this is a temporary trend or a structural shift. Be it as it may, some long-term damage has been done. The gold standard and its variants have been around for millennia, outliving several disastrous monetary experiments. Fiat money has been with us for just over four decades. Why should this time be different? The experience of the last four decades makes the historian in me fear for the future of fiat money.

To conclude, the current global financial crisis has reopened an old debate on the international monetary system by baring weaknesses and flaws that have long been known. The debate is centred on both stability and equity. International co-operation is necessary to resolve a complex interplay of several interrelated problems. The G20 seems better positioned than the IMF to arrive at some international consensus on these issues. However, while there has been some progress, the big issues of moral hazard and inequity deriving from the global reserve currency seem intractable at this point in time. With the macro-economic framework under great strain, we may indeed be poised for a leap into the dark going forward. Since solutions seem elusive, even as everybody is agreed that there is a major problem, this conference is very timely. I am confident that it will be a fertile breeding ground for new ideas to take root.

Endnotes

1   The ideas articulated in this chapter were first made in a 'Keynote Speech' delivered at the 5th ICRIER GIZ Annual Conference on Reforming the International Monetary System, A Dialogue on Challenges and Cooperation, December 5–6, 2011, Indian Habitat Centre, New Delhi. An earlier version of this chapter was published as *ICRIER Policy Series No.11*, 8 December 2011.

2   Secretary, Prime Minister's Economic Advisory Council, India. The views expressed in this chapter are personal and do not represent those of the Government of India. (aloksheel@ aloksheel.com www.aloksheel.com).

3   Vijay Joshi and Robert Skidelsky, 'Keynes, Global Imbalances, and Internal Monetary System Reform, Today', in ed. Stijn Claessens, Simon Evenett and Bernard Hoekman *Rebalancing the Global Economy: A Primer for Policymaking* Chapter 24. http://www.voxeu. org/index.php?q=node/5219 Centre for Economic Policy Research, 2010.

4   *The Turner Review*, UK Financial Stability Authority, March 2009. www.fsa.gov.uk/pubs/ other/turner_review.pd G20 Finance Ministers and Central Bank Governors had identified these root causes in Sao Paulo, Brazil on November 8–9, 2008. http://www.g20.org/ Documents/2008_communique_saopaulo_brazil.pdf.

5   Vijay Joshi and Robert Skidelsky, op.cit.

6   Lorenzo Bini Smaghi, 'The Triffin Dilemma Revisited', European Central Bank Conference on the International Monetary System: Sustainability and Reform Proposals, October 3,

2011, 100th birth anniversary of Robert Triffin, Triffin International Foundation, Brussels. http://www.ecb.int/press/key/date/2011/html/sp111003.en.html.

7   Robert I. McKinnon, 'Why Exchange Rate Changes Will Not Correct Global Trade Imbalances' in Ed. Claessens, Evenett and Hoekman, *Rebalancing the Global Economy: A Primer for Policymaking,* op. cit, Chapter 12. Fred Bergsten, 'The Dollar and the Deficits: How Washington Can Prevent the Next Crisis', *Foreign Affairs,* Volume 88 No. 6, November/December 2009. http://www.iie.com/publications/papers/paper.cfm?ResearchID=1312.

8   National Income = Consumption + Investment + (Exports – Imports).

9   Angela Merkel, the German Chancellor, has drawn attention to the thrifty the Swabian housewife who always balances her budget by force of habit. http://www.ft.com/intl/cms/s/0/21dddea4-7d60-11df-a0f5-00144feabdc0.html#axzz1gmIUE17m   Trends in the Distribution of Household Income Between 1979 and 2007, Congressional Budget Office,The Congress of the United States. http://www.cbo.gov/ftpdocs/124xx/doc12485/10-25-HouseholdIncome.pdf.

10 Jared Bernstein and Lawrence Mishel, Economy's Gains Fail to Reach Most Workers' Paychecks, Economic Policy Institute, April 30, 2007, http://www.epi.org/publication/bp195/.

11 The IMF's Consultative Group on Exchange Rate issues (CGER), has been evaluating the exchange rates of industrialized countries, and more recently of major developing countries as well.

12 The IMF had sounded a warning on the build up of unsustainable global imbalances as early as in its 2002 *World Economic Outlook,* even prior to the Chinese current account surpluses, and more specifically In its June 29, 2007 Staff Report on the Multilateral Consultations on Global Imbalances with China, the Euro Area, Japan, Saudi Arabia and the United States. http://www.imf.org/external/np/pp/2007/eng/062907.pdf. See also Maurice Obstfled and Kenneth Rogoff, 'The Unsustainable US Current Account Position Revisited'. NBER Working Paper 10869, October 2004. http://www.nber.org/papers/w10869.

13 Abdul Abiad, Prakash Kannan, and Jungjin Le, 'Evaluating Historical CGER Assessments: How Well Have They Predicted Subsequent Exchange Rate Movements?' IMF Working Paper WP 09/32, February 2009.

14 IMF Performance in the Run-Up to the Financial and Economic Crisis. IMF Surveillance in 2004–07 http://www.ieo-imf.org/ieo/pages/IEOPreview.aspx?img=i6nZpr3iSlU per cent3d&mappingid=dRx2VaDG7EY per cent3d Independent Evaluation Office of the IMF, 2011.

15 Leaders' Statement, Pittsburgh, September 25, 2009. http://www.g20.org/Documents/pittsburgh_summit_leaders_statement_250909.pdf.

16 The Los Cabos Growth and Jobs Action Plan. Annex B: The Los Cabos Accountability Assessment. http://www.g20.utoronto.ca/2012/2012-0619-loscabos-actionplan.pdf. St. Petersburg Action Plan, September 6, 2013. Annex 4: The St. Petersburg Accountability Assessment and Progress Towards Strong, Sustainable and Balanced Growth. http://www.g20.utoronto.ca/2013/Accountabilty_Assessment_FINAL.pdf.

17 Claudio Borio and Andrew Filardo, 'Globalisation and Inflation: New Cross-Country Evidence on the Global Determinants of Domestic Inflation', Bank of International Settlements, Working Paper # 227, May 2007. http://www.bis.org/publ/work227.pdf?noframes=1.

[18] US Urban CPI rose by just 10 per cent between June 2000 and March 2004. The US Case Shiller Housing index rose by 60 per cent during the same period. The US FED serially lowered the Fed Funds rate from 6.5 per cent to 1 per cent over this period.

[19] Popularly known as the 'Greenspan doctrine'. See his Remarks at the Economic Club of New York, New York City, 19 December 2002. http://www.federalreserve.gov/boarddocs/speeches/2002/20021219/default.htm.

[20] John B. Taylor, 'Does the Crisis Experience Call for a New Paradigm in Monetary Policy?', CASE Network Studies and Analyses # 402/2010 http://www.case.com.pl/strona–ID-publikacje,publikacja_id-30086909,nlang-710.html *The Economist* of 18 October 2007, carried a graph showing just how much the Fed Funds rate deviated from the 'Taylor Rule' in the run up to the crisis. The Taylor Rule itself was deduced from an evaluation of past policy decisions of the US Fed that had worked well.

[21] Alan Greenspan, The Age of Turbulence. Adventures in a New World. Allen Lane, 2007, 381. Greenspan was specifically referring to the impact of cross-border capital flows. We now know that much of this mobility was on account of the shadow banking system.

[22] Financial Stability Board, Strengthening Oversight and Regulation of Shadow Banking. An Overview of Policy Recommendations. August 29, 2013. http://www.financialstabilityboard.org/publications/r_130829a.pdf.

[23] Government securities provide much of the risk-free collateral in the repo market which is a major source of funding in the shadow banking system. This system could be destabilized should these securities lose their risk free status. Gillian Tett, 'Debt impasse exposes Achilles' heel of finance', *Financial Times*, October 11, 2013. http://www.ft.com/intl/cms/s/0/2fa2f0ec-31c1-11e3-a16d-00144feab7de.html?siteedition=intl#axzz2hCW2FvCo.

[24] Jörg Bibow, 'The Global Crisis and the Future of the Dollar: Toward Bretton Woods III?' Levy Economics Institute of Bard College and Skidmore College, Working Paper No. 584, February, 2010. http://www.levy.org/pubs/wp_584.pdf See also *Financial globalization: Reset or Retreat? Global Capital Markets 2013*, Mckinsey Global Institute, March 2013. For data on the shifting structure of leverage in western financial systems. http://www.mckinsey.com/insights/global_capital_markets/financial_globalization.

[25] Cannes Summit Final Declaration, 4 November 2011. http://www.g20.org/pub_communiques.aspx Paragraphs 9–21.

[26] Maurice Obstfeld, 'International Macroeconomics: Beyond the Mundell-Fleming Model', IMF Staff Papers, Vol. 47 Special Issue, 2001 http://www.imf.org/external/pubs/ft/staffp/2000/00-00/o.pdf.

[27] IMF, World Economic Outlook, September 2011, 25. http://www.imf.org/external/pubs/ft/weo/2011/02/index.htm.

[28] McKinsey Global Institute, *Financial Globalization: Retreat or Reset?*, March 2013.

[29] Jonathan D. Ostry, Atish R. Ghosh, Karl Habermeier, Marcos Chamon, Mahvash S. Qureshi, and Dennis B. S. Reinhardt, 'Capital Inflows: The Role of Controls', IMF Staff Position Note SPN/10/04, 19 February 2010. http://www.imf.org/external/pubs/ft/spn/2010/spn1004.pdf.

[30] G20 Coherent Conclusions for the Management of Capital Flows Drawing on Country Experiences as endorsed by G20 Finance Ministers and Central Bank Governors, October 15, 2011. http://www.g20.utoronto.ca/2011/2011-finance-capital-flows-111015-en.pdf.

[31]   R Hausmann and F Sturzenegger, *U.S. and Global Imbalances: Can Dark Matter Prevent a Big Bang?* Harvard University, 13 November 2005. http://www.cid.harvard.edu/cidpublications/darkmatter_051130.pdf.

[32]   One of the earliest concerns in this regard was articulated in the 1960s by Valéry Giscard d'Estaing, then French Minister of Finance, to whom is attributed the origin of the phrase 'exorbitant privelege'.

[33]   One of the most publicised recent statements was a speech by Zhou Xiaochuan, Governor of the Bank of China, at the Bank for International Settlements on 23 March 2009. http://www.bis.org/review/r090402c.pdf.

[34]   Stephen Jen and Alexandra Dreisin, The USD's Hegemonic International Currency Status, SLJ Macro Partners, September 11, 2013. http://research.sljmacro.com/rp//521/process.clsp?EmailId=179889&Token=20228271CE54C7EC69DE041C97831318D.

[35]   Barry Eichengreen, 'The Dollar Dilemma. The World's Top Currency Faces Competition', *Foreign Affairs,* September/October 2009.

[36]   This was the view of both Milton Friedman and the current chairman of the US Federal Reserve, Ben Bernanke, http://www.federalreserve.gov/boarddocs/speeches/2004/200403022/default.htm. Liaquat Ahmed's recent study of the policies of three central bankers during the Great Depression arrived at a similar conclusion that 'for all of Norman's enormous prestige and Schacht's creativity, they were both hamstrung by the dictates of the gold standard', Liaquat Ahmed, Lords of Finance. 1929, The Great Depression, and the Bankers Who Broke the World, William Heinemann, London, 2009, 503.

[37]   Olivier Blanchard, Giovanni Dell'Ariccia, and Paolo Mauro, 'Rethinking Macroeconomic Policy', IMF Staff Position Note, SPN/10/03, 12 February 12 2010. http://www.imf.org/external/pubs/ft/spn/2010/spn1003.pdf.

[38]   Robert Zoellick, 'The G20 must look Beyond Bretton Woods II', *Financial Times,* 7 November 7, 2010. http://www.ft.com/cms/s/0/5bb39488-ea99-11df-b28d-00144feab49a.html# axzz14dKEeR16.

The Chiang Mai Initiative and its Relevance for India[1]

Sheetal K. Chand

Introduction

The Asian currency crisis of 1997–98 was a traumatic experience, and especially for Indonesia, the Republic of Korea (henceforth Korea), Malaysia, and Thailand. The crisis hit suddenly and with unprecedented ferocity. The affected countries were ill prepared for it. Their responses failed to contain the crisis, and may even have aggravated it. According to many observers, these policies, except for those that Malaysia adopted, were heavily influenced by the US treasury and the IMF.[2] One consequence has been a loss of trust on the part of many Asian countries in the ability of the global mechanism and its key institutions to anticipate crises, to manage them when they occur and to formulate policy prescriptions that would protect the interests of the affected countries. This has led to demands for a comprehensive reform of the global mechanism. The call is for reforms of global governance, accompanied with major improvements in the surveillance and crisis management functions of its principal institutions, especially the IMF, and a greatly enhanced capacity to provide emergency liquidity assistance. In the interim, most Asian countries have put their trust in self-insurance involving large international reserve accumulations. They have also initiated a regional balance of payments self-help arrangement, the Chiang Mai initiative (CMI), which was transformed in 2010 into the Chiang Mai Initiative Multilateralization (CMIM).[3]

In the aftermath of the Asian currency crisis, the US, as the principle stakeholder of the international monetary system, and the IMF have both acknowledged the need for some reforms.[4] However, they have questioned the need for regional self-help institutions, expressing concern that these could unnecessarily duplicate and interfere with the efficient workings of the global mechanism.[5] They also point out that self-insurance is expensive, since it involves allocating savings that could be put to better use. They urge the Asian countries to rely more on the global mechanism, centred on the IMF and an enhanced G20 body; to limit their recourse to expensive self-insurance and regional self-help institutions; to contemplate reserve pooling at the global level and to further liberalize their economies so as to give more room to market-based solutions.

However, these recommendations and proposed solutions are problematic. They do not address the highly volatile capital flows and exchange rate movements that the present set-up of the international monetary system permits. The fear of many Asian countries is that their growth-oriented development goals could be undermined should such externally induced factors turn adverse. Hence, they seek additional solutions, with the CMIM as a potential source of protection. A key issue for the Asian countries is whether the CMIM could promote intra-regional stability of exchange rates and cope with various types of balance of payments shocks and liquidity crises that may arise. Could it, for example, provide liquidity as needed to help cushion the adverse impacts of volatile capital flows? Could it provide a pooling service that reduces the costs to the individual member country of international reserve accumulations for self-insurance? Could it assist with a required balance of payments adjustment for a member country without inflicting an excessive cost on the country? Not least, could it pave the way for an appropriate reform of the global institutions? The purpose of this chapter is to examine these issues and the possible appeal that the CMIM could have for India.

This chapter is organized as follows: Section 2 briefly describes the CMI and its successor the CMIM. Section 3 examines the Asian currency crisis, which motivated the CMI. Section 4 provides an overview of the various types of balance of payments problems that could arise and their current mode of resolution. Section 5 considers how the CMIM could contribute to resolving balance of payments and liquidity problems. Section 6 examines the CMIM's potential usefulness for India and raises issues of an essentially political economy nature were it to seek membership of the CMIM.

The CMI and its Successor, CMIM

Background to the Launching of the CMI and its Successor CMIM

The CMI and CMIM are products of the Asian currency and financial crisis. At the height of the crisis in 1997, Japan had proposed an Asian Monetary Fund (AMF) that would provide rapidly disbursing liquidity support with minimal conditionality. Under the initial AMF proposal Japan had offered to commit US$50 billion for a total fund of US$100 billion. This was intended as a gesture of support in recognition of the difficulties that several Asian countries had experienced from the rapid depreciation of the yen and also some reflux of capital back to Japan.

However, the US and the IMF succeeded in demolishing the proposal. They regarded the AMF as unnecessary and counter-productive. The US treasury pushed strongly instead for addressing the crisis through IMF-supported programmes, arguing that these could be supplemented with substantial loans from both IMF and G7 sources, and unlike the AMF accompanied by rigorous and extensive conditionality. The latter they contended was needed to secure essential reforms such as the liberalization of various markets, including the financial ones, which the US treasury and the IMF argued would help promote sustainable recovery. Furthermore, stringent conditional lending would help avoid moral hazard. The alternative Japanese proposal, with its focus on rapidly disbursing liquidity support and low conditionality, was dismissed as interfering with the adjustment process, impeding essential reforms and encouraging moral hazard. Evidently, the US and the IMF viewed the AMF as a threat to their global financial hegemony and managed to quash the proposal.

During the crisis the affected national authorities lacked adequate international reserves or access to international liquidity to deal with the sudden onset of massive capital outflows. They were subjected to a fundamental and classic policy conflict. To protect exchange rate pegs, liquidity needed to be tightened and interest rates increased. However, rapidly evolving recessionary conditions and the deteriorating liquidity position of the banks called for the opposite. A contributory factor for the recession was the slowdown of exports as a consequence of increasingly overvalued exchange rates following rising domestic inflation and both the appreciation of the dollar to which they were pegged and the depreciation of the yen, the currency of their biggest trading partner.[6] This tension fed one-way speculation that exchange rate pegs were unsustainable, and foreign hedge funds whose activities had hitherto been relatively muted became very active in exploiting the opportunities present. In July 1997, Thailand was forced off its dollar peg. This triggered a regional contagion effect, especially among trading competitors who were forced to abandon their original pegs and adopt floating exchange rate arrangements or to re-peg at a much devalued rate as did Malaysia.

With the exception of Malaysia, which under the leadership of Prime Minister Mahathir Mohammed resisted pressure from the US treasury and the IMF, the other Asian countries experiencing the brunt of the crisis, in particular, Indonesia, Korea and Thailand adopted IMF-supported programmes. However, their experiences with these programmes were not satisfactory. A key contention was that the reform and stabilization measures of the programs addressed the wrong problem, which unnecessarily worsened their crises. They viewed their problems as essentially emanating from sudden capital outflows, liquidity shortages and increasingly over-valued exchange rates for which the remedies would be capital controls, liquidity injections and controlled exchange rate adjustment. Instead, the US treasury and the IMF insisted on fiscal consolidation, deregulation and liberalization of various markets including the foreign exchange system and the avoidance of capital controls. As a result, their economies became highly destabilized; exchange rates overshot on the downside, and the economies underwent excessive deflation with acute social costs. All this, they believed, could and should have been avoided. In their view, after several years of rapidly expanding foreign financial capital inflows as a result of capital market liberalization at the behest of the international community, they experienced a sudden and massive capital outflow, which caused an acute bank liquidity crisis that triggered a currency crisis.

The perceived failure of the global mechanism to adequately address their plight led the Asian countries to engage in self-insurance. Ironically, the very stringency and content of the IMF-supported programmes, which was introduced ostensibly to avert moral hazard on the part of concerned countries, was found to be so damaging that they resolved never again to be in a situation that required recourse to the IMF. Accordingly, they allowed exchange rates to be undervalued and large current account surpluses to develop and accumulated massive foreign exchange reserves.

The affected countries, together with China and Japan, also embarked on an Asian regional collaborative initiative. Recognizing from the strong US and IMF opposition, and the earlier backing down of the Japanese, that an AMF was not immediately attainable, they proceeded cautiously. The first stage involved the launching of the CMI arrangement in 2000, which consisted of a cumbersome network of bilateral swap arrangements. It is noteworthy that China, while initially hesitant with regard to the earlier proposal of an AMF, became an eager proponent of both the CMI and its successor CMIM, as regional self-help institutions.

Present Nature of the CMIM

The CMIM, which succeeded the earlier CMI, became effective on 24

March 2010. It comprises the ASEAN countries plus China, Japan and Korea (ASEAN+3). Its core objectives are (i) to address balance-of-payments and short-term liquidity difficulties in the region, and (ii) to supplement the existing international financial arrangements. It is yet to be tested and till date no drawings have been made.[7]

In order to pursue its mandate, the CMIM has set up a fund of US$120 billion in US dollars that is now to be doubled, and which is accessible through currency swap transactions to participants. The maximum any participant can draw is determined by an agreed purchasing multiplier applied to their assessed contributions. The multipliers exhibit steep progressivity, ranging from 0.5 for the biggest contributors like China and Japan to 5 for smaller contributors such as Vietnam. While China and Japan each contribute 32 per cent, their maximum drawings are limited to 16 per cent each, whereas Vietnam can draw up to 5 per cent even though its contribution is only 1 per cent. The swaps are for 90 days at a time and can be renewed up to seven times, implying a maximum borrowing duration of approximately two years. Interest is charged at LIBOR+150 basis points for the first drawing and the first renewal, but increases by 50 basis points for every two renewals for a maximum of 300 basis points. Drawings that exceed 20 per cent of the maximum amount disbursable are linked to an IMF-supported programme.

A two-thirds majority of the CMIM's executive body is needed for a drawing to be approved. Voting power is distributed to members according to the amounts they contributed, supplemented by basic votes that are allocated equally. Given the present distribution of votes, no single country can exercise veto power, although China and Japan come close to it.

The CMIM arrangement provides the basis for the establishment of a monetary research unit to conduct relevant macroeconomic research for promoting its objectives. There is also provision for a regional surveillance unit. Once the latter is operational, it is intended to de-link the IMF programme requirement for drawings above 20 per cent. However, the issue of what conditionality to apply thereafter remains to be determined.

The Asian Currency Crisis, its Costly Aftermath and Some Lessons

The Asian currency crisis heralded a new and virulent form of balance of payments problem that is associated with highly volatile foreign portfolio capital flows. This section considers some aspects of this problem and its economic aftermath for the affected countries.

Origins

Table 9.1 indicates key underlying trends of the Asian currency crisis. In the years building up to the crisis, the environment became increasingly deregulated and liberalized and non-residents were able to readily acquire domestic financial claims in these countries. This was attractive since the returns to be obtained were substantially higher than in the source countries. For example, short-term interest rates in the Asian countries were, for several years prior to the crisis, some 5 per cent higher than in international money centres. With pegged exchange rates and low exchange rate risk perceptions, foreign banks and funds found it attractive to lend and invest locally. There was a massive increase in portfolio investment inflows, especially in 1995 and 1996, which were primarily directed to the stock exchanges and to lending to local banks and firms. The rapid build-up in the inflows expanded domestic liquidity, which the local banks leveraged further. There was a large increase in the pool of investment financing, and much of it was directed to areas that yielded the prospect of quick capital gains such as real estate.[8] The economies boomed, and investment exceeded the generally high levels of domestic savings. This was essentially the result of private sector behaviour as the governments were generally operating tight fiscal policies (Table 9.2). Current account deficits increased, but the size of foreign capital inflows was such that the countries still managed to register modest increases in international reserve holdings. Table 9.3 indicates that going into the crisis external debt levels of the concerned countries were not unduly high.

Table 9.1: Asian Crisis Countries: Net Private Capital Inflows*

(In billions of US dollars)

	1994	1995	1996	1997	1998	1999
Total net private capital inflows	36.1	74.2	65.8	-20.4	-25.6	-24.6
Net foreign direct investment	8.8	7.5	8.4	10.3	8.6	10.2
Net portfolio investment	9.9	17.4	20.3	12.9	-6.0	6.3
Bank loans and other	17.4	49.2	37.2	-43.6	-28.2	-41.1
Memo:						
Current account balance	-23.2	-40.4	-53.0	-25.0	69.7	61.7
Change in reserves (- is increase)	-6.1	-18.5	-5.6	39.5	-47.0	-38.8

*Indonesia, Korea, Malaysia, Philippines and Thailand
Source: IMF Annual Report, 1999.

Table 9.2: Asian Crisis Countries – General Government Balance
(Per cent of GDP)

	1995	1996	1997	1998	1999
Indonesia	0.8	1.2	-0.7	-1.9	-1.5
Korea	1.3	1.0	-0.9	-3.8	-2.7
Malaysia	2.2	2.3	4.1	-0.4	-3.8
Philippines	-1.4	-0.6	-0.8	-2.7	-4.4
Thailand	3.0	2.5	-0.9	-2.5	-2.9
Of which: central government					
Indonesia	0.8	1.2	-0.7	-1.9	-1.5
Korea	0.3	0.0	-1.7	-4.3	-3.3
Malaysia	1.3	1.1	2.5	-1.5	-4.1
Philippines	-1.4	-0.6	-0.8	-2.7	-4.4
Thailand	2.5	1.0	-1.7	-2.9	-3.7

Source: IMF Annual Reports

Table 9.3: Asian Crisis Countries – External Debt
(Per cent of GDP)

	1995	1996	1997	1998	1999
Indonesia	56.3	53.4	63.9	149.4	96.5
Korea	37.6	38.4	43.8	58.8	-53.4
Malaysia	54.9	55.0	61.6	81.7	75.7
Philippines	26.0	31.6	33.4	46.9	33.4
Thailand	49.1	49.8	62.0	76.9	61.4
Of which: short-term debt					
Indonesia	8.7	17.5	27.5	76.4	5.9
Korea	7.2	9.9	11.1	11.7	7.6
Malaysia	8.3	12.0	14.0	15.6	11.3
Philippines	14.6	17.9	13.3	9.7	9.3
Thailand	24.5	20.7	23.1	21.0	11.4

Source: IMF Annual Reports

As the boom petered out in 1996, asset prices began to decline, the prospect of quick capital gains waned and foreign creditors began to reduce their local investment exposures, starting with Thailand. They also became increasingly reluctant to renew maturing obligations of local banks with the Japanese banks, who were the largest creditors in Thailand, in the forefront.[9] Restructuring of Japan's domestic financial system which, in part, required Japanese banks to increase their capital to comply with newly mandated BIS capital requirements, restrained their lending abroad. They were also experiencing the effects of a sharp depreciation in the yen relative to the dollar, which eroded their ability to service their dollar liabilities and placed added pressure on them to reduce their external loans. As a result, they abandoned their traditional informal agreements in countries such as Thailand for more or less automatically renewing credit. This generated a liquidity problem for the local Asian banks which, in turn, restricted loans to their customers, while increasing their recourse to international financial markets for funding.

Signs that the banks were experiencing difficulties caused a massive outflow of deposits. Attempts on the part of the authorities to provide domestic liquidity and to meet international foreign currency obligations rapidly depleted international reserves, and perceptions of exchange risk, which had hitherto been muted, intensified. These perceptions of growing exchange risk were not confined to Thailand and rapidly spread to other Asian countries.

The only countries that avoided the contagion effects that the outflow of funds unleashed were those that operated capital controls and managed their exchange rates, notably China and India.

Aftermath for Affected Countries' Economies

The IMF programmes were premised on the expectation that massive exchange rate depreciations, together with structural reforms and stabilization policies in line with the 'Washington Consensus', would pave the way for a resumption of their previous high rates of growth. However, with the exception of the Philippines, which had an enduring semi-permanent programme relationship with the IMF and exhibited virtually no change in its relatively low growth trajectory both before and after the crisis, the others experienced sharp drops in their formerly high growth rates. It is noteworthy that this poor performance appears to have lasted for much longer than the programmes envisaged (Figure 9.1a). In contrast, China and India continued to experience rapid economic growth, which in the case of India even accelerated (Figure 9.1b).

Figure 9.1a: Asian Crisis Countries – Annual Growth Rates, 1991–2010

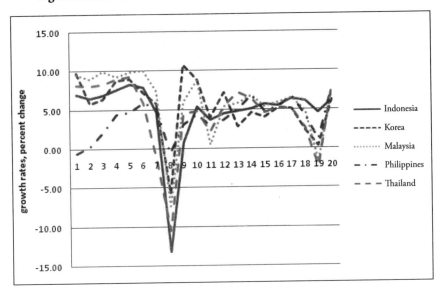

Figure 9.1b: China and India – Annual Growth Rates, 1991–2010

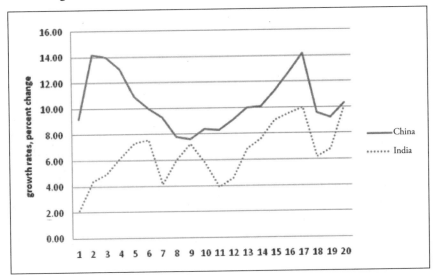

Statistical tests confirm Figure 9.1a's indications of long-term shifts in growth rate performance. The procedure adopted here is to divide the time series on growth rates into two sub-samples: a pre-crisis one running from 1990–97 and a post-crisis one from 1999–2010. The year 1998 is taken as the excluded year since it straddles the crisis periods for each country. The results reported in Table 9.4 indicate that for Indonesia, Malaysia and Thailand post-crisis mean growth rates fell by substantial amounts from the pre-crisis period levels. In the case of Thailand, the fall was from an average of 7.3 per cent annual growth rate to an average of only 4.4 per cent annual growth in the post-crisis period; for Malaysia the fall was from 9.2 per cent to 5.1 per cent while for Indonesia the fall was from 7.3 per cent to 3.5 per cent. Korea's post-crisis performance was only slightly better with the fall from 7.0 per cent to 4.9 per cent.

Table 9.4: Selected Asian Countries' Growth Rates, 1990–2010:
Testing for Structural Break

	Indonesia		Korea		Malaysia		Philippines		Thailand		China		India	
	A	B	A	B	A	B	A	B	A	B	A	B	A	B
Mean	7.0	4.9	7.7	5.1	9.2	5.1	3.1	4.6	7.4	4.4	10.6	10.1	5.3	7.3
Variance	1.2	2.2	2.7	8.1	0.8	8.2	5.5	3.3	14.9	7.1	11.6	3.6	3.2	4.2
t-Stat	3.7*		2.6*		4.7*		-1.5		1.9*		0.4		-2.3*	

A refers to period 1990–97; B refers to period 1999–2010.

* indicates rejection of no significant difference between period means at the 5 per cent level of significance.

Source: IMF World Economic Outlook, September 2011 and author's calculations.

For the most part there was a marked increase in growth rate variance, which could affect conclusions regarding shifts in mean growth rates. Allowing for unequal variances in the tests, Table 9.4 presents the results from testing the hypothesis that a structural break occurred in growth rates around 1998. The test statistic and procedure rejected the null hypothesis that there was no change in mean growth rates for several of the countries, even after allowing for the marked increase in post-crisis variances.[10]

The precipitous decline in the performance of the crisis-affected countries contrasts sharply with the situation for China and India. For China, the pre- and post-crisis average growth rates amounted to 10.6 and 10.1, respectively, which the test statistic showed to be an insignificant difference. The comparable mean growth rates for India were 5.3 and 7.3 per cent, respectively, with the test statistic here showing a significant increase for the post-crisis period.

Decline in Post-crisis Growth Rates

In order to explain secular growth rates, emphasis is usually placed on productive factors such as the rate of capital accumulation, technological progress and growth in the labour force. These three factors are expressed in the following general production function which conveys that aggregate output Y results from applying labour L to the stock of capital K for a given set of techniques A.

$$Y = f(K, L, A) \tag{9.1}$$

To derive a relationship for the growth rate of output, equation 9.1 is first linearized and the resultant expressed in first difference terms (Δ denotes the first difference operator)

$$\Delta Y = \alpha \Delta K + \beta \Delta L + \gamma \Delta A \tag{9.2}$$

The coefficients, α, β, and γ relate changes in output to changes in the productive factors. Dividing through by the preceding period's output Y_{-1} and re-arranging, yields the output growth rate as a function of changes in the underlying factors:

$$\frac{\Delta Y}{Y_{-1}} = \gamma \frac{\Delta A}{Y_{-1}} + \alpha \frac{\Delta K}{Y_{-1}} + \beta \frac{\Delta L}{Y_{-1}} \tag{9.3[11]}$$

In what follows the focus will be on the capital stock change term, i.e., investment or $\frac{\Delta K}{Y_{-1}}$. Note that the coefficient α is the inverse of the incremental capital–output ratio $\alpha = \frac{Y_{-1}}{\Delta K} \frac{\Delta Y}{Y_{-1}} \equiv \frac{\Delta Y}{\Delta K}$.

Figure 9.2, which plots the annual growth rates of the sample countries against the investment ratio, indicates that the two series are related. Of particular interest is that the charts point to a pronounced fall in the investment ratios at about the same time as the decline in growth rates. Testing for structural breaks in investment behaviour between the pre- and post-crisis periods confirms the visual impressions of association from the Figure. The results reported in Table 9.5 show that for Indonesia the fall in the investment ratio was from an average of nearly 40 per cent before the crisis to about 25 per cent after the crisis year, with similar large falls taking place in Malaysia and Thailand. Although for Korea and the Philippines, the falls in the investment ratios were less pronounced, they were significant.[12]

However, turning to China, the investment ratio did not exhibit any significant change, while for India there was even a pronounced increase

Figure 9.2: Selected Asian Countries, Investment Ratios and Growth rates, 1991–2010

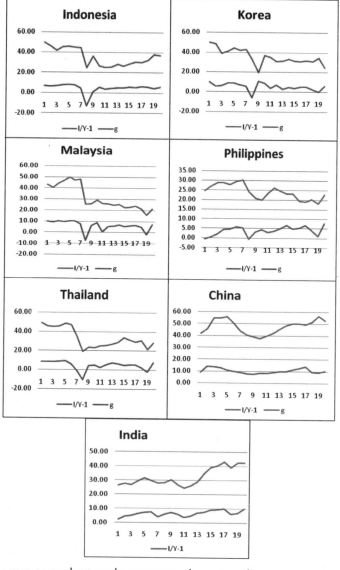

Y-axis is per cent growth rate and per cent growth rate in real investment weighted by the preceding year's investment-to-GDP ratio.

Table 9.5: Asian Crisis Countries' Investment Ratios, 1990–2010:
Testing for Structural Break in 1998

	Indonesia		Korea		Malaysia		Philippines		Thailand		China		India	
	A	*B*	*A*	*B*	*A*	*B*	*A*	*B*	*A*	*B*	*A*	*B*	*A*	*B*
Mean (per cent of GDP)	39.2	25.3	37.3	29.4	39.3	21.8	24.9	19.8	40.2	25.5	39.6	41.5	24.9	30.9
Variance	2.7	13.3	2.0	1.4	14.3	10.0	2.8	5.6	8.1	10.4	9.7	18.9	2.1	33.2
t-Stat	11.6**		12.9**		10.8**		5.7**		10.8**		-1.1		-3.4**	

A refers to period 1990–97; B refers to period 1998–2010
** indicates rejection of no significant difference between period means at the 1 per cent level of significance
Source: IMF World Economic Outlook, September 2011 and author's calculations.

during the post-crisis period. These developments paralleled those found earlier regarding differences in growth rates between the crisis-affected countries and China–India.

The next step is to estimate a statistical relationship between the investment ratios and the growth rates. Table 9.6 reports the results from regressing growth

Table 9.6: Selected Asian Countries' Growth Rate Regressions, 1990–2010

	Indonesia	Korea	Malaysia	Philippines	Thailand	China	India
Intercept	-3.83 (0.36) (0.05)	-9.53 (0.01) (-2.83)*	-1.27 (0.62) (-0.50)	4.67 (0.21) (1.31)	-5.18 (0.11) -1.70)	0.96 (0.77) (0.30)	-2.06 (0.20) (-1.34)
I	0.24 (0.05) (2.15)*	0.51 (0.00) (4.50)**	0.23 (0.01) (2.92)**	-0.03 (0.81) (-0.24)	0.29 (0.00) (3.31)**	0.20 (0.01) (2.95)**	0.27 (0.05) (5.68)**
R^2	0.5	0.53	0.33	0.00	0.38	0.33	0.64
S.E	4.13	2.61	3.66	2.41	3.82	1.79	1.32
Obs.	18	20	20	20	20	20	20

Investment ratio is defined as total investment divided by previous year's GDP, all in real terms. First item in parentheses is the p-ratio, and the second item in parentheses is the t-test.
* indicates significance of the t-test at 5 per cent confidence level, and ** at the 1 per cent confidence level.
Source: International Monetary Fund World Economic Outlook September 2011, and author's calculations.

Figure 9.3: Selected Asian Countries, 1991–2010: Fit of Growth Model

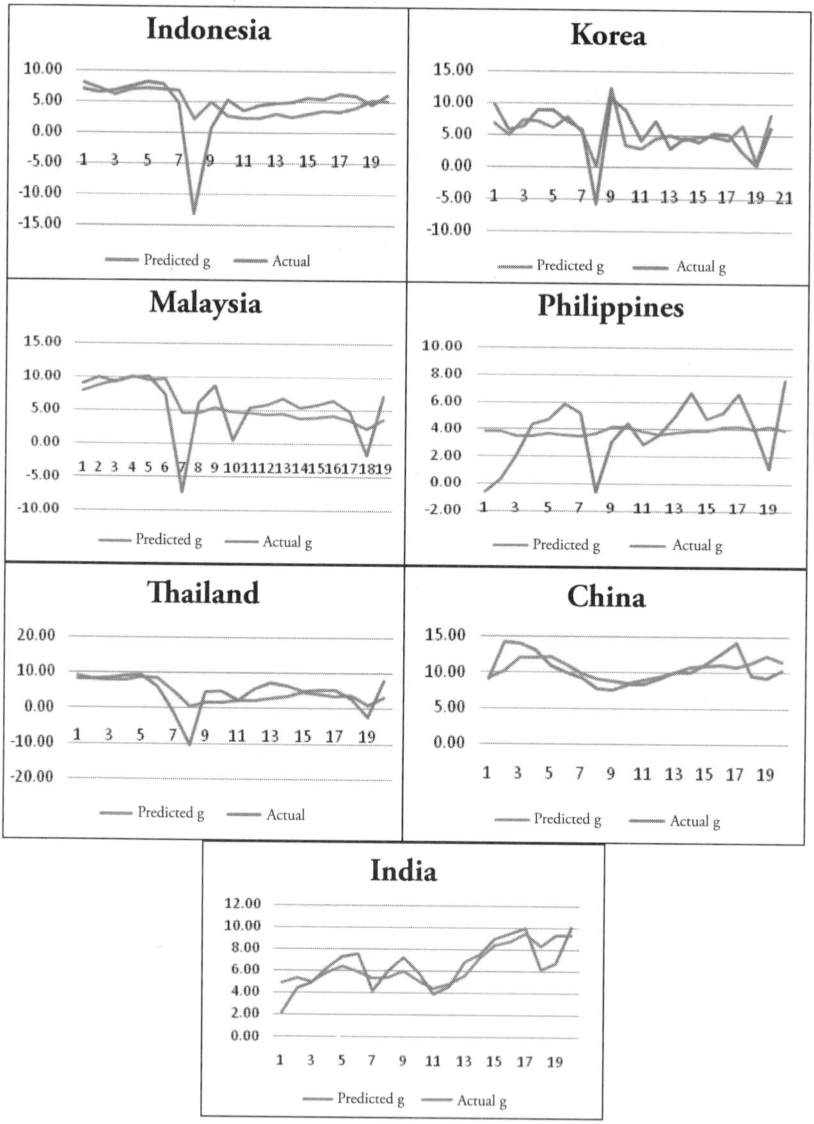

Source: WEO data and author's computations.

rates on the investment ratios. The results indicate significant correlations between the two variables, with the exception of Philippines. For most of the sample countries, the coefficient relating the growth rate to the investment ratio is around 0.25, indicating an incremental capital-output ratio of around

4. However, the latter ratio for Korea is around 2, which suggests a highly efficient use of capital, while for China it is about 5, which could reflect the very large role played by infrastructural investment. Figure 9.3 shows that the fit of this simplified growth model appears to be quite good especially for Indonesia, Korea and India.

Investment clearly appears to be an important determinant of growth performance. A key question is why did investment ratios fall so much for the crisis-affected countries, but not for China and India? As was noted above, a major difference between the two groups is that the latter applied capital controls to greatly restrain footloose portfolio capital inflows, while allowing the more enduring FDI. This enabled China and India to escape the pronounced capital outflows that afflicted the others, with the consequence that there was less pressure on their exchange rates. Balance sheets of financial intermediaries and firms in these two countries were therefore much less impacted. Nor were the foreign-denominated components of government debt ratios subject to the ravages of extreme exchange rate depreciations, while in general there were no requirements for government bailing out financial institutions. Furthermore, with balance sheets relatively unscathed, there was less need for domestic savings to be diverted away from internal investment to meeting the externally imposed exigencies of having to service foreign debt in highly depreciated local currencies. On this score, the cash flow position of firms in China and India would be less constraining than in the crisis-affected countries. Financial intermediation in China and India continued to channel savings towards domestic investments, for which the demand was high. This has not been the experience of the Asian crisis-affected countries for several years after the crisis hit.

Judging from the long-term decline in growth rates it would appear that free flowing and highly volatile portfolio capital can inflict much higher costs in the form of a long-term decline in growth rates when capital flows out than standard cost-benefit evaluations of portfolio flows indicate. Capital flow proponents claim that the benefits of a free flow of portfolio capital to the recipient country are not just that it supplements inadequate savings but that it adds to local expertise in evaluating projects. It is also claimed that the unimpeded flow of portfolio capital brings in efficiency enhancing competition. Furthermore, it helps in the correct pricing of assets. However, opponents to unregulated free flow of portfolio capital argue that Asian economies already have high rates of saving and do not need supplementation, while the technical efficiency enhancing benefits are at best marginal. They pale in comparison to the potential costs from excessive overshooting of asset prices and enhanced volatility. They also regard as dubious claims that free capital flows promote correct asset pricing and, thus, the efficient global allocation of capital. This might be valid under ideal textbook conditions, but the real world is characterized by information asymmetries, differing perceptions of risk and uncertainty, diverse strategic behaviours to promote various interests, speculative gain motives and not least several impediments to smooth functioning of markets across borders. The very fact of rapid capital flow reversal, which is often underpinned by emotion, can undermine domestic asset prices to such an extent as to negate the value of the claimed asset pricing function.

In sum, it would appear that the benefits from the free flow of portfolio capital are likely to be far greater for the financial sector itself, and, in particular, for hedge funds that thrive on volatility than for the real sector. However, it is the latter that is of greater interest and concern to the recipient country.

Balance-of-Payment Problems and their Resolution under the Current Global Mechanism

The core objective of the CMIM is to assist its members to address balance-of-payment problems and to mediate short-term liquidity difficulties. This section reviews a range of balance of payments problems that can arise as a backdrop to the subsequent discussion.

Traditional Setting

A balance of payments problem is encountered when a country becomes unable to meet its foreign exchange payment obligations.[13] Traditionally, the problems involved flows such as domestic overspending, adverse shocks to foreign exchange earnings or higher external debt service costs. Since not being able to meet foreign exchange payment obligations can impose high costs both for the economy and the wider international community, much attention has been directed to developing institutions and policies to contain these costs. However, the issues involved are complicated and the history of efforts to address them show mixed results.

At one extreme, a country could adopt autarkic methods for dealing with a balance-of-payments problem through exchange rate manipulation and controls on trade and capital flows. However, these self-serving policies inflict beggar-thy-neighbour effects on other countries, which can lead to retaliatory responses as was observed during the turmoil of the inter-war period. A good deal has been done in the post-war period to develop institutions such as Bretton Woods to restrain autarkic self-serving policies, to coordinate movements in exchange rates and establish rules to govern the conduct and interactions of its members. However, the collapse of the Bretton Woods mandate on exchange rates in 1971 led to a greatly watered down system in which countries are free to choose their exchange rate system, which could vary from a pure float to a fixed rate that is pegged to another currency or basket, the main stipulation being that once an exchange rate regime was selected the country would stick to it. This opened the possibility of countries manipulating their exchange rates for their own advantage, but it was believed that surveillance by the IMF and peer pressure from other countries would contain the problem.

The initial expectation after the collapse of the Bretton Woods exchange rate system was that floating exchange rates and the pursuit of appropriate macroeconomic policies would ensure exchange rate convergence. It was also expected that the IMF would exercise firm surveillance, which would prevent countries from taking undue advantage of the more flexible exchange rate environment. However, these expectations have not been met. Exchange rates between the major currencies have gyrated wildly, sometimes involving excessive depreciation and at other times an excessive appreciation. Since the major currencies appear to be floating relatively unimpeded *vis-à-vis* each other, the observed gyrations can represent the effects of several different factors such as current account imbalances and portfolio shifts, rather than sheer manipulation. Nonetheless, these exchange rate movements pose a dilemma for many countries even if they choose to peg to one of the major currencies, or a basket of such currencies, as fluctuations in cross-rates can exert whipsaw effects. This was observed during the Asian crisis when the depreciation of the yen relative to the dollar created cross-effect difficulties for those Asian countries which were pegged to the dollar.

Many countries, experiencing difficulties in this much more complex and less rule-based environment, yearn for a more stable exchange rate environment in which to promote their development objectives. They have attempted to attain this through various forms of interventions, but with mixed success and often subjected to accusations that they were manipulating their exchange rates to gain an unfair trade advantage.[14]

Although the strict exchange rate discipline of the Bretton Woods system was abandoned, an important feature of that system that was retained was the balance of payments adjustment support mechanism. The IMF provides temporary balance-of-payment financing through various facilities that have evolved over time so as to give the country some breathing room to apply adjustment methods that are internationally more palatable.

In the traditional world dominated by flows the core strategy for restoring external balance is to curb domestic overspending, irrespective of its origin or composition. This would usually be through reducing the domestic rate of credit creation and, in particular, its financing of any fiscal deficit, which would also be cut back.[15] As a *quid pro quo*, the country would be required to further liberalize its external trade and related foreign exchange payments.

Onset of Liberalized Foreign Exchange Markets: First- and Second-generation Currency Crises

The IMF, through the programmes it supported and the required Article IV consultations, was successful in promoting its mandate of liberalizing the international payments process. Countries were urged to attain Article VIII status, which involves the complete removal of current account payment restrictions. This paves the way for broader foreign exchange markets in which transactors could take positions and engage in speculative trades.

However, broader and more active foreign exchange markets unleash new destabilizing forces. Whereas in the traditional Bretton Woods approach an adjustment of the fixed peg would be countenanced only if it reflected a 'fundamental disequilibrium', pressures from the foreign exchange market could undermine that principle. They could lead to a currency crisis well before the country exhausted its international reserves and before a fundamental disequilibrium became entrenched. Krugman (1979) and other economists formulated so-called first-generation currency crisis models to demonstrate that a country running a fiscal deficit and losing foreign exchange reserves did not have the luxury of waiting until its reserves were nearly exhausted to take remedial actions, unlike with the traditional and much more restrictive forex setup. Forward-looking transactors in the forex markets could anticipate the likelihood of eventual devaluation, and when international reserves crossed some belief-based threshold level they would head for the exits, which would precipitate a collapse of the peg. Allowing speculators to engage in short sales of the country's currency further accelerates this dynamic.

Speculators could borrow the local currency, and sell it short for foreign exchange in the hope of buying the local currency later at a more depreciated rate. The greater the short sales the greater the pressure on the spot market, and the bigger the decline in the central bank's foreign exchange reserves, should it intervene to stave off the depreciation pressure. Greater the pressure, sooner too would the speculator be able to reap profits from the forced depreciation of the exchange rate. The speculator takes some risk but often when dealing with rigid exchange rates the speculation acquires the character of a one-way-bet, especially if speculators command sizable resources or can trigger bandwagon effects so that others join in the speculation.

Subsequent developments showed that even if the poor fundamentals such as an excessive fiscal deficit of the first generation of currency crisis models are not present, a currency crisis could still be triggered, provided there are indications of policy inconsistency. This led to the so-called second generation of currency crisis models (Obstfeld, 1994). All that is needed are beliefs that the central bank would not be willing or able to maintain its exchange rate commitment. For example, speculators might believe, with good reason, that when confronted with the choice of preserving an exchange rate level requiring tight monetary policies, and stimulating the domestic economy in the face of recession and rising unemployment through looser policies, political considerations might induce them to choose the latter.[16]

Free Capital Mobility and Third-generation Currency Crisis Problems

As domestic financial and credit markets were further liberalized, a new source of volatility and pressure on exchange rates was added. Beginning in the early 1990s, there was growing impetus to liberalize domestic financial markets and to integrate them with international markets by allowing cross-border capital flows.[17] This created the conditions for the so-called 'third generation' variety of currency crisis (Krugman, 1999). The distinguishing feature here is that it involves cross-border effects on balance sheets of both financial intermediaries and of their customers, which were formerly insulated from international influences. This increases the potential for financial disorders, since it could now originate from abroad. Furthermore, since it involves balance sheets and transactions in stocks that dwarf flows, the damage on the real sector could well exceed that inflicted by the other categories of balance-of-payment problems so far reviewed.

On opening up the financial sector, local banks will attract foreign funding, especially if they offer higher rates of interest. Local firms may also find it attractive to borrow abroad at lower interest rates than those charged locally. Unlike traditional foreign direct investments, which often involve taking an equity position in domestic firms, financial liberalization enables domestic entities to acquire greater leverage through foreign borrowing. Foreign funds, which for tax and regulatory reasons are typically registered in offshore havens, are also free to operate in the local stock exchanges. Not surprisingly, the flow of such foreign lending is greatly stimulated if exchange rate guarantees are provided, even if only implicit, and especially if domestic entities assume any exchange rate risk. The greater foreign exposure of the domestic financial sector that ensues, raises the possibility of a local financial and currency crisis, which could be triggered either by foreign financial developments or domestic events. Depending on the extent of their unhedged leveraging in foreign currency denominated instruments there could be severe balance sheet effects on local entities. As a result, the entities would be forced to liquidate their assets and deleverage, with possibly long-lasting adverse effects on their future investment outlays, as was observed in the previous section for the Asian crisis countries.

To bring out some of the key issues, consider the following simplified balance sheet for a financial intermediary (FI) operating in a deregulated and internationally liberalized setting:

Table 9.7: Balance Sheet: Financial Intermediary (FI)
(Local currency equivalent, end of period)

Assets	Liabilities
Loans to private residents	Deposits
	Residents
Loans to government	Non-residents
	Funds
Loans to non-residents	Local
Banks	Non-residents
Funds	Other banks
	Local
	Non-residents
Reserves with Central Bank	Net worth/equity

The potential problems that the FI faces can occur on both sides of its balance sheet, and many scenarios are possible. For example, loans to firms, especially after a period of buoyant leveraged lending could constitute a serious problem, if the firms suffer an adverse blow to their cash flow. Indeed, some analysts regarded problem loans to domestic firms as the main trigger for the Asian currency crisis. According to this view poor quality, low return investments had been encouraged in an environment of 'crony capitalism', with a lack of due diligence on the part of financial intermediaries, if not their active connivance.[18] Many of these firms contracted unhedged foreign currency liabilities. Foreign creditors, fearing that these firms lacked the ability to service their loans, attempted to call in the loans and stop roll-overs. Local FIs were reluctant to act as replacement sources of finance. The failure of firms to renew their financing compounds their inability to adequately service their borrowings, forcing them to engage in distress sales of their assets. As more and more firms sell, the market conditions begin to resemble those at a fire sale. With the sales proceeds increasingly inadequate to cover their liabilities, firms would be forced into insolvency. At the same time, regulatory requirements to maintain adequate capital reserves would force the FI's to call in loans to other, perhaps healthier firms, thereby, forcing additional fire sales, if they are unable to raise funds elsewhere.

In turn, a big rise in non-performing loans (NPL) in the FI's portfolio, together with inadequate loss provisioning, raises concerns about the safety of deposits and loans on the liability side of the FI's balance sheet. Foreign creditors, for example, non-resident banks engaged in inter-bank lending, would be concerned about the safety of their funds and might choose not to renew their loans. Leverage now works in reverse for the local FI, which would have to call in some more loans. But this could prove difficult and further add to its stock of NPLs. A lack of access to funding impairs the viability of the FI as a solvent institution. Thus, what may have started out as a cash-flow problem for a number of firms ends up as a full-fledged banking crisis.

The authorities might try to stem the loss of funding to the banks and act as lenders of the last resort. In a financially closed economy, the local central bank should be able to stem the banking crisis. However, in an open financial setting the central bank's provision of funds may be dissipated if the FIs have significant foreign loans and are required to pay off foreign creditors. This puts pressure on the central bank's foreign exchange resources and erodes its ability to prevent the exchange rate from depreciating. Yet it is the latter that is of importance in stabilizing balance sheets containing foreign linkages.

Growing recognition of the problems being encountered by the central bank could lead to an even bigger outflow of funds from the banks, including those normally held by residents who now try to hedge against exchange rate depreciation or the possibility of capital controls. The process is further aggravated by hedge funds short selling the local currency. As reserves become depleted, the central bank's ability to act as lender of the last resort diminishes, ultimately forcing a capitulation. The ensuing currency crisis forces the floating of the exchange rate. Alternatively, or in tandem, the country could choose to default and also apply controls on outward capital flows.

This stylized asset and liability table of the FI indicates other possible scenarios with different initial triggers. However, the precise nature of the trigger may be less important if successive components of the balance sheet can feed off each other and some of these happen to be weak. It is, thus, relatively easy to generate the conditions for an extended banking and currency crisis, as transactors seek to protect their holdings through deposit withdrawals and capital outflows.[19]

Approaches to Resolving Balance-of-payments Crises

Broadly, and following the order of the discussion in the last section, corrective policies may be summarized as follows. In the traditional Bretton Woods set-up, the adjustment strategy would focus on determining the sustainable level of domestic expenditures, especially that of government. Account would be taken of various considerations including such matters as the structure and productivity of taxation, the debt profile and essential expenditures. An appropriate strategy would be formulated for reducing unsustainable expenditures in a phased manner. If the exchange rate indicated a fundamental disequilibrium, which usually meant that it was grossly overvalued and a disincentive for exports, this too would be adjusted. The IMF would provide the funds needed to smooth the adjustment, while having in place a credible IMF programme was usually expected to exert a catalytic effect, unlocking additional financing for the balance-of-payments and for investment. Sooner or later, depending on the programme details and their implementation, growth would resume.

However, with the onset of forex liberalization and the greater scope for foreign exchange speculation, balance-of-payment problems initially acquired characteristics generally associated with the first- and second-generation currency crisis models. It became more important now to exercise appropriate regulation to restrain unnecessary and potentially destabilizing speculation, but this may not always be possible. Speculative forces may be so strong that they may force the de-pegging of the exchange rate even if its level is judged appropriate for trade flows. This would be the case if the speculation is being driven by poor fundamentals such as excessive and unsustainable domestic spending, for which the traditional solution would be to cut expenditures but not necessarily to depreciate the exchange rate. The appropriate adjustment strategy in these new circumstances would need to include measures that would curb or otherwise offset destabilizing speculation. One of the latter measures could be to float the exchange rate temporarily. A potential problem is that portfolio transactions may force an excessive depreciation of the exchange rate, while any attempt at restoring a level better aligned to balancing trade flows triggers another bout of destabilizing speculation. Preventing excessive depreciation and ensuring that the new level prevails will require countervailing actions such as deploying quick disbursing international funds that are drawn from reserves or immediate access to international sources, so as to offset speculative activity. In principle, considerably larger access to international liquidity is needed than for traditional, flow-related balance-of-payment problems.

However, if available international financial resources are inadequate, it could be advisable to introduce controls on foreign exchange speculation, including curbing access to local credit sources, rather than rely wholly on potentially debilitating big increases in real interest rates. Ideally, measures addressing problems with fundamentals on the side of flows and interventions in the foreign exchange and credit markets to deal with stock side issues should be undertaken early. Just as speculators in the first- and second-generation currency crisis models act on anticipations and bring forward the crisis, the authorities need to act on anticipations of such destabilizing speculation so as to delay the onset of a crisis. This may be difficult, since there is likely to be a great deal of political and commercial resistance both from domestic and external sources, who may regard anticipatory actions as premature. This is likely to be especially the case if trading partners are undergoing conflicting exchange rate movements.

The room for manoeuvre is further reduced when domestic financial markets have been opened up and integrated with foreign markets, generating the third kind of currency crisis. On the one hand, domestic monetary policy looses traction, since transactors can bypass its effects by contracting abroad. A bigger dose of domestic monetary policy has to be applied than in the less integrated market setting if it is to have an effect. On the other hand, open financial markets give greater scope to destabilizing speculative activities and in markets additional to the foreign exchange one.

The ease with which bank deposits and portfolio investments can leave the country puts added pressure on the country's international reserves, making it much more difficult to defend a peg even if the fundamentals are sound. It is often thought, and indeed counselled, that in these circumstances the country has no other choice but to implement a draconian monetary policy with exceptionally high interest rates, float the exchange rate, and to tighten fiscal policy further. Such policies can exert excessive contractionary effects on the economy as was witnessed during the Asian currency crisis.

As a general rule, given the extent to which portfolio stock and foreign exchange movements have become dominant, the focus should be on addressing the stock-side implications of rapid portfolio movements, since these can dwarf the deterioration on the flow-side.[20] To prevent an excessive overshooting of the currency associated with a capital outflow and restrain adverse effects on balance sheets, some monetary tightening will be required. But as noted earlier this is a two-edged weapon, since it will compound the effects of local liquidity shortage that the capital outflow engenders. To break the impasse, the two measures noted above in connection with the first- and second-generation crisis models could also be applied but more intensively. The first requires international cooperation and takes the form of rapid and decisive international financial support, which could be made available both through international institutions such as the IMF and in the form of swap lines with major central banks. The second measure could be undertaken immediately at the discretion of the affected country and involve the introduction or intensification of capital controls. It could be viewed as the stock-side counterpart of the traditional use of financing and trade restrictions to protect the current account flows of the balance of payments.[21]

Relying on the Global Mechanism

In general, as suggested in the preceding review, a country's balance-of-payments problems are the outcome of shocks that are specific to the country such as terms of trade and capital flight to which are added more general shocks such as those that emanate from the working of the international monetary system and its impact on international liquidity. Hence, the nature of the balance-of-payments problem that a country may encounter and its resolution will depend in part on the international monetary system in place.

The Bretton Woods system was based on countries operating fixed but adjustable exchange rate pegs with reference to the dollar. The performance of the US balance of payments was therefore critical to the supply of international liquidity. As long as restrictions were maintained on capital market transactions, the general shocks emanating from US domestic monetary and fiscal policies were felt through the current accounts of the balance of payments. In such a set-up, balance-of-payments problems were largely associated with excessive domestic expenditures, external trade shocks and/or misaligned exchange rates. The amount of financing needed to promote satisfactory adjustment is limited and determined by such issues as the extent and phasing of the excess expenditure adjustment and the amount of time it takes to reorient production to exports.

However, with freely floating exchange rates between the major currencies, the adjustment requirements for other countries can be more daunting, and even more so if some happen to be pegging. As markets, and especially foreign exchange and other financial markets, become more globalized the potential and intensity of balance-of-payments problems increases sharply. There is now added a potentially dominant stock dimension to the traditional problems that largely concerned flows and the need for financing is potentially much greater. The failure of the global mechanism to provide the needed liquidity with which to fend off destabilizing speculative behaviour, while counselling against the introduction of capital controls, is contradictory and does not lead to viable solutions.[22] Placing the onus of adjustment entirely on the affected country, while letting speculators make off with their gains, is unlikely to be a sustainable strategy.

The CMIM and its Potential

This section considers how the CMIM can be made to function in a manner that promotes the interests of its members, as well as, regional and global interests.

Two Alternative Views following the Asian Crisis

To obtain some insight on the roles that the CMIM could play it is useful to begin with two leading views as to the causes and remedies of the Asian currency and financial crisis. The first, referred to here as the US treasury/IMF view, is that structural deficiencies, together with weak surveillance and regulatory capabilities in the Asian countries precipitated the crisis.[23] Solutions that are consistent with this viewpoint tend to emphasize reforms such as greater financial market liberalization, the avoidance of any recourse to capital controls, strengthened oversight, improved prudential regulation and market-friendly macro management.[24] From this vantage point the role of the CMIM would be the more modest one of supporting and furthering these reforms, while working closely in tandem with the IMF. Some reserve pooling through the CMIM might be useful but again only as an addendum to the financial assistance channelled through the IMF.

The alternative view is more radical. It places blame squarely on global finance in search of quick yielding higher returns as the major factor that destabilized the Asian economies. According to this view, pressure from the main international financial centres, their governments, and the IMF, persuaded Asian countries to prematurely open up their domestic financial markets to global finance. Perceiving quick-yielding profit opportunities led international banks, hedge funds, mutual funds and others to engage in a massive inward liquidity flow. The authorities were ill equipped both to cope with this capital inflow and to restrain the ensuing domestic boom and the subsequent sudden capital outflow when the boom petered out.[25] Proponents of this view, while accepting the need to improve domestic regulatory capabilities, argue that the more globalized the economy the more limited is likely to be the contribution of domestic regulation, however well designed and implemented. Accordingly, more weight should be placed on supranational and global mechanisms so as to ensure that global finance acts more beneficially. This will require several measures to supplement domestic ones, ranging from introducing international disincentives to rapid capital movements to the provision of sufficient international liquidity. In particular, an adequate international lender-of -last resort function is needed to supplement domestic lender-of–last-resort functions that are rendered increasingly ineffective as the economy becomes more open. The required supranational control mechanisms could include or even rely on regional initiatives such as the CMI.

The two sets of explanations appear to agree in one respect. Had internal financial markets been better regulated, excessive capital flows could have been dampened. Drawing on both sets of explanations, the potential roles for the CMIM would be more encompassing. They would include those of enhancing domestic regulatory capabilities, promoting suitable structural reforms, improving surveillance, encouraging the adoption of timely and appropriate stabilization and adjustment policies and providing needed liquidity, while functioning as a supportive but critical watchdog of the global mechanisms.[26]

Limited Use of the CMIM to Date

The CMIM has yet to be tested. To date, there have been no drawings from the CMIM. When Korea experienced a capital flow crisis in 2009, it was the US Federal Reserve that offered a US$30 billion swap to the Korean authorities, which did not draw on the CMIM. For it to function successfully as a regional reserve pooling arrangement that helps its members cope with balance of payments shocks, several criteria will have to be observed. The arrangement should have sufficient funds but the CMIM appears to fall short in this regard. It should have a functioning surveillance capacity that enables it to monitor, closely, developments affecting its members, both individually and regionally, but this is embryonic. While responding to the aid of a member, it should have the technical expertise to design and monitor adjustment programmes, which remains to be developed. It should have sufficient authority and legitimacy to be the first recourse of its members when in difficulty, but as noted here this was upstaged by the US Federal Reserve and their swap arrangement with Korea. A further indication of its limited authority is that its members have assigned only a small part of their substantial international reserves to the CMIM. Although one of its core objectives is to supplement international financial agencies, the formulation of coordination mechanisms with them, and especially the IMF, appears nascent. Nor has it played a role in the international deliberations concerning the resolution of global imbalances involving several of its members, and in particular China. Perhaps, the most important requirement is to have a clear understanding of the types of balance-of-payment problems that its members may encounter, and the objectives it wishes to serve in addressing them.

As long as its members continue to have very large international reserves, and the region is in reasonably good shape, the CMIM is unlikely to be tested. It could be contended that only when the occasion arises for it to be tested will its current limitations become manifest. Steps would presumably be taken then to address them, with the easiest probably being that of increasing the size of its fund. Until such time the CMIM would likely function as a relatively low-powered institution. However, this underestimates the importance of the CMIM and its future potential.

A More Significant Potential Role

A potentially important use of the CMIM would be as a model of governance, which aside from fulfilling the needs of its members could provide guidelines for the reform of IMF's governance. For example, if the CMIM's reliance on majority voting, with no member having a veto, is found to be satisfactory this could be a pointer to the IMF. Another aspect concerns the relationship between contributions and possible drawings, with the largest contributions giving a proportionately smaller draw, unlike at the IMF, where voting rights are basically in accordance with established economic power. This gives effect to the underlying motivation of having a reserve pooling institution that would be of particular benefit to smaller members. These do not have the financial and economic resources of the bigger and stronger members with which to handle the exigencies of opening up. Such an arrangement would be more 'democratic' and caring of the weaker and poorer members. It would also be a concrete expression of leadership exercised by the larger, more powerful members.

The CMIM could be useful in developing forms and modalities of surveillance that would help identify serious threats before they materialize. Standard IMF methods may not be the most appropriate in the Asian context. For instance, it is conceivable that better results could be obtained if low-key, non-intrusive 'Asian Way' characteristics were taken into account. The IMF's approach tends to emphasize 'objective indicators' both to warn of impending crises and to monitor progress in adjusting. Much of the policy dialogue between the IMF staff and the authorities focuses on what the objective indicators reveal. But the objective indicators can be misleading and may even misdirect attention away from the true underlying problems. The IMF's experience with surveillance has not been felicitous – for example, it failed to warn of impending Mexican crises, or the duration and seriousness of the Asian currency crisis or even the sub-prime crisis in the US despite being based there.

Properly designed objective indicators have an important role to play but in the Asian context they especially should be supplemented with a broader-ranging dialogue and enquiry. To enhance the quality of the surveillance, it would also be advisable to give consideration to adapting the conceptual framework underlying the IMF's surveillance work to better suit Asian conditions. The IMF's conceptual framework reflects the dominant views of its major shareholders and puts much stress on neoclassical modes of organization and their reliance on market forces. Thus, the counterfactual and default setting for the IMF would be a situation without market interferences, and surveillance is directed to monitoring the extent of deviation from the default setting. However, many Asian countries have a more paternalistic approach, which provides the default setting, and surveillance here would monitor deviations from the latter.

Efficient surveillance should establish causes of the balance-of-payment problems being encountered by members which, in turn, will help determine the appropriate remedies to apply. For example, in the case of a sudden outflow of capital, surveillance should determine whether this indicates some deeper underlying structural or policy problems that require addressing, or whether it is simply the result of exchange rate and interest rate developments elsewhere in the world that triggered an arbitraging outflow. It would be inappropriate to use the 'opportunity' of crisis conditions to press for reforms that have no direct bearing to the genesis of the problem, as was done during the Asian crisis. The CMIM could help guard against the preceding type of temptations on the part of interested parties who may superficially express a desire for reform to help the affected countries, but are really interested in the opportunities that may be created for promoting their own commercial and financial interests. The Asian experience with the Asian crisis reform initiatives, in particular the scope provided for foreign funds to profit from the induced volatilities in exchange rates and interest rates and also the foreign acquisition of local banks and other entities at fire sale prices, has led to considerable cynicism about the true motives of the international financial community and core institutions.

IMF and the CMI Initiative

IMF's Role during the 1997–98 Crisis

Many observers contend that the IMF was ineffective in its surveillance prior to the crisis; deficient in its pre-crisis policy advice and inept in dealing with the crisis when it broke.[27] The IMF and its G7 core had strongly pressed for capital market liberalization in the years leading up to the crisis. However, they did not adequately warn of the potential dangers or of the regulatory and other steps that need to be taken in order to prevent a crisis from breaking out. Furthermore, when the crisis did break out, they did not have in place adequate and quick disbursing international liquidity support mechanisms to help douse the flames. Instead, they misread the nature of the crisis and recommended erroneous policies and proposed cumbersome and onerous financing facilities. These are serious charges that challenge the competence of the global mechanisms.

As noted earlier the countries undergoing IMF-supported programmes performed relatively poorly.[28] They were required to apply policy instruments of restraint as if they were experiencing a traditional balance-of-payments crisis of the type associated with overspending and excessive fiscal deficits. Even though their fiscal situations were generally in surplus when the crisis hit in the latter half of 1997, the countries were required to engage in fiscal retrenchment. However, despite enacting additional revenue measures and cutting expenditures, the erosion in real GDP growth rates was so severe that revenues fell, with the result that the fiscal situation of the affected countries worsened significantly (Table 9.2). As shown in this table, the external debt levels of the affected governments were also generally satisfactory before the crisis. Nonetheless, and despite the subsequent relatively small fiscal deficits, there was a much bigger increase in external debt levels as a per cent of GDP. This was largely a result of exchange rate adjustments and the requirements of financial sector re-capitalization. It was especially severe for Indonesia.

The IMF-supported programmes that were put in place did not insulate the affected countries from exchange rates overshooting by wide margins or domestic asset values from undershooting (Figure 9.4). The overshooting of the exchange rate had devastating effects on balance sheets, since a substantial part of liabilities were denominated in foreign currency, the local values of which increased sharply. At the same time the tighter monetary policy, the much higher interest rates and the general drying up of liquidity badly eroded cash flows and led to forced 'fire sales' of assets. The consequence was a much lower valuation of the asset side of balance sheets. Thus, a situation that was initially perceived to be a liquidity crisis, initiated by deposit withdrawals from local banks, quickly turned into a solvency issue and the net worths of many banks and firms were wiped out. The rapidity with which this transformation occurred was the result of the high leverage that characterized the balance sheets of many firms. Banks, which were already experiencing grave liquidity problems, now had to contend with a cascade of non-performing loans and effectively ceased lending. These developments had serious effects on the real economy: investment collapsed, private consumption declined steeply while the fiscal sector became contractionary as taxes were raised and government expenditures slashed. Not surprisingly, the affected economies experienced huge GDP contractions, which were comparable to those during the Great Depression.

Figure 9.4: Exchange Rates per US Dollar, 1992–2010: Period Averages

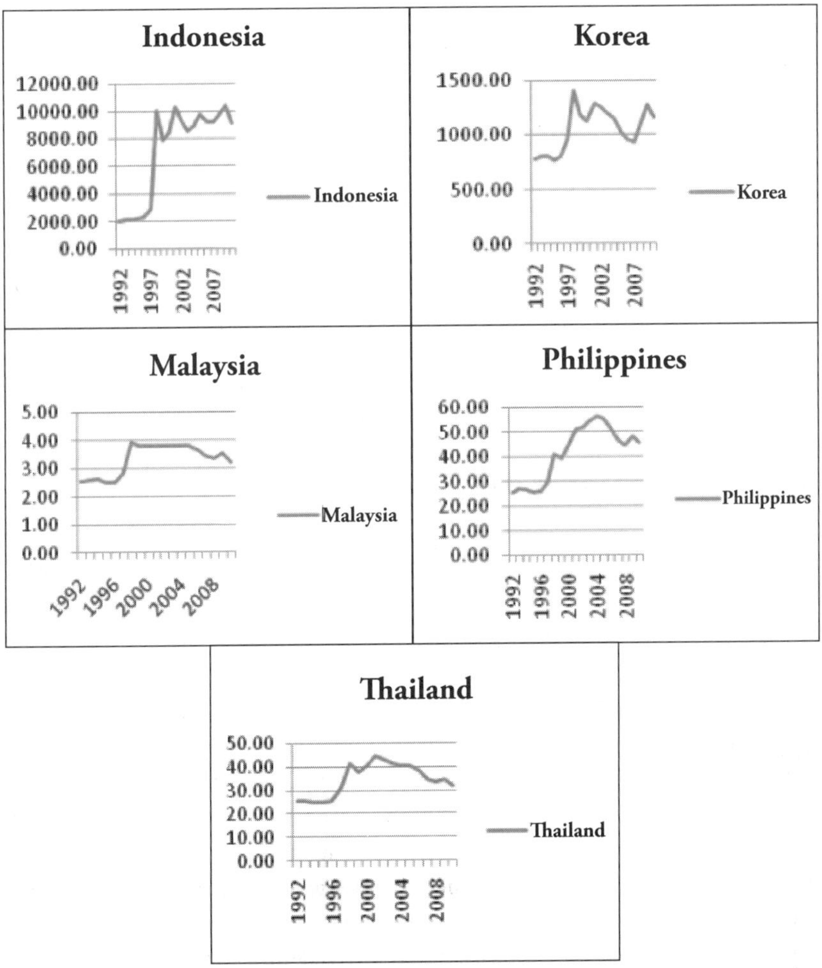

Source: International Monetary Fund, IFS

The devastating effects of the crisis on balance sheets and the deterioration in cash flows were so severe that they needed to be recapitalized. During this process of enforced increased saving, outlays such as investment would inevitably suffer resulting in an increase in the current account of the balance of payments (Figure 9.5). Greater credit allocations could have provided some relief, but local financial institutions, having become seriously compromised with regard to their own cash flows and balance sheets, instead reduced their lending exposure. Owing to the severity of the crisis this period of enforced increase in net saving became a long-drawn-out process, which would help

Figure 9.5: Selected Asian Countries: Current Account of Balance of Payments

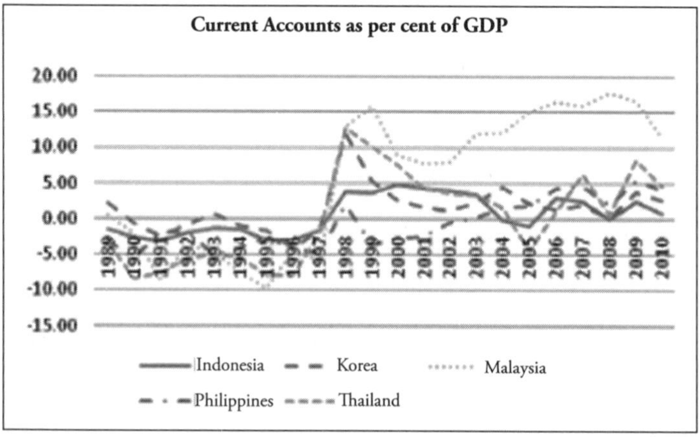

Source: International Monetary Fund, World Economic Outlook, September 2011 and author's calculations

explain the observed long-term declines in investment ratios. Contributory factors to the latter would also be the lower rates of return obtainable on capital in a situation of acute recession in the face of higher rates of return needed to service loan finance.

An alternative solution would have been to rely on capital controls to impede overshooting of exchange rates. However, both the US treasury and the IMF were resolutely opposed to introducing or intensifying capital controls and, while cautious in their comments on China and India, heavily criticized Malaysia for doing so. They argued that maintaining and improving the efficiency of capital markets and allowing unimpeded movement of portfolio finance was part of the solution to the crisis and not the cause. The latter they attributed to crony capitalism that thrived in an inadequate domestic regulatory environment and to weak macroeconomic policies. Furthermore, they argued that capital controls were in any case unworkable, and that transactors would find ways of circumventing them. Instead they advocated a market-friendly approach of floating exchange rates, further liberalization of goods and financial markets and policy reliance on higher interest rates and monetary tightening and fiscal retrenchment.

In the aftermath of the crisis the US treasury and the IMF, fearing loss of influence, responded to the Asian post-crisis initiatives with overtures rather than the antagonisms they had exhibited during the Asian financial crisis. They have put forward several arguments, such as, self-insurance is inefficient and costly and if that the countries relied more on the IMF they could do with fewer costly reserves which would be to their advantage. They have also claimed that the IMF has learnt its lessons and that it would improve its surveillance while working to ensure that programmes are relevant and better tailored to the circumstances of countries. Furthermore, the IMF would become more responsive to regional concerns and improve its own governance to give a greater voice to emerging economies whose voting shares would be increased.

The IMF has taken several steps towards fulfilling its pledges. It has adjusted its surveillance procedures, for example, introducing regional surveillance in addition to country surveillance and streamlined its Article IV consultation reports. It has proposed new facilities with enhanced and more automatic drawings and modified the conditionality that it applies, which is now more tightly focussed on key macroeconomic variables. Some of these developments are being operationalized in the recent programmes with countries in Europe, which also serves as an evolving blueprint of cooperation between the IMF and regional agencies such as the EU. The IMF now welcomes regional fund initiatives such as the CMIM, provided they maintain links with the IMF. In particular, the IMF and its G7 core contend that the regional funds should take their cues from the IMF, and they should view themselves as complementary to the IMF rather than as alternatives. One argument that is generally presented for continued linkages is that the IMF can exercise superior surveillance because of its greater reservoir of expertise. The IMF also claims that it is better able to impose rigorous conditionality than regional funds which may be more reluctant because of their closer relationship with countries in their region.

However, the steps taken so far, while significant, do not go far enough. Emerging economies continue to be under-represented both on the Board and among the staff. The US retains sole veto power; small European countries still exercise disproportionately large votes and quota sizes; the managing director's selection continues to be restricted to a European; the staffing of the organization, especially at its senior levels, continues to reflect a predominantly western bias and the conceptual underpinnings remain heavily market oriented with a heavy emphasis on open financial markets, notwithstanding a grudging acceptance of temporary capital controls.

Some Issues of Political Economy

Asian views about the future of the CMIM have yet to fully coalesce. This is partly because of a perceived need to tread carefully vis-a-vis the US and the IMF based on historical experience, but also because of likely underlying tensions between its two principal members, China and Japan. The two appear to have different visions of the functions of the CMIM. Japan seems to have abandoned the earlier notion of an AMF as an alternative to the IMF and its goal of exercising financial hegemony through such an institution.[29] Between 1997, when that prospect held greatest promise, and the present, China has quadrupled its GDP, which is now bigger than that of Japan's and accumulated vastly larger reserves. In the context of the growing regional and indeed global dominance of China, Japan seems to have responded by placing more emphasis on its G7 credentials and interests and essentially to follow the lead of the US. This would lead to a view that downplays the role of the CMIM, for example, treating it as a limited reserve pooling arrangement that brings a regional dimension to matters such as the members' exchange rate levels, which are of concern to Japan, in light of its extensive trade links with the region. As for promoting balance-of-payments adjustment in the region, it would appear that Japan's preference would be for the CMIM to work in close conformity with the IMF. An example of the latter model of cooperation would be the collaboration between the IMF, the ECB and the EU, in formulating adjustment programmes for European countries experiencing payments difficulties and with the IMF playing the key role.

China's Strategic Interests and the CMIM

China's strategic interests appear quite different from those that may plausibly be attributed to Japan. Although there is no overt rift between the two in the CMIM, in which both are equal partners, it can be expected that over time their differing strategic interests will lead to more open dissension regarding the direction and role of the CMIM. China has voiced several concerns, and in casting around for ways to address them it is likely that China would look upon the CMIM as a potential instrument. At the most fundamental level, China challenges the present structure of the international monetary system and its dependence on the dollar, while Japan appears more accepting of the *status quo*. China's concern is that the present system has led to highly volatile swings in exchange rates as exemplified, for example, by the dollar–euro exchange rates or the dollar-yen rates, and that these fluctuations are injurious to trade and investment. Since these exchange rate gyrations result from the global dependence on the dollar and its subjection to contradictory domestic US considerations and global requirements, China has floated the proposal of a world fiat currency that would be globally administered, and with seigniorage shared equitably among the members (Zhou, 2009). Such proposals have been strongly resisted in the past by the US, which stands to lose greatly. Replacing the dollar would only be feasible if the US agrees, which it is unlikely to do for the foreseeable future. The main recourse that is left to countries seeking currency stability, other than pegging to the dollar and being subject to volatile cross-rates, is to set up currency blocs. The Europeans selected this option when they established the European Monetary Union (EMU) and the subsequent Eurozone, indicating a potential direction for the CMIM.

However, the Chinese would appear to want to go beyond the EU model of cooperation with the IMF. They are, for instance, critical of the governance of the IMF, which they regard as excessively subject to American and European control and its biased role in exercising surveillance and in promoting balance-of-payment adjustment. In contrast, Japan, which wields considerable influence at the IMF, appears more accepting of the present IMF framework and operations. China has several other concerns with the IMF. First, China does not accept that its role in the IMF corresponds to the size of its economy and pre-eminence in trade as the world's largest exporter, notwithstanding the recent revision of IMF voting rights in its favour that have partially addressed the matter. From China's perspective as long as the IMF is perceived as being over-represented by European countries, while subject to US veto, it lacks legitimacy. Second, China regards itself as the natural hegemon of Asia and in particular of the ASEAN+3 grouping. China is the largest trading partner of the region and is rapidly emerging as the dominant external influence. Hence it is natural for China to believe that it should have a decisive voice in matters pertaining to the region. But this raises potential conflicts not only with Japan but also with the US, which has major geopolitical interests in the region and has taken several initiatives to bolster them, such as setting up Asia-Pacific Economic Cooperation (APEC). Third, China is dubious about the quality and objectivity of the surveillance that the IMF exercises and its ability to prevent crises from occurring.[30] Fourth, China harbours doubts about the appropriateness of IMF balance-of-payments adjustment strategies, as was exemplified for instance during the Asian crisis. The fear is that IMF programmes tend to be excessively deflationary with injurious effects on both the countries undergoing them and on trading partners, among whom China is the largest.

The CMIM provides China with a potential instrument to at least partially address the concerns raised above. Regarding currency instability, China may want to go beyond reserve pooling and move in the direction of a common currency area or at least an EMU-type arrangement of fixed exchange rates among members. This would promote stability in the region and pre-empt competitive depreciations of exchange rates. In a way, this was achieved when the other Asian countries were pegged to the dollar. However, Japan which by then had become their most or next most important trading partner was not pegged to the dollar, and the Asian crisis of 1997 was partly precipitated by the sharp depreciation of the yen relative to the dollar. This impacted adversely on the Asian countries' trade with Japan and followed an earlier boom that was associated with a sharp appreciation of the yen against the dollar.

China, the region's most important trading partner, has pre-empted a repeat of the earlier yen scenario since it essentially pegs its exchange rate to the dollar, while allowing for progressive appreciation. Nonetheless, some volatility remains vis-a-vis the euro and the yen, as seen from dollar's perspective, which could adversely affect their trade, investment and growth. The CMIM provides scope for further mitigating adverse exchange rate effects insofar as it is able to persuade Japan to join in a stable regional currency area. Given the gyrations that Japan has experienced as a result of its floating exchange rate it might be in its interest to work out an arrangement with China and other CMIM members for a broader regional zone of stability. Consideration would also have to be given to replacing the dollar as the anchor, one possibility being that of a currency composite that would include the renminbi and the yen. However, such collaboration for the present is problematic insofar as Japan, in keeping with the G7 viewpoint, strongly advocates the free floating of the renminbi, which China resists. In any event China is likely to proceed cautiously. China's preferred approach to reforms is to study the available options through lengthy deliberations and to undertake pilot projects so as to better ascertain benefits and risks. Once the net benefits have been determined and found to be in accord with the interests of the State, implementation is usually swift. This is likely to characterize its handling of the CMIM, which holds promise as a pilot project for the eventual reform of the international monetary system and its operational institutions.

India and the CMIM

From India's perspective and indeed that of the CMIM members, the ideal situation would be to have a well-functioning international monetary system. Such a system would be based on a set of rules and would function through well-governed and efficient, supporting institutions. It would ensure a stable and dynamic environment that promotes trade, capital investment and growth in an equitable manner. It would avoid excessive volatilities and overshooting of exchange rates, interest rates, stock exchanges and commodity exchanges. It would cope with the liquidity implications of aggregate shocks and promote satisfactory adjustments. In particular, it would avoid the inherent contradictions resulting from reliance on a single country's currency, whose issuance is a compromise between competing internal and external requirements. In such an environment and with an appropriately revamped IMF as custodian of the system, there would be no need for rival regional organizations. The latter, if needed, would operate as agents of the IMF, for example, in a manner similar to that of the regional Federal Reserve Boards in the US.

However, the present situation is a long way from that ideal and nor has the governance of the IMF accorded India an adequate role commensurate with its size and potential. It would therefore be prudent for India to hedge its bets and look upon the CMIM as a means for attaining its longer-term goal of an appropriately revamped IMF.

As was noted earlier, the CMI initiative has stimulated welcome changes at the IMF, which is an externality that India has enjoyed without being a member of CMIM. Free-riding remains an option for India. However, it might be more productive to join the CMIM, not so much because of the reserve pooling facilities which are as yet small compared to India's reserves, but to be in a position to influence its development both as a regional zone of stability and as an international reform instrument. In turn, by joining and being identified with the CMIM India could benefit from regional synergies in other areas such as trade and be awarded a greater role in institutions of global governance because of the support that it can draw upon in Asia.

However, India is likely to encounter some difficulty in joining the CMIM. At present CMIM is delicately poised between China and Japan. Their strategic visions for this institution appear to be at odds, with that of China as a rapidly growing developing country possibly more in tune with the rest of the membership. Memories of the Asian currency crisis debacle are still fresh in the minds of the smaller members, as is Japan's capitulation over the AMF proposal. The delicate balance between China and Japan could be disrupted if Asia's third largest economic power were to join. A question of major interest to the members would be whether India sides with China or Japan, and how India exercises this choice could well determine whether China's or Japan's strategic visions prevail in the CMIM. Membership could thus enable India to exercise the role of a tie-breaker, which it could use to tilt the CMIM in the direction of which one of the two's strategic interests come closest to India's. Hence, both China and Japan are likely to approach the issue of India's membership with great caution. In particular, they will wish to ascertain where India stands on CMIM strategic issues before backing India's membership.

A further complicating factor is that Japan, having now been overtaken by China and with bleaker economic prospects, is concerned over China acquiring too much power and influence in the region. This fear is likely to be shared by the other members of CMIM, and in China's eyes if India too shares this fear, a natural bond would be created between India and Japan. China's concern would then be that India is more likely to side with Japan, even if the latter two entertain different strategic visions for the CMIM. When combined with uncertainty over India's strategic interests, it is likely that China will conclude that the standpoint, of a more self-reliant Asian region that promotes global reforms under Chinese leadership, would stand a better chance if India were kept out of the CMIM. Given these perceived risks of accepting India, China is therefore likely to oppose India's participation, whereas Japan is more likely to welcome it despite any incipient differences in strategic visions.

India will have to persuade China that they share common interests with respect to regional stability and international reforms and on the role of the CMIM as a potentially valuable tool. In particular, India will need to demonstrate that if it were to join the CMIM that would increase the status and reach of the organization and improve the prospects for international reform. India will also need to take steps to defuse Chinese fears that once the irrevocable decision is taken to admit India into the CMIM, India would engage in coalition building activities, especially with Japan, that would thwart the ultimate goal of international monetary reform. All these steps will require enhanced contacts and discussions with China, jointly commissioned studies and public statements and commitments from India that are specifically directed at allaying China's fears.

Conclusion

This chapter has examined the origins of the CMIM in the context of the present organization of the international monetary system. While there have been some improvements, global response mechanisms are still inadequate; autarkic reliance on self-insurance is too costly indicating that regional arrangements could be a useful solution. It was argued that on balance, the CMIM has considerable potential to further the development interests of its members by creating a more stable regional trade, exchange rate and capital transaction environment and that India should consider joining it.

Endnotes

[1] In preparing this chapter I have benefitted from discussions with several persons and especially Partho Shome, while claiming sole responsibility for any errors or omissions.

[2] See especially Feldstein (1998), Khatkhate (1998) and Wade (1998).

[3] The initiative comprises the ASEAN countries plus China, Japan and Korea.

[4] See, for example, Grimes (2011) and Henning (2009).

[5] Eichengreen (2007) reproduces these arguments.

[6] Fluctuations in cross-border exchange rates were another source of instability.

[7] For discussions on its potential role reflecting different viewpoints see Grimes (2011), Henning (2009), Kawai (2010), McKay et al. (2010) and Sussangkarn (2011).

[8] Kawai (2010).

[9] King (2001).

[10] Use of the t-test statistic assumes that the variable is normally distributed. A visual examination of the normal probability plots for each of the countries shows that with the exception of Philippines they were broadly linear indicating that the assumption is at least not grossly violated.

[11] Terms such as $\frac{\Delta K}{\Delta Y_{-1}}$ are identical to the growth rate of capital weighted by the preceding year's capital output ratio $\frac{\Delta K}{K_{-1}} \frac{K_{-1}}{Y_{-1}}$. The former is more convenient for use in the regressions since it retains the interpretation of the coefficients in equation 9.2.

[12] Zhou (2013) shows that the puzzling decline in investment ratios is concentrated in the non-tradable sector, where smaller firms operate and that these are financially constrained and heavily dependent on credit from the banking sector.

[13] This is readily seen using the standard national income accounting identity for sectoral balances: $(S - I) + (T - G) = (X - M)$. Here $(S - I)$ is the private sector net saving balance, S being saving and I denoting investment; $(T - G)$ is the government sector fiscal balance, with T representing fiscal revenue and G government expenditures and $(X - M)$ is the balance with the rest of the world, i.e., the current account of the balance of payments, with X denoting exports of goods and services and M indicating imports of goods and services. Improving the current account of the balance of payments to better meet external payments requires attending to the left-hand side of the preceding equation. Direct intervention through fiscal means involves raising T and reducing G.

[14] Dooley et al. (2003) refer to this as Bretton Woods II.

[15] The focus on overspending was irrespective of the source of the country's balance of payments problem, whether external shocks or domestic mismanagement, the argument

being that even if the country was not overspending at the time the adverse external shock struck, it could now be construed as doing so as evidenced by the current account deficit.

[16] Exploiting such conflicts was famously exemplified in 1991 when the UK was forced out of the ERM fixed exchange rate mechanism by speculative short selling bets of the Soros-managed Quantum Fund.

[17] The IMF in 1997 had even proposed an amendment to its Articles to enjoin capital market liberalization. This was laid to rest when the Asian crisis unfolded in that year.

[18] Corsetti *et al.* (1999).

[19] One should also note that a possible trigger for a currency crisis and associated balance sheet problems could be the behaviour of cross-exchange rates. If some trading partners experience depreciation relative to a partner's currency this could stoke speculation as to the future behaviour of that currency and precipitate a crisis for it.

[20] However, this assumes that the fundamentals on the side of flows are reasonably sound and not themselves the source of the stock-side movements.

[21] Bhagwati (2004) notes some parallels.

[22] Following the 2008 crisis there has been an improvement in the availability of larger amounts of more quickly disbursing IMF funds, but these are still inadequate. However, capital controls are now more readily countenanced, provided they are of temporary duration.

[23] In the US this view was jointly held by the Treasury and the Federal Reserve.

[24] These requirements form part of the well named 'Washington Consensus' that Williamson (1989) enunciated.

[25] See Kawai (2009).

[26] The last is needed because the present set-up of the international monetary system favours globalized financial institutions such as international banks and hedge funds. These have the resources to exploit market volatilities and constitute a powerful interest group who lobby strenuously against the introduction of institutions that would limit market volatility and thereby reduce the potential for profits. Thus, a useful role for the CMIM would be that of a countervailing lobby that recommends institutions and practices more in line with the Asian countries' objectives of growth, development and stability.

[27] See, for example, the references cited in footnote 2.

[28] Malaysia is an anomaly, since it introduced capital controls and avoided an IMF programme but engaged in IMF-style policies of containment.

[29] See Amyx (2002).

[30] The IMF's Independent Evaluation Office (IEO) has in a recently released report expressed similar concerns on the organization's failure to anticipate and pre-empt the recent major financial crisis.

References

Amyx, J. 2002. 'Moving Beyond Bilateralism?' Japan and the Asian Monetary Fund. *Pacific Economic Papers* No. 331.

ASEAN+3. 2009. Joint media statement of the 12th ASEAN+3 Finance Ministers' Meeting, May.

Bhagwati, J. 2004. *In Defense of Globalization*. Oxford: Oxford University Press.

Corsetti, G., P. Pesenti and N. Roubini. 1999. 'What Caused the Asian Currency and Financial Crisis'. *Japan and the World Economy* 11 (3): 305–73.

Dooley, M., D. Folkerts-Landau and P. Garber. 2003. 'An Essay on the Revived Bretton Woods System'. NBER Working Paper No. W9971.

Eichengreen, B. 2009. 'Out of the Box thoughts About the International Financial Architecture'. IMF Working Paper 09/116. Washington: International Monetary Fund.

Eichengreen, B. 2007. 'A Blueprint for IMF Reform: More than just a Lender'. *International Finance* 10(2): 153–75.

Feldstein, M. 1998. 'Refocusing the IMF'. *Foreign Affairs* 77 (2): 20–33.

Grimes, E. W. 2011. 'The Asian Monetary Fund Reborn? Implications of Chiang Mai Initiative Multilateralization'. *Asia Policy* 11: 79–104.

Henning, C. R. 2009. 'The Future of the Chiang Mai Monetary Initiative: An Asian Monetary Fund'. *Policy Brief OB09-5*. Washington, D.C: Peterson Institute for International Economics, PB09-05.

IMF. 2009. 'The Debate on the International Monetary System'. Washington: International Monetary Fund.

IMF IEO (Independent Evaluation Office). 2011. 'IMF Performance in the Run-up to the Financial and Economic Crisis: IMF Surveillance in 2004–07'. Washington: IMF.

Kawai, M. 2010. 'From the Chiang Mai Initiative to an Asian Monetary Fund'. *Mimeo*. ADBI, Tokyo.

Kawai, M. 2009. 'Reform of the International Monetary Architecture: An Asian Perspective'. ADBI Working Paper, No. 167. Tokyo.

King, M. R. 2001. 'Who Triggered the Asian Financial Crisis?'. *Review of International Political Economy* 8(3): 438–66.

Khatkhate, D. 1998. 'Chasing Shadows: East Asian Financial Crisis and the IMF'. *Economic and Political Weekly* 33(17): 963–69.

Krugman, P. 1978. 'A Model of Balance of Payments Crisis'. *Journal of Money, Credit, and Banking* 11: 311–25.

Krugman, P. 1998. 'What happened to Asia?'. *Mimeo*. Cambridge: MIT.

Krugman, P. 1999. 'Balance Sheets, the Transfer Problem, and Financial Crises'. *International Tax and Public Finance* 6: 459–72.

Lipscy, P. Y. 2003. 'Japan's Asian Monetary Fund Proposal'. *Stanford Journal of East Asian Affairs* 3(1): 93–102.

McKay, J., U. Volz and R. Wolfinger. 2010. 'Regional Financing Arrangements and the Stability of the International Monetary System'. DIE (Discussion paper 13/2010) Bonn.

Obstfeld, M. 1994. 'The Logic of Currency Crises'. *Cahiers Economique et Monetaires*, 43: 189–212.

Radelet, S. and J. Sachs. 1998'. East Asian Financial Crisis: Diagnosis, Remedies, Prospects'. *Brookings Paper* 28(1): 1–74.

Sussangkarn, C. 2012. 'Prevention and Resolution of Foreign Exchange Crisis in East Asia'. ADBI Working Paper 363 Tokyo.

Sussangkarn, C. 2011. 'The Chiang Mai Initiative Multilateralization: Origin, Development, and Outlook'. *Asian Economic Policy Review* 6(2): 203–20.

Zhou, Y. S. 2013. 'Explaining ASEAN-3's Investment Puzzle: A Tale of Two Sectors'. IMF Working Paper No. 13/13.

Zhou, X. 2009. 'Reform the International Monetary System. Bank for International Settlements (BIS)'. *BIS Review* 41.

Wade, R. 1998. 'The Asian Debt-and-Development Crisis of 1997: Causes and Consequences'. *World Development* 26(8): 1535–53

Williamson, J. 1989. 'What Washington Means by Policy Reform'. In *Latin American Readjustment: How Much has Happened*, edited by Williamson, J. Washington: Institute for International Economics.

Contributors

Parthasarathi Shome is Advisor (Minister of State) to the Indian Finance Minister, 2013. He was Chairman, Expert Committee on General Anti-Avoidance Rules (GAAR), Government of India, July–October 2012, Director and Chief Executive of Indian Council for Research on International Economic Relations (ICRIER), New Delhi, 2011–12, Chief Economist of Her Majesty's Revenue and Customs, United Kingdom, 2008–11 and Advisor to the Indian Finance Minister (Secretary) 2004–08. He received the highest civilian honour of the Government of Brazil, *Commander of the Order of the Southern Cross*, in 2000, for his contributions to Brazilian tax reform.

Shome began his career in academia in 1975, becoming Professor of Economics at American University, Washington DC. He joined the IMF in 1983, holding various positions, including Senior Economist in the Office of the Managing Director, 1989–90, Chief of Tax Policy, 1992–95, and Director, IMF Singapore Institute, 2001–03. He chaired India's Ninth and Tenth Five-Year Plan Advisory Groups on Tax Policy and Administration and was Director, National Institute of Public Finance and Policy, New Delhi, 1995–97.

He has published in *Journal of Economic Theory, Journal of Public Economics, National Tax Journal, Oxford Economic Papers, Oxford Review of Economic Policy, Public Finance, Public Finance Quarterly, Staff Papers IMF* and others.

Ashima Goyal, Professor at the Indira Gandhi Institute of Development Research, Mumbai is widely published in institutional and open economy macroeconomics, international finance and governance and has been a consultant to ADB, DEA, GDN, UNDP, RBI, UN ESCAP and WB. She is the author of *Developing Economy Macroeconomics* (Allied, New Delhi, 1999), and editor of *Macroeconomics and Markets in India: Good luck or Good Policy?*

(Routledge – UK, 2012), *Handbook of the Indian Economy in the 21st Century: Understanding the Inherent Dynamism* (OUP – India, 2014, forthcoming). She is active in the Indian policy debate and has served on several government committees, boards of educational and financial institutions. She is a member of the Monetary Policy Technical Advisory Committee of the RBI, a Public Interest Director at MCX-SX Stock Exchange and Chairperson of the IMC Committee on Economic Policy. She was a visiting fellow at the Economic Growth Centre, Yale University, USA, and a Fulbright Senior Research Fellow at Claremont Graduate University, USA. She was the first Professor P.B. Brahmananda Memorial Research Grant Awardee for a study on *History of Monetary Policy in India since Independence* (2011).

Poonam Gupta is currently Senior Economist in the office of the Chief Economist of the World Bank in Washington DC. Prior to this, she was holding the Reserve Bank of India Chair of Economics at the National Institute of Public Finance and Policy, Delhi. Also, she has previously worked at the International Monetary Fund, Delhi School of Economics and ICRIER. Her research interests span issues related to macroeconomic management, causes and recovery after financial crises, implications of financial sector liberalization for developing countries, role of the services sector in growth and political economy issues in the context of India. Her work has been published in leading academic journals and in collected volumes.

David Vines is Professor of Economics, and a Fellow of Balliol College, at Oxford University. He is also an Adjunct Professor at the Australian National University and a Research Fellow of the Centre for Economic Policy Research. Vines writes on international macroeconomic policymaking, and recently published, with Peter Temin, *The Leaderless Economy: Why the World Economic System Fell Apart and How to Fix It* (Princeton University Press, 2013). He has been working on the role of the International Monetary Fund, and the G20, in the reform of the international financial system. He has also published papers on the macroeconomic instability within the European Monetary Union in the build-up to the financial crisis in Europe, and on macroeconomic policy reforms within Europe. From 2008 to 2012, Vines was the Research Director of the European Union's Framework Seven PEGGED Research Program, which analysed the Politics and Economics of Global Governance: the European Dimension. From 1978 to 1985, he worked in Cambridge with the Nobel Prize-winner James Meade. From 1985 to 1992, Vines was Adam Smith Professor of Political Economy at the University of Glasgow.

T. N. Srinivasan is Samuel C. Park, Jr. Professor of Economics (Emeritus) and Professor Emeritus in International and Area Studies at Yale University. He was Yong Pung How Chair Professor at the Lee Kuan Yew School of Public Policy at National University of Singapore (2001–12) and a Research Professor at the Indian Statistical Institute, Delhi (1964–77).

His research interests include the Indian Economy, International Trade, Development, Agricultural Economics and Microeconomic Theory. Some of his publications include *Growth, Sustainability and India's Economic Reforms* (2011); *Economic Reform in India* (co-edited, 2013) and *Reintegrating India with the World Economy* (co-authored, 2003), *Agriculture, Growth and Redistribution of Income: Policy Analysis with a General Equilibrium Model of India,* (co-authored, 1991) and *Foreign Trade Regimes and Economic Development: India,* (co-authored, 1975).

He is a Foreign Associate of the National Academy of Sciences, USA, and Fellow of the American Philosophical Society, the Econometric Society and the American Academy of Arts and Sciences, a Distinguished Fellow of the American Economic Association. He received the Padma Bhushan, the third highest civilian award of the Government of India in 2007 and the Mahalanobis Memorial Medal of the Indian Econometric Society in 1975.

Jyotirmoy Bhattacharya is Assistant Professor of Economics at the School of Liberal Studies, Bharat Ratna Dr B.R. Ambedkar University, New Delhi (AUD). Dr Bhattacharya has been associated with AUD since 2011. From 2009 to 2011, he was a Fellow at the Indian Council for Research in International Economic Relations (ICRIER) where he was part of the teams that worked on G20 issues and on the macroeconomics of the Indian economy. He has also taught at the Indian Institute of Management Kozhikode. His current research interests include the empirics of sticky prices and economic models of learning and expectations.

Shuheb Khan is a Research Associate at ICRIER since December 2009. Before joining ICRIER, he worked with Finance Commission for Union Territories constituted by the Ministry of Home Affairs. His broad areas of interest include macroeconomics, finance, monetary economics and issues related to ownership in the banking sector.

Renu Kohli is a New-Delhi-based macroeconomist. Currently *Lead Economist*, International Financial Architecture, DEA-ICRIER G20 Research Programme, she frequently consults with foreign investors on Indian macro and financial sector issues. A former staff member of the International

Monetary Fund and Reserve Bank of India, she has published in a number of refereed journals; she has also authored a book – *India's Experience with Capital Account Liberalization* (2005). She has several academic distinctions/honours to her credit, including the Commonwealth Award in 1992.

Alok Sheel is currently Secretary of the Prime Minister's Economic Advisory Council that advises the Prime Minister on critical economic issues referred to it by the Indian Prime Minister. He joined the Indian Administrative Service in 1982. He has 25 years of experience in public administration including project management, exercising judicial authority, diplomatic exchanges and interface with democratic representative institutions. His experience lies in the global economy, macroeconomic policy, public finance and economic management, particularly understanding the Global Financial Crisis and the Great Recession and negotiating the coordinated global policy response within the G20.

Sheetal K. Chand resides in Cyprus, where he chairs Mwezi LLC, a newly founded management and economic consultancy service. After some years as an economist with the Ministry of Economic Planning, Uganda Government, he joined the International Monetary Fund (IMF), where he eventually served as an advisor and chief of the Fiscal Analysis Division. On retiring from the IMF he has taught and researched at the University of Oslo's Department of Economics. In addition, he held visiting professorships at universities in different countries and provided consultancy services to certain governments in the area of public finance. His primary interest lies in the theory and design of policy applications with particular reference to macroeconomics, public finance and pension issues. Some of his recent publications include 'Stabilizing poverty in the context of the IMF's monetary model' (*Journal of Poverty Alleviation and International Development*, 2012) and 'The relevance of Haavelmo's macroeconomic theorizing for contemporary macro policy making' (*Nordic Journal of Political Economy*, 2012).

Index